Literacy

The Creative Curriculum® Approach

Cate Heroman

Candy Jones

Teaching
Strategies® Inc.
Washington, DC

Editors: Toni S. Bickart and Laurie Taub
Cover and book design: Carla Uriona
Production: Carla Uriona and Jennifer Love King

Teaching Strategies, Inc.
P.O. Box 42243
Washington, DC 20015
www.TeachingStrategies.com
ISBN 1-879537-87-7

Teaching Strategies and *The Creative Curriculum* names and logos are
registered trademarks of Teaching Strategies, Inc., Washington, DC.

The publisher and the authors cannot be held responsible for injury, mishap,
or damages incurred during the use of or because of the information in this
book. The authors recommend appropriate and reasonable supervision at all
times based on the age and capability of each child.

Library of Congress Cataloging-in-Publication Data

Heroman, Cate.
  Literacy : the creative curriculum approach / Cate Heroman, Candy Jones.
    p. cm.
  Includes bibliographical references.
  ISBN 1-879537-87-7
  1. Language arts (Preschool) 2. Education, Preschool--Curriculum. 3.
Language experience approach in education. I. Jones, Candy, 1956- II. Title.
  LB1140.5.L3H47 2004
  372.6--dc22
                              2004014460

Printed and bound in the United States of America
2010   2009   2008   2007   2006   2005   2004
10 9 8 7 6 5 4 3 2 1

Acknowledgments

This book required the efforts of a team of talented people. We want to thank our expert literacy panel for their work in reviewing our research and providing specific feedback and suggestions, particularly about meeting the needs of English language learners and modifying activities to accommodate children with disabilities: Linda Espinosa, Ph.D., associate professor, Early Childhood Education, University of Missouri-Columbia, and formerly co-director of the National Institute for Early Education Research at Rutgers University; Kathy Lathrop, pre-kindergarten director, California Reading and Literature Project, UCSC-Monterey Region; and Elizabeth Villaseñor, a teacher of children with disabilities in Los Angeles, CA.

Diane Trister Dodge, president of Teaching Strategies, and Jan Greenberg, recently of Reading Is Fundamental and now training manager at Teaching Strategies, reviewed an early draft and gave us valuable suggestions. Bonnie Blagojevic, research associate, Center for Inclusion and Disabilities Studies at the University of Maine, and associate editor of *Information Technology in Childhood Education*, helped us enhance the Computer interest area section with up-to-date information.

We especially want to thank Toni Bickart, vice president, publishing, at Teaching Strategies for the direction she provided in the thinking and editing process, and Laurie Taub, editorial assistant, for challenging our choice of words and probing for meaning in everything we wrote. Thanks to Carla Uriona, design and production manager, for her excellent work; our new production specialist, Jennifer Love King; and everyone at Teaching Strategies for their help and support.

In our ongoing efforts to meet the needs of teachers in the field, we have been focusing on the importance of the teacher's role in literacy learning for several years. Over the last three years we have introduced the concepts in this book to thousands of teachers who have used them with many thousands of children. We thank our colleagues for their inspiration and commitment. Finally, we thank the many teachers, and the members of the Staff Development Network at Teaching Strategies, who have crafted literacy-related activities. We deeply appreciate their sharing ideas and expertise and their trying many of these strategies in a wide range of settings.

Table of Contents

Chapter 4–Literacy Learning in Interest Areas 133

Foreword

Strong language and literacy skills are essential for children's success in school and in life. Children who do not learn to read and write by the end of the primary grades are at risk for school failure. Effective instruction in the preschool years can make all the difference, and the children who are most at risk for school failure stand to benefit the most.

Literacy learning begins at birth, but too many children are not receiving a steady diet of rich language and literacy experiences. Recent research has confirmed what early childhood educators have long known: by age three, differences in children's understanding and use of language and literacy skills are enormous. Some children, for example, have twice the vocabulary of other children. This is a significant finding because the number of words a child knows and uses is a good predictor of reading ability. Preschool teachers have from one to two years to address this gap. They have the power to give every child a solid foundation in language and literacy skills, and to inspire children to read and write to learn.

I'm delighted to introduce this new resource from Teaching Strategies by my colleagues, Cate Heroman and Candy Jones. *Literacy: The Creative Curriculum Approach* is designed for programs using *The Creative Curriculum® for Preschool*, but the content is applicable to all teachers working with preschool children. Building on the comprehensive approach of the Curriculum, the purpose of this book is to empower teachers to use the latest research-based strategies so that they intentionally teach children critically important skills and incorporate language and literacy learning in their everyday work with children.

New Expectations and Mandates

The bar for literacy learning has been raised for preschool children and their teachers. While the early childhood years—birth to age 8—are a critical period for developing language and literacy skills, early childhood educators know that normal development is very individualized and uneven. Despite this knowledge about developmental variations, expectations about what *every* child should know and be able to do before kindergarten have changed. The Head Start Outcomes Framework outlines what every 4-year-old should know and be able to do before entering kindergarten. Today, every state has developed or is in the process of developing Early Learning Standards, and every one includes specific literacy skills and knowledge. Wherever children are served—in child care, Head Start, pre-k, preschool, and family child care—teachers are accountable for ensuring that children develop these skills.

Along with changing expectations for children and mandates for programs, there is an increasing body of research on literacy and school readiness. This research confirms that teachers must be intentional about how they talk with children and the kinds of activities and experiences they plan to help children acquire critically important attitudes, skills, and knowledge about language and literacy.

While a simple solution to building a solid foundation in language and literacy skills for all children would be nice, none exists. There is no magic formula or single approach to teaching language and literacy skills that will address every child's individual needs and learning style. A language and literacy curriculum is not an isolated subject that can be dropped into the ongoing curriculum or addressed only at specific times of the day.

Language and literacy instruction is most effective when it is built into a comprehensive approach that gives equal attention to all aspects of a child's development: social and emotional, physical, cognitive, and language development. There are times for direct teaching—one-on-one, in small groups, and in large groups. In addition, children practice and use language and literacy skills during daily routines and during the active learning that takes place in interest areas and outdoors. It is essential to have in place an assessment system linked to the curriculum goals and objectives so that teachers can pinpoint each child's progress in developing skills, plan instruction on the basis of this information, and ensure that every child is learning. This is the *Creative Curriculum* approach.

The *Creative Curriculum* Approach

A distinguishing feature of *The Creative Curriculum* is the framework, with five components, that rests on a solid foundation of theory and research. This framework applies to all decisions teachers make about when, how, and what to teach.

- **How Children Develop and Learn:** Teachers must know what preschool children are like, developmentally and individually, and the ways culture affects how they relate to others and learn. They use this knowledge to make decisions about appropriate activities, what will interest individual children, how to interact and ask questions, and how to motivate each child. Because some children are advanced language learners and others have special challenges (because of inexperience with language, identified disabilities, or because they are just learning English), special attention must be given to meeting the needs of all children.

- **The Learning Environment:** Children are excited about learning to read and write when they have reasons for using these skills. That is why the context in which skills are taught is as important as the specific skills and knowledge teachers want children to acquire.

  The physical environment is organized in eleven interest areas: Blocks, Dramatic Play, Toys & Games, Art, Library, Discovery, Sand and Water, Music & Movement, Cooking, Computers, and Outdoors. This is because preschool children learn best when they can make choices about where to work and engage in activities independently or with a few other children.

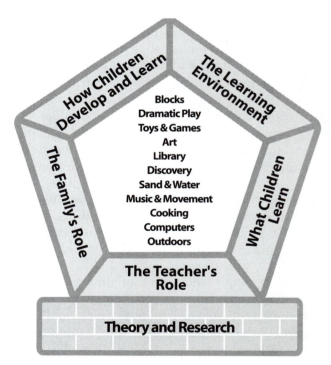

Literacy materials can and should be part of every area so that children use them in their play to learn. The daily schedule and routines offer more opportunities to involve children in meaningful reading and writing experiences. Because language and literacy skills are tools for communicating with others, the social environment of the classroom is of paramount importance in promoting these skills and in motivating children to use them. The positive relationships teachers build with each child, and the ability of every child to make friends and cooperate with others, lead to lasting, positive outcomes.

- **What Children Learn:** This component of the Curriculum framework describes the knowledge and skills that are essential for children to learn in all content areas: literacy, math, science, social studies, the arts, and technology. In order for teachers to be intentional about the literacy instruction and experiences they plan for children, teachers must know what the research shows about the seven components of literacy.

  This book therefore builds on the information offered in the Curriculum. It provides an extensive definition and description of each component of literacy, a summary of related research, and a thorough description of the teacher's role in supporting the development of skills and concepts related to each component: 1) literacy as a source of enjoyment, 2) vocabulary and language, 3) phonological awareness, 4) knowledge of print, 5) letters and words, 6) comprehension, and 7) books and other texts.

- **The Teacher's Role:** After families, teachers are the single most important influence on children's learning. Teachers are role models for language and literacy learning. They demonstrate literacy behaviors throughout the day, engage children in conversations, ask questions that encourage children verbalize their ideas, and show children how much they enjoy reading and writing. In order to address the learning needs of every child, teachers must know how to observe children purposefully. They keep the goals and objectives of the Curriculum in mind when they observe children and document the observations that demonstrate a child's abilities related to a variety of objectives.

  For language development, 13 objectives apply to speaking and listening, reading and writing. *The Creative Curriculum® Developmental Continuum for Ages 3–5* shows teachers the steps children typically go through in accomplishing each objective. By pinpointing where children are on the *Developmental Continuum*, teachers can plan the introduction of new knowledge and skills to children. They help children apply and practice these skills during small-group activities, in interest areas, and by engaging them in studying a topic that has meaning to them. The strong link between a systematic approach to assessment and a comprehensive curriculum enables teachers to scaffold and support each child's learning.

- **The Family's Role:** Language and literacy experiences begin at birth, and family members are children's first and life-long teachers. As stated earlier, children enter preschool with widely different language and literacy experiences. Teachers can share with families the importance of talking with their children, teaching them new words, asking questions, and engaging in conversations. They may help them learn how to obtain children's books and strategies to use in sharing books with their children. When teachers form partnerships with families, children do better in school. The *Creative Curriculum* approach describes ways of building strong partnerships and offers practical ways for families and teachers to support children's learning.

What This Book Offers

To build on the comprehensive approach of the *Creative Curriculum* framework and the *Developmental Continuum* Assessment System, this book offers teachers a wealth of practical ideas and strategies. It has a clear and practical format that makes it easy for teachers to access the information and incorporate the ideas into their ongoing programs. By describing the research in practical terms, teachers learn not only *what* to do but *why* these strategies are effective.

Effective Teaching Strategies

The book details the use of seven research-based teaching strategies: 1) talking, singing and playing with language; 2) reading aloud; 3) storytelling; 4) story retelling; 5) writing; 6) scaffolding children's literacy learning through play; and 7) using studies to promote literacy. It offers explicit guidance on how to begin the activities, ways intentionally to promote children's language and literacy development and learning, and tips to share with families on how to use related strategies at home. The delightful vignettes that illustrate each of the teaching strategies bring teachers' use of the strategies and activities to life.

A Strong Emphasis on Language

Readers will find a strong emphasis on promoting language skills with children because all literacy depends on language development. Some teachers are natural talkers; it's easy for them to think of what to say to a child to promote vocabulary and language development. They know how to ask the kinds of questions that encourage children to talk and express their ideas.

Other teachers need more practice in posing questions and making statements that will build children's thinking and language. A central goal of this book is therefore to help all teachers become good talkers who are able to take advantage of every opportunity to engage children in conversations, teach new words, and model effective language skills. Developing this ability will make a profound difference. It will promote both children's language skills and positive relationships.

Purposeful Use of Interest Areas

Another goal of this book is to empower teachers to infuse language and literacy in all aspects of daily life in the classroom and to make them interesting and engaging. Rather than asking teachers to add something else to their programs, it takes a fresh look at what is already taking place in a *Creative Curriculum* classroom through the lens of literacy. The interest areas provide the context where children practice the language and literacy skills they are learning.

There are many ideas for bringing literacy into all interest areas and hundreds of examples of what teachers can say and do. Each interest area discussion describes how everyday, child-initiated experiences contribute to children's literacy learning in relation to other Curriculum objectives as well as to the language objectives. Suggestions are made for adding books, props, and other reading and writing materials and tools to the areas, to build children's oral language skills and encourage them to explore independently the many functions and forms of literacy they experience through planned activities and interactions with teachers. It shows how teachers intentionally teach literacy skills and encourage critical thinking by talking, modeling, demonstrating, and coaching.

Language and Literacy Activities

The last chapter includes a wide variety of rich and enjoyable activities that can be implemented using readily available materials. Once an activity has been tried, the teacher can expand upon it and apply the approach with other materials and books. Each activity is structured so that the user can identify the *Creative Curriculum* goals and objectives for language development addressed by the activity, the necessary materials and preparation, and the preferred or recommended setting. Specific strategies are outlined for extending the activity and adapting it for English language learners or children with disabilities. Finally, suggestions are given for incorporating literacy into the overall physical environment, as well as the eleven interest areas, so that children can *practice and use* the literacy concepts and skills learned in teacher-directed activities

I am confident that *Literacy: The Creative Curriculum Approach* will inspire and empower teachers with the many examples, activities, and ideas that they can easily incorporate in their daily program. When teachers enjoy their work, children sense their pleasure. Children who find language and literacy experiences enjoyable and satisfying are more likely to become good readers and writers.

Diane Trister Dodge
Founder and President
Teaching Strategies, Inc.

How to Use This Book

Literacy: The Creative Curriculum Approach is a critical part of Teaching Strategies' language and literacy program. While teachers can use the book by itself, it is a valuable part of a comprehensive approach to curriculum and assessment for children ages 3–5. This new supplement expands on the information provided in *The Creative Curriculum for Preschool*, showing how and why language and literacy can and should be part of children's everyday experiences and activities. It explains early literacy learning and describes when and how to teach directly the skills and knowledge children need to become successful readers and writers.

Chapter 1, The Components of Literacy, describes the essential skills, knowledge, and understandings that preschool children need in order to become competent and confident readers and writers. It reviews the research about each component and describes what teachers can do to help children progress. The seven components are literacy as a source of enjoyment, vocabulary and language, phonological awareness, knowledge of print, letters and words, comprehension, and books and other texts. Readers who want to learn even more than what this book presents can use the research citations in the Appendix as a starting point for further study.

Chapter 2, Planning Your Literacy Program, helps you get started. To plan, you have to know exactly what you want children to learn. This chapter therefore begins with the 13 *Creative Curriculum* objectives that address speaking, listening, reading, and writing. Throughout the book you will see references to these objectives, to guide your observation and planning. Because the physical environment is a powerful teaching strategy, the next step is to create a literacy-rich classroom, including a wide range of materials that encourage children to engage in oral language experiences, reading, and writing. We show how every event in the day, from children's arrival to their departure, is an opportunity to promote language and literacy skills. Because some children have special needs, this chapter offers specific strategies for children with disabilities, children with advanced abilities or experience, those who are just learning English, and children who have not yet had rich language and literacy experiences. The chapter concludes with a step-by-step roadmap for planning your literacy program.

Chapter 3, Teaching Strategies, introduces the seven strategies for teaching literacy: talking, singing, and playing with language; reading aloud; storytelling; story retelling; writing; supporting children's literacy learning through play; and using studies to promote literacy. As you read these strategies, reflect on your current teaching practices. While most of these strategies are probably familiar to you, think about how you are using them. Consider how you can use these strategies throughout your day in a more intentional way.

Chapter 4, Literacy Learning in Interest Areas, invites you to reconsider your interest areas as the context for literacy learning. The chapter begins with a discussion of the Library Area, the hub of literacy learning in a *Creative Curriculum* classroom. The discussions of the remaining ten interest areas are formatted in the same way. The first section of each discussion looks at everyday experiences that typically occur in the area—whether it is working a puzzle or pounding clay—and points out their relationship to literacy learning. As you evaluate your interest areas, use the suggestions from this chapter to include literacy-related materials and books. The discussions also include suggestions about how to scaffold children's learning as they are engaged in everyday experiences in the area. A final section helps you to observe children's progress while working in the area.

Chapter 5, Literacy Activities, offers specific instructions for activities for whole groups, small groups, or individual children. First, look at your daily schedule and think about the best opportunities to include the activities. Next, think about the children's developmental levels in the areas of language and literacy. With this information in mind, select activities that meet the particular needs of the children. We encourage you to think of ways to adapt or extend the activities by asking yourself:

- How can I use this activity with available resources?

- What other books can I use for this activity?

- How can I adapt this activity to make it easier or more challenging?

- Can I modify the activity so that all children can participate in some way?

In addition to the activities included in this book, subscribers can find an ever-growing bank of activities on CreativeCurriculum.net, Teaching Strategies' Web-based assessment system.

The Appendix includes tools to help you with various aspects of your language and literacy program. The Literacy Implementation Checklist may be used to guide an evaluation of your program and help you consider changes. The Language Development section of *The Creative Curriculum Developmental Continuum for Ages 3–5* is a useful planning tool that enables you to offer instruction on the basis of each child's development. It is also a useful tool to assess children's progress toward the objectives. The Matrix of Activities gives you a list of all the activities in the chapter, shows which components of literacy they address, and suggests the interest areas in which you might choose to do them. We prepared the Literacy Observation Forms (Alphabet Knowledge Observation Form, Phonological Awareness Observation Form, and Print and Book Concepts Observation Form) as reproducible forms for tracking aspects of each child's learning and development.

Literacy: The Creative Curriculum Approach can be used in a variety of ways. Teachers can use it independently to broaden their understanding of literacy and to learn appropriate strategies to enhance children's literacy learning. It can also serve as the content for focused professional development, either in study groups or learning teams, or as part of ongoing training. Teachers could learn about a specific component and accompanying strategies and then practice them in the classroom. These classroom experiences can be discussed at future sessions with colleagues. In addition, teacher mentors can model a particular strategy, demonstrate how the key components of literacy are addressed, and then coach teachers using the techniques described in this book.

inside this chapter

Components of Literacy

1

As an early childhood teacher, you know the importance of language and literacy learning in your program. You know that literacy learning depends upon more than teaching the ABCs, introducing children to environmental print, setting up a Library Area, or clapping out syllables in a word. Language and literacy are tools for thinking and communicating. When teachers plan meaningful ways for children to use language and literacy as tools, children are motivated to become readers and writers, and they learn about the features, forms, and functions of written and spoken language.

Young children seek to be part of a social group and to communicate with the important people in their lives, first orally and later through print. While young children may not use sophisticated communication strategies, they are definitely eager to share urgent thoughts, ideas, needs, and feelings. This desire to communicate and participate in the classroom community motivates young children to persist in the often challenging tasks of early literacy. Because it is based on continuous interactions with knowledgeable adults, literacy learning is integrated into the overall, comprehensive program in a *Creative Curriculum* classroom.

This approach recognizes that play is an essential part of learning for preschool children. The skills children learn through purposeful, productive, and high-level play—skills in verbalization, vocabulary, language comprehension, problem solving, observation, empathy, imagination, assuming another's perspective, using symbols, and learning to cooperate with others—are foundational skills for all cognitive development (Olfman, 2003). A teacher in a *Creative Curriculum* classroom knows how to maximize children's learning opportunities as they play by thoughtfully observing children, reflecting on what children are doing, and planning ways to guide and extend learning. This process is also used to plan appropriate direct instruction.

In order to create a high-quality literacy program, teachers must understand the components of literacy. The components of literacy described in this chapter and in the research literature are the basis for the intentional teaching strategies and activities described later. An understanding of the components is necessary in order for teachers to observe children effectively and to analyze and evaluate their development. Then the teacher can decide which strategies and activities will best support the literacy development of a particular child or group of children. These are the seven components of literacy: literacy as a source of enjoyment, vocabulary and language, phonological awareness, knowledge of print, letters and words, comprehension, and books and other texts.

Literacy as a Source of Enjoyment

When children enjoy having books read to them, and when they are excited about what they are hearing and learning, children are motivated to learn to read and, later, to read to learn. Children's vocabularies increase as they are introduced to new words in meaningful contexts, and then they have an easier time reading those words when they encounter them in print. Children practice reading more often when they find it enjoyable and useful. When they practice reading a lot, children increase their fluency, or the speed at which they recognize words and comprehend the text.

Most preschoolers are not yet reading. A central goal for these emergent readers is to introduce them to the power and pleasure of literacy. A love of reading can begin long before children start formal schooling. When a parent holds a child and reads aloud, the child begins to experience reading as a pleasurable activity. Later, these memories inspire them to persist through the often difficult early stages of literacy learning. Not all children have had these enjoyable experiences, so it is essential to provide positive literacy experiences in the preschool classroom.

A child who enjoys literacy activities will more than likely participate during interactive read aloud times, notice print in the environment, ask questions about the meaning of print (e.g., *What does that say?*), and spend time reading once he or she is able. Teachers consider a variety of ways to motivate children and help them experience the power and pleasure of literacy learning.

Role models

- Do children see adults enjoying reading and writing?

- Do teachers show enthusiasm during read aloud times and talk about why they enjoyed a book?

- Do children see adults reading and writing to accomplish meaningful tasks?

- Do children hear adults communicating effectively?

- Do adults interact with children in meaningful ways in the Library Area, periodically during choice time?

- Do teachers encourage families to enjoy reading and writing together?

Attractive and Inviting Library Area

- Is the area attractive, with comfortable furniture that helps children relax as they look at books?

- Is the area furnished with cozy, homelike touches such as plants, rugs, pillows, pictures, stuffed animals, and dolls?

- Is attention drawn to special books by displaying them with their covers facing out?

- Is there quality literature of interest to children?

- Are story retelling props located near the related book? Are books and tapes stored together?

- Are books in good condition and rotated periodically?

Literacy Linked With Play

- Do teachers observe children and offer materials and real-life reasons to use literacy in their play?

- Are there literacy materials in interest areas to inspire children's play?

- Do teachers encourage children to talk about their play?

Choices

- Are children able to choose the reading and writing materials they want?

- Are sufficient choices of literacy materials available to children?

- Are children able to choose the friend they would like to work with?

Challenging, Yet Achievable, Literacy Experiences

- Are children's literacy efforts successful?

- Are the literacy activities age-appropriate?

- Are the literacy experiences and activities appropriate for each child's interests and abilities?

- Do teachers observe children's literacy behaviors and scaffold their learning by gently challenging them?

When adults observe and interact with children and provide stimulating opportunities for language and literacy learning, children begin to experience literacy as a source of enjoyment. They are motivated to engage in language and literacy experiences.

What Does Research Say?

Use of literature

Literature use increased dramatically when teachers incorporated enjoyable literature activities into the daily program, when library centers were created in classrooms, and when recreational reading was scheduled on a daily basis (Morrow & Weinstein, 1982, 1986).

Literature-based programs positively affect children's attitudes toward reading (Goatley, Brock, & Raphael, 1992).

Children want to read more often when they have a choice in what they read, have the opportunity to interact with others to discuss what they have read, and feel successful about reading (Gambrell, Palmer, & Coding, 1993).

Kindergarteners who demonstrated a strong interest in books scored significantly higher on standardized reading readiness tests and were rated higher on work habits, general school performance, and social and emotional development than those whose book interest was lower (Morrow, 1983).

Children who have never experienced the pleasure of literacy are likely to be unenthusiastic about learning to read and write (Snow, Barnes, Chandler, Goodman, & Hemphill, 1991).

Role of adults

Children tend to go the book corner when teachers are there intermittently, not when they were never there or when they were always there (Rawson & Goetz, 1983).

Children benefit when teachers provide children with daily opportunities to experience literature pleasurably, to discuss stories, to relate literature activities with content, and to share the books they read or look at (Galda & Cullinan, 1991; Huck, 1976; Stewig & Sebesta, 1978).

Reading to children at school or at home leads them to associate reading with pleasure and provides them with models of reading (Morrow, 2001).

Good feelings gained in story readings transfer to the act of reading, itself (Hiebert, 1981; Taylor, 1983).

When materials only and materials coupled with adult scaffolding were compared, children engaged in significantly more literacy-related play when adults were present and involved (Pickett, 1998).

Children are more likely to be fluent readers and enjoy reading more if parents have fun reading to them and if they show children that reading books is a source of enjoyment (Snow, Burns, & Griffin, 1998).

Environment

Before entering school, children who have access to books choose to look at them independently. They appear to value literacy as a source of entertainment (Baker, Scher, & Mackler, 1997).

Literacy-enriched play centers increase, often dramatically, the amount of literacy-related activities in which children engage during play (Neuman & Roskos, 1990; Vukelich, 1990; Noble & Foster, 1993).

What Is the Teacher's Role in Literacy as a Source of Enjoyment?

Teachers play a key role in encouraging children's positive attitudes toward reading and writing. What you do and say help promote a lifelong habit of reading and writing for pleasure and for information.

Model literacy behaviors that you enjoy.
When you read a story to children, talk about why you chose the book and why you love it. Talk about getting good news from a friend in a letter or an e-mail message. Share a greeting card you received and explain why it is special to you.

Make story time pleasurable.
Demonstrate your enthusiasm and excitement about reading. Create a warm, nurturing atmosphere for reading aloud, so that the children look forward to participating. Select quality literature that the children will want to hear read. Invite visitors—parents, directors, community volunteers—to read stories to children individually or in groups. Read books that you enjoy. Your love of the stories will show in the expressions on your face and in the tone of your voice.

Capture children's interest before beginning to read aloud.
Set the stage for the story by connecting it with an experience familiar to the children. For example, you might introduce a story by asking, *Have you ever thought about what you could do with a magic pebble? In our story today, Sylvester, the donkey, finds one.* Use objects, sounds, fingerplays, games, or personal recollections as ways of motivating children to listen and respond to a story.

Invite children to choose books to look at independently and to request titles for story time.
Encourage children to talk about their favorite books and share their recommendations with others. Keep Post-its and pencils in the Library Area so children can identify their favorite books by writing their names and placing the papers on the covers.

Include books and reading strategies that invite active participation during story time.
Involving children in read aloud times not only motivates them, but it also promotes their language skills and comprehension.

Make your Library Area attractive and inviting.
Draw children to this area by spotlighting special books with props for retelling and by displaying other interesting books with their covers facing out. Use homelike touches, such as rugs, rocking chairs, plants, pillows, framed pictures and beanbag chairs, to make the area one that the children want to visit and where they can relax as they read. Rotate the books periodically to add fresh reading material and maintain interest. Include books related to the topic you are studying, as well as others of special interest to the children.

Add books made by the children, themselves, to the Library Area.
Children can dictate the text to you or write independently. A photo album with captions written beneath the pictures is also a nice addition to the area.

During choice time, go to the Library Area periodically.
Children enjoy interacting with their teachers by discussing what they are reading or doing. Your presence in the Library Area will attract children to it. However, if some children enjoy reading alone, your presence may deter them. The best solution is to go to the Library Area periodically during choice time, but do not remain there the entire time.

Create opportunities for children to work together during literacy experiences.
Children are motivated when they work together. Children can work cooperatively as they retell stories, write and illustrate books, clap rhymes, use literacy-related computer programs, and create and play with signs and other literacy props.

Work with families to make literacy experiences at home pleasurable.
Emphasize to families the importance of reading and talking about books with their children every day. Through newsletters, conversations, family workshops, and conferences, show families how to make literacy a fun activity rather than something children are forced to do. Suggest that families take their children to the library and obtain a library card. Offer opportunities for children to take books home from the Library Area. Encourage families to keep story time warm, nurturing, and enjoyable.

Vocabulary and Language

Oral language is the foundation of literacy. Literacy learning begins with listening and speaking. Infants listen to familiar voices and then learn to babble and later speak. Through speech, children learn to organize their thoughts and ideas. They construct their own understanding of the rules of language as they interact with adults and others in meaningful exchanges. They gradually learn the rules for ordering sounds and using language in standard forms. To acquire literacy skills, children transition from oral language to written language. Written language, both reading and writing, requires a well-developed vocabulary and a good understanding of the rules and structure of oral language. Literacy learning also requires the insight that written language is different from spoken language.

Language is a system of words with rules for their use in listening, speaking, reading, and writing. Language can be divided into two areas: *receptive language* and *expressive language*. *Receptive language* refers to the language that a person takes in, the language one hears and reads. *Expressive language* is the language that a person speaks and writes. Children acquire language by moving through predictable stages, but the pace differs from child to child.

There are four kinds of vocabulary:

1) *Listening vocabulary*—the words we need to know in order to understand the language we hear.

2) *Speaking vocabulary*—the words we use to express ourselves orally.

3) *Reading vocabulary*—the words we need to know in order to understand what we read.

4) *Writing vocabulary*—the words we use to express ourselves in writing.

When children are learning to read, they use their listening and speaking vocabularies to make sense of printed words. Later, their experience with reading and writing helps them to expand all of their vocabularies.

Children learn new words and learn about the structure of language in four different ways:

- talking with peers and adults throughout the day through informal and guided conversations

- songs, rhymes, fingerplays, and movement activities

- hearing new words to describe what they are experiencing firsthand

- listening to print read aloud and talking about new words

These important experiences can encourage the rapid language development of children who come to preschool with limited language skills. When teachers guide conversations and use particular words to describe children's experiences, they intentionally teach the vocabulary and language rules that children need to think and communicate more effectively.

If you have children whose primary language is not English, recognize that a strong base in a first language promotes school achievement in a second language (Snow, Burns, & Griffin, 1998). English language learners are more likely to become readers and writers of English if they understand the vocabulary and concepts in their primary language first. These children need special attention to increase their vocabularies and other language skills. The long-term goal is for children to be able to understand, speak, read, and write in both the primary language and English. You therefore want to support children's first language as you help them acquire proficiency in English.

What Does Research Say?

Vocabulary development

Children learn the meaning of most words indirectly, through everyday experiences with oral and written language. In addition, there are times when teaching children the meaning of words directly can be effective (National Reading Panel, 2000).

Conversations matter when children are young. Talking with children provides them with experiences that are important to both their cognitive and their social/emotional learning (Hart & Risley, 1995).

When children are engaged in tasks in which they are learning vocabulary, they have larger vocabulary gains (Dickinson & Smith, 1994; Senechal, 1997; Drevno et al., 1994; Daniels, 1994, 1996).

Exposing children to new vocabulary words often and in various ways can have a significant effect (Senechal, 1997; Leung, 1992; Daniels, 1994, 1996; Dole, Sloan, & Trathen, 1995).

The context in which new vocabulary words is learned is critical. Vocabulary words should be words that the child will find useful in many different contexts (McKeown, Beck, Omanson, & Pople, 1985; Kameenui, Carnine, & Freschi, 1982; Dole, Sloan, & Trathen, 1995).

Children with larger vocabularies have more developed phonological sensitivity (Wagner et al., 1993, 1997), and this can be noticed early in the preschool years (Burgess & Lonigan, 1998; Chaney, 1992; Lonigan, Burgess, Anthony, & Barker, 1998; Lonigan, Burgess, & Anthony, 2000).

Children benefit from teacher-child conversations that include varied vocabulary and deal with topics that challenge children's thinking (Dickinson & Tabors, 2001).

Reading development

The majority of reading problems could be prevented by, among other things, increasing children's oral language skills (Snow, Burns, & Griffin, 1998).

There is a positive correlation between individual differences in oral language skills and later differences in reading (Bishop & Adams, 1990; Butler, Marsh, Sheppard, & Sheppard, 1985; Pikulski & Tobin, 1989; Scarborough, 1989; Share, Jorm, MacLean, & Mathews, 1984).

Vocabulary is critically important in oral reading instruction (National Institute of Child Health and Human Development, 2000b).

Vocabulary is the strongest predictor of later reading and literacy ability (Chall, Jacobs, & Baldwin, 1990).

Reading aloud

Storybook readings help teach children meanings of unfamiliar words (Robbins & Ehri, 1994).

The frequency of a target word in a story influenced the occurrence of the word in the child's retellings, and read aloud events seemed to help children to learn new words by incidental learning (Leung, 1992).

For 4- to 5-year-old children, one single book reading was enough to significantly improve new expressive vocabulary of ten target words in the story (Sénéchal & Cornell, 1993).

Teacher talk associated with storybook reading has an impact on the amount of child-initiated analytic talk important for vocabulary gains (Dickinson & Smith, 1994).

Repeated readings of a story to prekindergarten children enhanced vocabulary gains. Children learned more from answering questions during readings than they did when simply listening to the narrative (Sénéchal, 1997).

What Is the Teacher's Role in Promoting Vocabulary and Language Development?

The best way to help children increase their vocabularies and learn other language skills is to provide opportunities for them to hear different forms of language. You do this by modeling language, having extended conversations, and reading aloud. While most children learn the language they hear easily, some children do not. For these children, more direct teaching is necessary.

Serve as a good language model.
When talking with children, use complete sentences. Expand children's language by building on what they say. Use the child's words and add more of your own. If a child says, *Go outside*, respond by saying, *Would you like to go outside today? We'll go outside right after we finish cleaning up.*

Give children something to talk about.
Provide interesting experiences that spark children's curiosity and wonder. Include many first-hand experiences where children can use their senses to explore and use language to communicate what they are thinking and doing. To encourage children to talk, make changes in the environment, bring in natural items, and share your own experiences. These give children important background knowledge for later learning.

Repeat and reinforce new words.
When a new word has been introduced to the children, use it in different contexts throughout the day. For example, after reading aloud the story *The Enormous Turnip*, talk about having an enormous appetite or how enormous a tree seems.

Observe, wait, and listen.
Pay close attention to what a child is trying to tell you or show you. Ask questions. Be patient and wait for the child to respond. Then listen attentively to what the child says so you can answer and model language appropriately.

Talk frequently with children.
Spend lots of time listening to what children have to say and then responding appropriately. Strive for at least five exchanges in each conversation with children, to encourage them to carry on lengthier conversations. During conversations, clarify the meaning of words and encourage higher-level thinking.

Go beyond the here-and-now in your conversations.
Discuss things that happened yesterday and last week and that might happen in the future. Invite children to use their imaginations and think creatively. Talk with children and pretend to be in another situation at another time. For example, ask a child, *If you could be any animal, what would you be? What would you do?* Challenge children's thinking.

Use open-ended questions and prompts.
Open-ended questions are those that can be answered in a number of different ways. They can't be answered with a simple yes or no. Prompts such as, *I wonder what would happen if...,* encourage children to think creatively and express their ideas.

Read to children daily and talk about the story before, during, and after reading.
Discussions while reading aloud not only help children practice their language skills and increase their vocabularies, but they also aid comprehension. Make sure you read aloud two or more times a day to individuals, small groups, and/or the whole class

Include songs, rhymes, and fingerplays throughout the day.
By doing so, children learn new words, hear different forms of language, and develop an awareness of the rhymes, rhythms, and patterns of language.

Play language games and provide language materials.
During small- and large-group activities, play games that focus on language. For example, a game of "20 Questions" helps children learn how to ask questions while also developing reasoning skills.

Offer models for children to hear their own language.
If you are not fluent in all of the languages spoken in your classroom, try to find people who are proficient in them. This could be your assistant, family members, resource persons, or volunteers. Encourage these individuals to converse, play, read, and sing with children who are learning English. Communicate with families about topics of study and activities and encourage them to discuss these topics with their children in their home languages.

Share informational books that relate to the children's particular interests.
Such books offer opportunities to introduce children to new ideas and information and extend children's vocabulary and language about topics that go beyond the here-and-now.

Phonological Awareness

Phonological awareness (sometimes referred to as phonological sensitivity) is hearing and understanding the different sounds and patterns of spoken language. It includes the different ways oral language can be broken down into individual parts, for instance, separate sounds and syllables. For some children, hearing these different parts of spoken language can be difficult, because it requires them to attend to the sounds of speech separately from meaning.

Phonological awareness develops along a continuum, from simple skills (e.g., listening) to very complex skills (e.g., manipulating individual sounds in words). Each phonological awareness skill involves varying levels of difficulty.

Phonological awareness begins with **listening** to sounds in the environment. These beginning listening skills help children later attend to the separate sounds in words. The next skills are **rhyming** and **alliteration**. For preschool children, rhyming requires recognizing the sounds in the endings of words. Alliteration involves hearing similar initial sounds, such as in *big beautiful buttons.*

As children begin to understand how language works, they become aware that language is made up of words that are grouped together. After becoming aware of the beginning and ending sounds in words, children can be helped to hear the separate **syllables** in words. In preschool, children can clap the words of a sentence or tap rhythm sticks to mark the syllables in their names.

Another way to explore how words are put together is by examining **onset** and **rime**. *Onset* refers to the sounds before the first vowel in a syllable. *Rime* is the rest of the syllable, from the first vowel to the end. For example, in the word *ball*, *b* is the onset, and *all* is the rime. Preschoolers can be taught to play with onset and rhyme while reciting the *Jack Sprat* nursery rhyme or similar verses. When older children learn about word families (e.g., *ball, call, fall, tall*), they are paying attention to onset and rime.

At the more complex end of the continuum of phonological awareness, the focus is on the smallest unit of sound, the **phoneme**. When preschoolers play with words, they usually play with phonemes. For example, if you sing, "Dow, dow, dow your boat, gently down the stream," more than likely the children will say, "No! That's not right! It's *row*." In this playful way, they are paying attention to phonemes.

As children's phonological awareness skills advance, they learn to manipulate phonemes in many different ways. They blend and segment phonemes, or substitute one phoneme for another. These manipulation skills found at the most complex end of the continuum are called **phonemic awareness**. Research shows that these advanced skills are one of the most powerful predictors of success in learning to read.

The following chart illustrates the difference between beginning phonological awareness skills and more advanced skills. Notice that, for listening, most of the behaviors are at the beginning level. At the phoneme level, most of the skills are more advanced.

	Beginning Phonological Awareness Skills	More Advanced Phonological Awareness Skills
Listening	Attends to sounds in the environment Discriminates sounds that are the same and different Remembers sounds heard Discriminates one sound from many	
Rhyming	Joins in and repeats rhyming songs, fingerplays, and poems Fills in the missing rhyming word of a song, fingerplay, or story	Decides whether two words rhyme Chooses rhymes from non-rhyming alternatives Generates rhyming words in isolation from context
Alliteration	Participates in songs, stories, and rhymes with alliterative text Recognizes the similar initial sounds of words that begin the same way Identifies the beginning sound of familiar words	Generates a group of words that begin the same way
Sentences and Words	Claps separate words in a sentence Listens for a particular word or phrase	Blends and segments compound words
Syllables	Claps syllables of own name Claps syllables of familiar words	Identifies the syllables in two- and three-syllable words Blends syllables to form words Deletes syllables
Onset and Rime	Recites rhymes, songs, or fingerplays that focus on onset and rime Begins to separate initial sound from rest of word	Separates initial sound from rest of word Blends onset and rime to make words
Phoneme	Plays with the sounds of words	Matches sounds Counts phonemes Identifies sounds in words (beginning, ending, medial) Blends phonemes Segments words into separate phonemes Deletes phonemes Substitutes phonemes

Phonological awareness skills are promoted by songs, stories and rhymes. Children also develop understanding about sounds, letters, and words as they attempt to write. You will notice this in their play. When attempting to write a shopping list, a child may initially write a single letter to stand for an entire word (e.g., *M* for *milk*). Later on, she will begin to add more letters (e.g., *MK* for *milk*). You may hear the child say the word slowly to listen for the sounds while writing.

Children with language delays may have deficits in their ability to hear or process language sounds. Of course this affects their language development. Phonological awareness skills are particularly difficult for these children, so they may need more repetition of activities than other children.

English language learners have to distinguish phonemes in English that may not be part of their native languages. This may mean a child has difficulty hearing and/or pronouncing the sounds of English. English language learners may need more repetition of the songs, rhymes, and fingerplays you use in the classroom. Repetition gives them opportunities to develop greater understanding of the meaning of the words as well as the sounds.

Phonological awareness lays the groundwork for **phonics**. After children have a good understanding of the sounds of language, they begin to connect printed symbols, e.g., *M*, to their corresponding sounds, e.g., /m/. Be aware that phonics is not the same as phonological awareness, which involves only auditory skills and not sound-symbol correspondence.

What Does Research Say?

Development of Skills

Phonological awareness plays a crucial role in learning to read, and the development of this ability typically begins by about age 3 and improves gradually over many years (Snow, Burns, & Griffin, 1998).

Young children's phonological sensitivity is a strong predictor of later reading, writing, and spelling ability (National Early Literacy Panel, 2004).

There is a developmental progression from phonological awareness of "large" units of speech (such as rhymes, words, and syllables) to the "small" units of speech (e.g., phonemes) (Goswami & Bryant, 1990).

Phonological awareness skills are less likely to develop through incidental exposure (Sulzby & Teale, 1991).

Phonological awareness can be facilitated, and that facilitation can lead to reading improvement (Alexander, Anderson, Heilman, Voeller, & Torgesen, 1991).

Rhyming

Rhyming is one of the first skills to develop in phonological awareness (Snyder & Downey, 1997).

Young children become sensitive to the sound of rhyming words at an early age (Apel, 1997; Ball, 1993; Braunger, Lewis, & Hagans, 1997).

Young children are typically able to detect words that rhyme, even when other phonological skills have not developed (Whitehurst & Lonigan, 1998).

Children develop a sense of the sound structure of language by saying rhymes, singing, and reciting fingerplays (Jenkins & Bowen, 1994).

Rhyming and alliteration are significantly related to later reading success (Snowling & Stackhouse, 1996; MacLean, Bryant, & Bradley, 1987; Bradley & Bryant, 1978, 1993).

Rhyming may be an initial step toward phonemic awareness (MacLean, Bryant, & Bradley, 1987).

Alliteration

Alliteration skills typically begin developing around age three (Apel, 1997; Ball, 1993; Moats, 1998, MacLean, Bryant, & Bradley, 1987).

Alliteration requires children to pay attention to parts of words that are smaller than a syllable (Ball, 1993).

Word, Syllable, Onset and Rime Segmentation and Blending

Young children are first able to represent and manipulate more holistic units of speech (e.g., syllables) before they become able to segment phonemes (Fowler, 1991).

Onset and rime develop earlier than phoneme awareness and also correlate to later reading ability. (Bradley & Bryant, 1983; MacLean, Bryant, & Bradley, 1987).

Onset and rime awareness may be the key to unlocking phonemic awareness (Adams, 1990).

Phonemes

Few children acquire phonemic awareness spontaneously (Adams, Treiman, & Pressley, 1998).

Phonemic awareness is the most potent predictor of success in learning to read. It is more highly related to reading than tests of general intelligence, reading readiness, and listening comprehension (Stanovich, 1986, 1994).

Phonemic awareness is central in learning to read and spell (Ehri, 1984).

Preschool, kindergarten, and primary grade teachers should provide linguistically rich classroom environments where children play with sounds (Adams, 1990; Griffith & Olson, 1992; Mattingly, 1984; Yopp, 1992).

What Is the Teacher's Role in Promoting Phonological Awareness?

Children differ in their need for instruction in developing phonological awareness. Teachers therefore need to use a range of strategies with individual children, small groups, and large groups. Remember that phonological awareness activities should be playful and engaging, as well as intentional.

Know each child's level of phonological awareness and provide appropriate experiences.
You may have some children who have already progressed beyond the very earliest stages of phonological awareness. They may demonstrate their skills during everyday activities and be ready for more advanced activities. However, you may have some children who have not been introduced to language play. They may need more direct teaching to progress along the continuum. As with all skills, it is important to know where each child is developmentally and to support his learning appropriately.

Use songs, stories, and rhymes that play with language.
Preschool teachers have always included songs, stories, and rhymes in their daily activities. Now research confirms the importance of these language forms in promoting phonological awareness. Be aware of the phonological awareness skills you can encourage by using particular songs, stories, and rhymes. Informally but intentionally, draw children's attention to the sounds of language when you share them.

Encourage children's curiosity about and experimentation with language.
When you model curiosity about language, it can be contagious! Demonstrate your enjoyment of words, and children will soon follow. Invite children to make up new verses to songs and rhymes.

Include phonological awareness activities in your daily schedule.
Throughout the day there are many opportunities to promote phonological awareness. Consider saying a chant during cleanup, dismissing children to go outside by the first sound in their names, reading a Dr. Seuss book at story time, tapping syllables with rhythm sticks during group time, or playing a game with sounds during small-group activities.

Explain to families the importance of sharing songs, stories, and rhymes with their children.
Suggest that they sing songs from their childhoods or familiar songs and rhymes that help build phonological awareness. Songs such as *This Old Man*, *Skitamarinky Dinky Dink*, *Polly Wolly Doodle*, *Baby Bumblebee*, and *Michael Finnegan* are examples of old favorites. There are also many "oldies but goodies" that families might remember and enjoy singing together. Encourage families of children who are English language learners to sing and to recite chants and rhymes in their home languages.

Knowledge of Print

Knowledge of print refers to all the concepts related to how print is organized and used to convey meaning. To make sense of written language, children need to understand how sounds, words, and sentences are represented in writing. They need to know that thoughts and feelings are written in a particular way.

Children's development of print knowledge varies according to their interests and experience with language. Children begin to understand that print carries meaning but that written language is different from oral language. They develop an understanding that print serves a number of purposes in our society (**functions of print**). They also learn that print has distinct features and forms (**forms of print**), and that print is organized in a particular way (**print conventions**). An important goal during the preschool years is therefore to introduce children to a variety of texts.

Functions of Print

Print has many purposes, and messages can be conveyed through many different forms of print. In the world around us, we read signs to find out where to go or what to do. We depend on print to show us where things are located in a store, and we fill out forms to provide information to others. We read messages, menus, instructions, and labels. In the classroom, print serves similar functions:

- Print is used to identify individuals and to show ownership (e.g., names on cubbies, sign-up sheets, personal signatures, authors' and illustrators' names on books).

- Print helps children and adults recall information and make choices (e.g., answer a question, choose a drink for snack).

- Print encourages interactions with others (e.g., thank-you notes, greeting cards, message boards).

- Print gives directions or tells someone what to do (e.g., recipes, instructions for hand-washing).

- Print is used to communicate information (e.g., class address book, observation logs).

- Print is a way for children to express their ideas and feelings (e.g., dictation, journal writing).

Most young children are very aware of environmental print, that is, the print that they see in their everyday surroundings. If not, teachers should call attention to this print, talk about it, and explain what it means. Children are often familiar with logos of businesses they visit frequently, such as restaurants and stores, as well as print on products they use often, such as toothpaste, snacks, and cereal. You can also help children read environmental print by designing learning activities that involve it.

Forms of Print

As children become more aware of print, they begin to notice that print has different forms. Letters and words have distinct features, different configurations, names, and sounds; a list requires a format that is different from a letter to a friend; you address an envelope in a particular way and create a sign in another. By planning experiences that involve different forms of written communication and offering children opportunities to read and write on their own during play, teachers promote children's understanding of the forms of print. The different forms of print that preschoolers use include:

- lists

- signs and labels

- newspapers, magazines, and pamphlets

- menus

- forms

- letters and envelopes

- greeting cards

- books

- directories, address books

- instructions

- charts and schedules

- recipes

- notes and messages

- e-mail

- journals

- captions

- calendars, appointment books

Conventions of Print

Rules govern the way in which print works. Readers must know these key concepts:

- Print is a form of language. Each spoken word can be written down and read, and each written word can be spoken aloud.

- Printed words function differently from pictures. Pictures support the print and can be used to predict and confirm the text.

- Books are read from the front cover to the back, page by page, in English and many other languages.

- Print is read from left to right and top to bottom, in English and many other languages.

- Letters are written in two forms, uppercase and lowercase.

- Letters represent sounds, letters are grouped together to form words, and words can be organized into sentences.

- Spaces are used between words.

- Punctuation serves a purpose.

Children learn the conventions of print by using environmental print, participating in interactive read aloud times, and seeing and hearing adults model reading and writing. Teachers call attention to these conventions every day, as they work with individual children and with small and large groups. For example, as children participate in read aloud times, teachers demonstrate that printed words function differently from pictures and that readers attend particularly to words to find meaning. Teachers call attention to the way print is organized on the page, that is, words are typically ordered from top to bottom and left to right on a page, and the text continues on the next page when it is turned. In addition to discussing the story, teachers talk about the title and the author's and illustrator's names.

When children see adults model writing, they see firsthand where to start writing on a page, how print is ordered from left to right, and how to return to the left side of the page after reading a line of writing. They listen to the teacher talk about using an uppercase (capital) letter to begin a sentence or a name and that a period tells the reader to stop.

What Does Research Say?

Development of print awareness

Children's knowledge of print concepts is an important predictor of later literacy achievement (Clay, 1979; McCormick & Mason, 1986, Wells, 1985).

Young children's concepts about print are a strong predictor of later reading, writing, and spelling ability (National Early Literacy Panel, 2004).

Children as young as three years old know that print carries a message (McGee, Richgels, Charlsworth, 1986).

Children learn the uses of written language before they learn the forms (Gundlach, McLane, Scott, & McNamee, 1985; Taylor, 1983).

Prior to entering kindergarten, many children begin to construct meaning from print (Downing, 1986).

Before entering kindergarten, children learn print conventions, including directionality, the concept of a word, and punctuation (Clay, 1993).

Children learn about print from a variety of sources, and, in the process, they come to realize that although print differs from speech, it carries messages just like speech (Morrow & Smith, 1990).

Knowledge of print conventions is children's understanding of the way text works (Johnston, 2002; Whitehurst & Lonigan, 1998).

Knowledge of print conventions is an integral part in the process of learning to read (Dickinson & Tabors, 1991; Mason, 1992).

Big books help children develop understandings about books, print, and the meaning of the text (Holdaway, 1979).

Role of adults

Knowledge of print concepts develops through direct contact with books and explicit modeling by skilled readers, as well as through exposure to environmental print. These experiences are lacking in some homes (Adams, 1990).

Reading to children contributes to their awareness of the functions, form, and conventions of print (Mason, 1980).

When adults supported children's learning in a print-rich environment, children were found to learn significantly more words in context than their peers who experienced a print-enriched environment without adult interactions (Vukelich, 1994).

Environment

Print exposure has substantial effects on the development of reading skills at older ages when children are already reading (Allen, Cipielewski, & Stanovich, 1992; Anderson & Freebody, 1981; Cunningham & Stanovich, 1991, 1998; Echols, West, Stanovich, & Zehr, 1996; Nagy, Anderson, & Herman, 1987).

Awareness of environmental print (e.g., signs and logos) in four-year-olds may be indicative of a print-rich home environment, a factor associated with early literacy development (Dickinson & DeTemple, 1998).

A central goal during the preschool years is to enhance children's exposure to and concepts about print (Clay, 1979, 1991; Holdaway, 1979; Teale, 1984; Stanovich & West, 1989).

What Is the Teacher's Role in Promoting Children's Knowledge of Print?

Print concepts are learned gradually over an extended period of time. Drawing children's attention to the features of print while sharing books, and supporting their efforts to use print in functional ways during everyday activities, will help children become readers and writers.

Create a print-rich environment.
Include print in the environment that is meaningful, functional, and interesting. Add common signs such as *Exit, Stop, Open,* and *Closed,* as well as printed logos from familiar products or businesses. Design relevant labels; signs; charts; and written-response activities, such as sign-in sheets or waiting lists. Use charts to take attendance and identify jobs on a daily basis. Draw children's attention to the letters and words as appropriate. It is important, however, not to clutter the environment with too much print.

Display print at a child's eye level.
Put yourself at a child's eye level in the classroom. Can you see the signs, charts, information, and other print in the room?

Use story and informational books and planned writing experiences to teach about print.
Children need materials to support their literacy development. Intentionally plan to read books aloud to large groups, small groups, and individuals and have books available for children's independent use. Place both fiction and non-fiction books in various interest areas so children can find the information they need and discover purposes for print. Stock the interest areas with writing tools so children can use symbols to express themselves.

Model literate behavior.
Intentionally model reading and writing in meaningful, purposeful ways. Talk about what you are doing and why you are doing it. Make it a practice to write classroom materials (posters, charts, schedules, recipes, labels, etc.) in the children's presence rather than when children are not around. Describe the process as children watch you write.

Make a point to distinguish between children's writing and drawing.
When you are talking to children about drawing and writing, use the words *drawing* and *writing* in your comments. For example, you might say, *You drew a red dress on your mom's picture. I see that you wrote her name over here.*

Draw children's attention to the conventions of print.
As you record a child's dictation, talk about where you are starting to write, why you are beginning a sentence with an uppercase letter, and what the punctuation mark means at the end of the sentence. When you read a book or a chart, move your finger under the words to help children learn directionality.

Talk about the uses of print.

Draw children's attention to the many ways print is used around them. Refer to the newspaper to check the day's weather. Read the lunch menu aloud. Talk about the note that a father sent about a classmate who is not feeling well.

Point out concepts about books each time you read to children.

Talk about where the writing starts on the page and which way to proceed when reading. Draw children's attention to the print on the page so they learn that readers attend particularly to the print, not the pictures.

Invite children to help you make signs and labels in the classroom.

By doing so, children will learn that print has a purpose. For instance, offer Ben markers and paper to create a *Do not touch* sign for his Lego creation. Ask Juwan help you make a feeding schedule for the class pet.

Structure times during the week when children use writing to anticipate a future experience.

They might write or draw about something they are looking forward to doing, such as going to a birthday party.

Encourage children to write words that are important to them.

The most important words to preschoolers are the ones that are in their hearts and heads. These include their own names and the names of family members, best friends, and pets. Encourage the children to write these words as they create drawings, messages, or greeting cards. As they do, they will be making a connection between spoken and printed words.

Observe children throughout the day and consider ways of supporting their play with print.

Think of ways you can enhance children's play with reading and writing. Offer paper and markers for making signs, writing tickets, or creating appointment books. Add books, newspapers, and magazines to pretend waiting rooms and home settings. Think of the many ways that print is a part of your life, and then offer print to children as they imitate real-life situations.

Letters and Words

Knowledge of letters and words is an important component of literacy, and it involves more than reciting the ABC song or recognizing individual letters. Readers must understand that a letter is a symbol that represents one or more sounds. A more complex level of understanding requires knowing that these symbols can be grouped together to form words and that words have meanings. The idea that written spellings correspond to spoken words is called the **alphabetic principle**. Children's understanding of the alphabetic principle is a predictor of future reading success.

Children demonstrate their understanding of the concept of a word when they match each spoken word to a printed word. You might notice children pretending to read and touching each word on the page as they recite a narrative. These children understand the concept of a word, and they realize that readers attend particularly to printed words rather than pictures.

Teachers help children learn specific skills related to letters and words. Children learn to

- recognize and name letters

- recognize beginning letters in familiar words, especially in their own names

- relate some letters to the sounds they represent

- match spoken words with written words, one-to-one

Most children learn to recite the alphabet at a young age by singing the ABC song. Then they learn the shapes of the letters made familiar by the song, in other words, they recognize the letters of the alphabet. Learning letter names helps children learn some of the sounds that letters represent. For example, if a child knows the name of the letter *e*, he also knows the long sound of *e*. Once children gain confidence in their ability to recognize letters, they begin to attend to their sounds. Then they group the letters together to write words, ordering the letters in the way they think the sounds are ordered.

Children tend to recognize the symbols of the alphabet in a particular developmental sequence.

- They first notice if a letter has straight lines or curved lines.

- Letters that are round (e.g., *O, C*) are usually recognized first.

- Letters that have curved lines (e.g., *P, S*) come next.

- Letters having curved lines with intersections (e.g., *B, R*) are distinguished from those without intersections (e.g., *S, J*).

- Letters with diagonal lines (e.g., *K, X*) are the last to be recognized.

While this progression is typical, children often recognize the letters in their own names first, because these are the letters of the words that are most important to them. Including activities with children's own names is an excellent way to make letters and words meaningful. After children learn the letters in their own names, they often learn the letters of other words that are significant to them, such as the names of family members and pets.

As children write, teachers can observe their understanding of letters and words. In their early writing attempts, children often use a single letter to represent a word, such as *S* for *soup*. This demonstrates their understanding of beginning sounds. Other children may write letters that represent beginning and ending sounds, such as *LV* for *love*. As their phonological awareness becomes more refined, they hear more sounds in words, and their invented spellings become more accurate and conventional. You will also notice their use of spaces between letters, groups of letters, and words, signifying an understanding of the concept of a word.

If you are working with English language learners, be aware that some letters in their native language may represent the same sounds in English and other letters may not. For example, while vowels look the same in Spanish (*a, e, i, o, u*), they are named differently and correspond to different sounds. Knowing this, teachers help children learn to say and understand words in English before expecting them to be able to distinguish the sounds accurately or use invented spelling (Peregoy & Boyle, 2000).

What Does Research Say?

Alphabet

 A pre-reader's alphabet knowledge is one of the single best predictors of eventual reading achievement (Adams, 1990; Stevenson & Newman, 1986).

Young children's alphabet knowledge is a strong predictor of later reading, writing, and spelling ability (National Early Literacy Panel, 2004).

The ability to name letters is a predictor of early reading success (Chall, 1967; Torgesen, 1998).

Letter names provide relevant information about the sounds they represent, and beginning readers appear to use this information in reading and writing (Ehri & Wilce, 1986; Read, 1971; Treiman, 1993).

Children's own names are highly motivating for learning letter names (Share & Jaffe-Gur, 1999; Bloodgood, 1999).

Preschool children's letter knowledge is a unique predictor of growth in phonological sensitivity across one year (Burgess & Lonigan, 1998).

Exposure to alphabet books may increase children's letter knowledge and phonological processing skills (Baker, Fernandez-Fein, Scher, & Williams, 1998; Murray, Stahl, & Ivey, 1996).

Children who can instantly and effortlessly recognize the letters of the alphabet are able to focus their attention on the other literacy tasks (Hall & Moats, 1999).

Alphabet books that use alliteration help increase phonemic awareness (Murray, Stahl, & Ivey, 1998).

The shapes of letters are learned by distinguishing one character from another by its type of spatial features (Gibson & Levin, 1975).

Letter-sound relationships

Familiarity of the letters of the alphabet and awareness of the speech sounds, or phonemes, to which they correspond are strong predictors of the ease or difficulty with which a child learns to read (Adams, 1990)

A beginning reader who has difficulty recognizing and distinguishing the individual letters of the alphabet will have difficulty learning the sounds those letters represent (Bond & Dykstra, 1967; Chall, 1967; Mason, 1980).

Before children learn to decode words in and out of context, they become able to use some letter-sound information to recognize, remember, and spell words. This is possible even if they are not taught the letter sounds, because the names of the alphabet letters provide clues to the phonemic representations in words (Mason & Allen, 1986).

What Is the Teacher's Role in Promoting Knowledge of Letters and Words?

Children gain knowledge of the alphabet when teachers plan meaningful activities and experiences that include letter recognition. These activities range from reading alphabet books; manipulating magnetic letters; playing alphabet matching games; singing the alphabet song; helping children learn to recognize the letters in their names; and writing, or attempting to write, letters and words.

Focus on letters and words as part of meaningful activities.

Talk about letters, sounds, and words as you take dictation and read it back, compose messages, and help children write during their daily activities. The alphabet is a system of symbols. Taken alone, each letter is of limited value. When letters are used in combination with other letters, words are created. For this reason, teaching the alphabet through "Letter of the Week" activities confuses some children about the purpose of letters in relation to written words. Such contrived activities are not the best use of classroom time.

Display the alphabet. Post the alphabet at the children's eye level.

Make it more meaningful by labeling each letter with a child's name that begins with that letter. Provide smaller alphabet strips or cards in the Library Area so a child can place a strip nearby and refer to it easily while writing.

Add alphabet books in the Library Area and other interest areas.

Some alphabet books with story lines are ideal for group reading, such as *Chicka Chicka Boom Boom* (Bill Martin, Jr.) and *The Alphabet Tree* (Leo Lionni). Other alphabet books are great for sharing one-on-one, but they are not ideal for group reading because there is no storyline. As you and the child explore an alphabet book together, talk about the letters, their shapes, and the names of pictured objects that begin with the letter. When selecting alphabet books, make sure that the pictures begin with a single letter sound, rather than a blend. Seeing "*S* is for *ship*" might confuse a child who is beginning to make the sound-symbol connection for *S*. Similarly, seeing "*C* is for *circle*" might also cause confusion, because most children learn the hard *c* sound (as in *cookie*) first. In addition, choose books that use upper- and lowercase letters. Make sure books have simple illustrations that children will recognize and that each pictured object has only one common name (not, for example, dog/puppy). English language learners benefit greatly from books that focus on a single word and picture per page.

Sing the alphabet song.
Singing the alphabet song helps familiarize children with the names and order of the letters. Sing it slowly enough so that the letter names do not run together. For example, pronounce *l, m, n, o* separately and not as one word, *elemeno.* For variety, sing it to a different tune, change the tempo, or start and stop at different parts of the song. Have a large alphabet chart handy so you can point to the letters as you sing them.

Teach about shapes.
Learning about shapes not only involves mathematical concepts, but it is also important in letter recognition. Written letters are combinations of straight lines, curved lines, slanted lines, circles, dots, and triangles. As you help children learn to recognize and write letters, describe their shapes; e.g., *Olivia, your name starts with an O. It looks like a circle, doesn't it?*

Encourage sensory exploration of the alphabet.
Children obtain and interpret information more readily when several of their senses are stimulated. They make important connections and understand concepts more easily when the learning experience includes sight, sound, and touch. By seeing and feeling letters, they not only learn the names of letters, but also their shapes and how they are formed. Offer children a variety of ways to explore the alphabet: by using sandpaper, salt trays, clay, magnetic letters, and felt letters and by forming letters with their bodies.

Provide opportunities and encourage children to write while they play.
Through their play, children explore writing for different purposes. As they write, observe their knowledge and use of the alphabet.

Help children create a personal word collection.
Write words that are important to each child on cards, such as the names of people in their lives and pets. Talk about the words as you write them. Store the word cards in a special box or envelope or on a ring. Children can refer to their personal word collections when creating greeting cards or writing captions for drawings.

Promote letter-sound association and phonological awareness when helping children learn about the alphabet.
As you look at alphabet books or guide children in their writing, talk about the sounds that correspond with them. Draw children's attention to the sounds of words: *This sentence has lots of words that begin with the /m/ sound:* merry, music, melody, *and* Max. *Can you think of someone in our class whose name begins the same way?*

Comprehension

Comprehension, the process of making meaning, is the goal of reading instruction. It is connecting what you read and hear with your experience. Your background knowledge helps you understand the meaning of the language. You connect the language you read and hear with personal experiences, information you have already learned, and concepts you remember. The more the language of a text relates to your prior knowledge, the more you will be able to make sense of what is being read. Each reader brings a broad range of background information to any text. Rather than merely calling words, the reader constructs understanding.

Although most preschoolers are not yet reading, comprehension is still important to them. They try to comprehend stories being read and told, oral directions and information, conversations, and subject area content (e.g., science, math, and music concepts). Listening comprehension skills are useful when children begin to read.

Through language-rich activities, such as read aloud times, conversations, and engaging in firsthand experiences, children develop comprehension skills in an integrated, meaningful way. Comprehension is enhanced when the content of an experience is interesting, relevant, and worth learning. Children who are learning to read must

- expand general background knowledge

- increase vocabulary

- understand the grammar, or structure, of the language

- make connections

  - construct, compare, and combine ideas

  - notice similarities and differences in information

  - recall and apply prior knowledge to new situations

- listen to and understand speech

- question, predict, hypothesize, and use language to process information

- judge the importance of particular information

- be motivated to learn

When preschoolers attempt to make connections between stories they hear, conversations, and personal experiences, they use some of the same cognitive processes that older children and adults use when they read. This ability to make connections to text strongly predicts future reading comprehension, even more than the other basic literacy skills (Van den Broek, 2001).

Encouraging children to find meaning should be the primary goal of all literacy activities. Comprehension skills begin to develop long before children learn to decode print. It begins with building background knowledge about the world and about language in order to understand and communicate.

Background Knowledge

Good readers have background knowledge that helps them to understand language. As they hear more language, they increase their background knowledge. A major goal in preschool is to provide many firsthand experiences to build children's knowledge of the world. Meaningful experiences are crucial to children's development, and talking about them promotes both language and cognitive development. Encouraging children to reflect on their experiences, ask questions, make predictions, hypothesize, and experiment helps them construct understandings about the world and about language.

As children engage in many varied experiences, they learn new words. They hear words, such as *squishy, damp, vehicle, experiment,* and *patterns,* in meaningful contexts. They not only hear the words, they experience the meaning of the words, using all of their senses to take in information and construct understandings. Later, as they encounter the words in print, they will be able to use those understandings to comprehend the text. The more you help children develop understandings through experience, the more likely they are to use their understandings in new contexts.

Comprehension of a story depends a great deal on the child's background knowledge. When selecting stories to read aloud, consider these questions:

- Do the children have the background knowledge needed to understand the story?

- Will the topic of the story interest the children?

- How complex is the language of the story?

- How many new words are introduced in the text?

- Is this book the right length for the children?

You can assess children's listening comprehension in many ways. You can observe how they ask questions, focus their attention, apply the information they hear, and incorporate what was heard in their play. You will know whether children are comprehending a story if, while listening, they

- describe the details of the story so far

- recognize the sequence of events

- predict outcomes

- make associations

- relate the story to personal experiences

Follow-up activities will also help you determine whether a child has comprehended a story. When you observe children retelling a story using props, note the complexity of the story details and sequence that they remember.

What Does Research Say?

Active experiences aid comprehension

Children who engage in frequent activities with books have larger, more literate vocabularies and learn to read better than children who have few book experiences (Dickinson & Tabors, 1991; Wells, 1986).

Dramatic play is related to comprehension in powerful, yet complex, ways. Metaplay is a significant factor in increasing story comprehension (Christie, 1983; Pellegrini & Galda, 1982; Saltz, Dixon, & Johnson, 1997; Silvern, Williamson, & Waters, 1983).

Story retelling helps children develop a sense of story structure and understandings about lanuguage that contribute to their comprehension of text (Morrow, 1985).

Reading aloud

Children who heard stories in small-group settings performed significantly better on comprehension tests than children who heard stories read one to one, who in turn performed significantly better than children who heard stories read to the whole class (Morrow, 1987, 1988; Morrow & Smith, 1990).

Children who heard stories read in a small group or one-to-one setting generated significantly more comments and questions than did children in the whole-class setting. Thus, reading to children in small groups offers as much interaction as one-to-one readings, and it appears to lead to greater comprehension than whole-class or even one-to-one readings (Morrow, 1987, 1988: Morrow & Smith, 1990).

Children's comments and questions increase and become more interpretive and evaluative when they have listened to repeated readings of the same story. Children also elaborated more and offered more interpretations after repeated readings of the same story (Pappas, 1991).

The primary goal of a read-aloud event is the construction of understanding from the interactive process between adult and child (Vygotsky, 1978).

A teacher's reading style has an impact on children's comprehension of stories (Roser & Martinez, 1985).

Familiarity that comes with repeated readings enables children to reenact stories or attempt to read them on their own (Sulzby, 1985).

Background knowledge

Comprehension is essential to future reading success because it enables children to process what they hear and read (Teale & Yokota, 2000).

Reader's background knowledge is important for understanding texts (Anderson & Pearson, 1984; Anderson, Spiro, & Montague, 1977; Bransford & Johnson, 1972).

Vocabulary knowledge is a major correlate of comprehension ability (Davis, 1968).

Children learn real-world knowledge from picture books (Crain-Thoreson & Dale, 1992).

Children identified as "low achievers" in school have limitations in their prior knowledge and understandings rather than any limitations in their ability to learn (Anderson, Spiro, & Montague, 1977).

What Is the Teacher's Role in Building Comprehension?

Preschoolers develop their comprehension skills through experiences that promote oral and written language skills, such as discussions, sociodramatic play, retellings, and interactive reading. Reading and re-reading many different types of books aid in building comprehension. Most important is the teacher's role in helping children make meaningful connections between new information and experiences and what they already know.

Building Background Knowledge and Vocabulary

Help children connect new information and ideas to what they already know.
Introduce and discuss new words in meaningful contexts. Provide experiences to help them learn what things are and how they work. Find out what children know about a topic and have them develop questions to guide their exploration. Discuss what they learn, helping them to link old and new knowledge. Use phrases such as *How is* ____ *like* ____? *Have you ever* ____? *What do you know about* _____? Promote their ability to solve problems and figure things out.

Encourage children to ask questions when they do not understand.
Many children ask *Why?* or *How come?* Others do not. Children who do not actively seek to understand are at a disadvantage as learners. You can model requests for clarification and more information. For example, you can say, *I'm not sure I understand,* and ask, *What do you mean?*

Extend and expand the topic.
Give children new information to expand their understandings about the world. When they talk about new words and ideas, actively listen to what they are saying. Respect their ideas and add new information to what they already know.

Promoting Listening Comprehension

Talk with children frequently throughout the day.
Use these opportunities to help children learn new information and clarify their thoughts and ideas. Talk about what you see and hear. Wonder aloud. Help children learn the give-and-take of conversations, that is, *I talk...you listen; you talk...I listen.*

Use language that is easy for children to understand.
As you introduce new words and ideas to children, explain meanings in language they can relate to and understand. This will help them connect new information with prior knowledge.

Help children understand language by rephrasing it when necessary.

When a visitor comes or when you are on a study trip, rephrase some of the conversation so children can understand what is being communicated. Rephrasing may also be necessary while reading stories.

Play listening games.

Games help children sharpen their listening comprehension skills. They learn to attend to particular sounds and words and focus on important information.

Help children learn to follow and give directions.

Play games with rules. Encourage children to create games and explain the directions to others. Use routines (e.g., setting the table, putting materials away, transitioning from one activity to another) to practice following directions. These games and routines sharpen children's listening comprehension.

Promoting Story Comprehension

Read aloud to small groups of children.

Children who listen to stories in small groups are able to share conversations about the stories. They learn from each other's comments and questions. In addition, a personal experience shared by one child in relation to a story may help other children make personal connections to it.

Prepare children for the reading by taking a *picture walk*.

Introduce the story by previewing the pictures. Ask the children to predict what the story is about by looking at the cover. Turn the pages slowly and encourage them to talk about what they see. As you read the story, talk about the characters, the setting, and the sequence of events, and help the children think about whether their predictions were correct.

Be sure to show children the pictures as you read.

Talk about the pictures informally as you read the story, to support children's comprehension of the narrative.

When reading to children, encourage them to ask questions, make predictions, talk about the story, and connect new ideas what they already know.

Ask questions and make comments, such as *Have you ever had a really bad day? Do you think a giant is real or make-believe? Where do you think Corduroy will find his button? This tugboat is just like the one we saw on our field trip.*

Facilitate story retellings.

Retelling stories requires children to think about what they have heard and to restate it in a way that others can understand. They must remember details of the story, such as the characters, setting, and order of events, and they must use their own language. (In chapter 3, Teaching Strategies, you will learn more about story retelling.)

Books and Other Texts

When children understand books and other texts, they learn that written language serves many purposes. They realize that written language is a valuable tool for learning about the world and a way to communicate with others.

To increase children's understanding of books and other texts, teachers give children experience with a wide variety of books from numerous categories, or genres, and help them develop concepts about books and book-handling skills.

Experience With Various Types of Books

Children need extensive experience with many different types, or genres, of books. Each type serves a different purpose and is read differently. The most familiar type of book in preschool classrooms is the **narrative picture book,** or **storybook.** As children learn to read, stories are an important part of their learning. They learn, for example, that to read a narrative book you start at the beginning and read through to the end, although not necessarily in one sitting. Experience with stories and discussions about them builds a solid foundation for literacy. Through storybooks, children learn story elements such as characters, setting, dialogue, and the sequence of events. While they may not know these terms, they talk about these elements during interactive read aloud times and story retellings. The more children hear narrative stories and discuss them, the more they will learn about how they are organized. Gaining this sense of story is very important to children's comprehension.

Other types of books offer other learning opportunities. **Wordless books** allow readers to use their imaginations to create their own narratives. **Poetry** is structured differently from prose. **Informational books** are used to learn new concepts and find answers to particular kinds of questions. Some informational books are structured as a story, while others are not read from beginning to end. As children gain an understanding of the purposes of different types of books, they learn basic rules about how each book genre is structured and how it is meant to be read.

When preschoolers have experience with different categories, or genres, of books, they begin to understand that language can be structured differently for various purposes. The language of print is usually different from that of conversations and from what is heard on television. Written language is usually more complex and abstract, and it makes different demands on the reader. The language of books usually has more formal grammatical structures and is more descriptive than casual speech. Usually, there is more varied vocabulary in books than in conversations. The language of children's books is also structured to help children attend to the sounds of language in ways that conversations do not.

With adult guidance, children notice how the language of picture books differs from that used in an informational books and poetry. In addition to narrative picture books, some examples of the various genres of early childhood literature include:

- informational, or nonfiction, books (*The Way Things Work* by David Macaulay; *Me on a Map* by Joan Sweeney)

- concept books (*What is Black and White?* by Petr Horacek; *Fish Eyes* and *Eating the Alphabet* by Lois Ehlert)

- wordless books (*Good Dog, Carl* by Alexandra Day; *Changes, Changes* by Pat Hutchins)

- contemporary fiction (*Uptown* by Brian Collier; *I Love My Hair* by Natasha Tarpley)

- fantasy (*Harold and the Purple Crayon* by Crockett Johnson; *Where the Wild Things Are* by Maurice Sendak)

- fairy tales and folktales (*Anansi the Spider* by Gerald McDermott; *Sleeping Beauty*)

- fables (*The Hare and The Tortoise* and *The Lion and the Mouse* by Aesop)

- historical fiction (*Giorgio's Village* by Tomie dePaola; *Tough Boris* by Mem Fox)

- biographies and autobiographies (*Martin's Big Words: The Life of Dr. Martin Luther King, Jr.* by Doreen Rappaport; *The Art Lesson* by Tomie dePaola)

- poetry (*Wake Up House! Rooms Full of Poems* by Dee Lillegard; *A Child's Garden of Verses* by Robert Louis Stevenson; *Mother Goose* by Blanche Fisher Wright)

- songbooks (*Cumbayah* by Floyd Cooper; *Philadelphia Chickens* by Sandra Boykin and Michael Ford)

Children also learn that there are other materials to read besides books. They can read magazines, message boards, menus, cookbooks, programs, lists, brochures, charts, signs, computer information, journals, letters and cards, circulars, billboards, and instruction books. Each serves a different purpose, is formatted in a different way, and is designed for a particular audience. When children are familiar with a particular form of text, they know how to approach a similar text.

What Does Research Say?

Reading aloud

When children are read to, they develop knowledge about books and the routines and language used to share them (Durkin, 1966; Ninio & Bruner, 1978; Pappas & Brown, 1987; Sulzby, 1985).

Through storybook reading, children begin to learn about narrative structure (Heath, Branscombe, & Thomas, 1986; Sulzby, 1985).

Reading to children enhances background information and a sense of story structure. It also familiarizes children with the language of books (Cullinan, 1992; Morrow, 1985).

Children with storybook experience learn how to handle a book and are familiar with its front-to-back progression. They also become familiar with story structure (beginning, middle, and end), as well as the concept of authorship (Smith, 1978).

Children who are read to frequently will "read" their favorite books by themselves, by trying to imitate the oral and written language routines of their literate models (Sulzby & Teale, 1987, 1991).

Book-reading interactions provide children an opportunity to understand stories in addition to models of literary language and structures not typically found in daily speech (Cochran-Smith, 1984; Purcell-Gates, 1988).

Children's initial questions and comments during story readings are related to pictures and the meaning of the story. Later, they pay more attention to the names of letters, the reading of individual words, or attempts to sound out words (Morrow, 1987; Roser & Martinez, 1985; Yaden, 1985).

Informational texts

Greater attention to informational texts will make children better readers and writers of informational text (Christie, 1984, 1987).

Children are able to respond to and learn from informational texts in sophisticated ways (Hicks, 1995).

Young children can learn about and from informational texts. Exposure to informational texts results in fast-developing knowledge of expository text structure and book language (Duke & Kays, 1998).

Engaging with books

Understanding the structure or characteristics of texts is a key to later reading and writing success (Gunn, Simmons, & Kameenui, 1995; Mason & Allen, 1986)

While young children consider each page of a book as a separate unit, older children respond to each page as part of a complete story (Sulzby, 1985).

What Is the Teacher's Role in Understanding Books and Other Texts?

First, teachers prepare an environment rich with children's literature from a wide range of genres. They intentionally teach concepts about books and help children understand that information and ideas can be found in many types of text.

Use a variety of genres when you read to children.
Give children experience with picture books, including folk- and fairy tales; poetry; and informational books. Call attention to how ideas are presented in different ways in various types of books. Talk about how these books are the same and different.

Include quality children's literature throughout the classroom.
Children benefit from experience with the rich language of books, beautiful illustrations, and stories that help them learn concepts and information about the world. In addition to reading books to children, make books available in interest areas where children may handle them.

Use books as sources of information.
Model how to search for information in a book. If a child sees a spider on the playground and wonders if it is poisonous, refer to an encyclopedia or book about spiders. Together, look in the index to find the page number. Read the information to the child and show him the picture. If you know that a child is interested in big machines, locate books related to that topic. By matching books to children's interests, teachers can build on children's natural curiosity.

Encourage children to become authors and illustrators and to produce different types of print materials.
Suggest that they make books of various genres, such as picture dictionaries and alphabet books, informational "how-to" books, and song books. Encourage them to make up their own versions of stories and add their names as the authors and illustrators.

Provide children with opportunities to use various other texts in the context of their play.
Observe children and brainstorm ways of adding literacy materials to extend their play. Offer children many forms of print, such as menus, cookbooks, directories, coupons, empty product containers, manuals, magazines, newspapers, schedules, brochures, catalogs, paper, pencils, and markers, and envelopes.

Increase children's general knowledge of the world with informational books.
Place these books throughout the classroom where children can refer to them in their play. Books about fish might be displayed next to the aquarium; a book about bridges or castles might inspire play in the Block Area; and a book on drawing will encourage children's exploration in the Art Area.

inside this chapter

2 Planning Your Literacy Program

Knowledge of the components of literacy prepares teachers to plan a literacy program. Planning for literacy learning is active and continuous, and it involves all staff members in finding ways to meet the individual needs of each child and the group as a whole.

Before teaching, think about these questions:

- What do I want children to know and be able to do?

- What essential dispositions am I fostering?

- How will I evaluate and assess the children's learning?

During teaching, think about these questions:

- Are children learning what I expected?

- Is unanticipated learning occurring?

- Are things going as planned?

After teaching, ask:

- What worked?

- What needs to be changed?

- What is the evidence?

When planning is careful and tailored to children's needs, children's efforts are more likely to be successful. Without ongoing planning, learning is left to chance.

In order to plan effectively and to address the questions mentioned above, teachers need to know the *goals and objectives of literacy learning*. The 2 goals and 13 objectives specifically related to language and literacy are listed below. Because children develop language and literacy skills as they work in many areas of the Curriculum, you will see a chart of the 50 objectives (Goals and Objectives at a Glance) as well. Many have implications for language development. For example, as you observe children's social/emotional development and consider objective 10, "Plays well with other children," there will probably be many opportunities to observe language development as well.

With these learning objectives in mind, teachers work to create a *literacy-rich physical environment* that supports and stimulates language and literacy use. Next, teachers think about how to incorporate *literacy experiences throughout the day* purposefully, in all routines and activities.

Because today's preschool classrooms are so diverse, teachers must think about ways to *meet the needs of all children*. They have to explore ways to challenge children with advanced skills, and to accommodate children with disabilities and those who are English language learners, so that they can benefit fully from the program. The final section of this chapter offers a guide to implementation to help you make language and literacy a central part of your program.

Goals and Objectives of Literacy Learning

Literacy: The Creative Curriculum Approach, includes goals for children ages 3–5 in the areas of listening and speaking, and reading and writing. They are 2 of the 10 goals for children from *The Creative Curriculum for Preschool* and include 13 of the 50 objectives.

The Creative Curriculum® Goals and Objectives at a Glance

SOCIAL/EMOTIONAL DEVELOPMENT	PHYSICAL DEVELOPMENT	COGNITIVE DEVELOPMENT	LANGUAGE DEVELOPMENT
Sense of Self 1. Shows ability to adjust to new situations 2. Demonstrates appropriate trust in adults 3. Recognizes own feelings and manages them appropriately 4. Stands up for rights **Responsibility for Self and Others** 5. Demonstrates self-direction and independence 6. Takes responsibility for own well-being 7. Respects and cares for classroom environment and materials 8. Follows classroom routines 9. Follows classroom rules **Prosocial Behavior** 10. Plays well with other children 11. Recognizes the feelings of others and responds appropriately 12. Shares and respects the rights of others 13. Uses thinking skills to resolve conflicts	**Gross Motor** 14. Demonstrates basic locomotor skills (running, jumping, hopping, galloping) 15. Shows balance while moving 16. Climbs up and down 17. Pedals and steers a tricycle (or other wheeled vehicle) 18. Demonstrates throwing, kicking, and catching skills **Fine Motor** 19. Controls small muscles in hands 20. Coordinates eye-hand movement 21. Uses tools for writing and drawing	**Learning and Problem Solving** 22. Observes objects and events with curiosity 23. Approaches problems flexibly 24. Shows persistence in approaching tasks 25. Explores cause and effect 26. Applies knowledge or experience to a new context **Logical Thinking** 27. Classifies objects 28. Compares/measures 29. Arranges objects in a series 30. Recognizes patterns and can repeat them 31. Shows awareness of time concepts and sequence 32. Shows awareness of position in space 33. Uses one-to-one correspondence 34. Uses numbers and counting **Representation and Symbolic Thinking** 35. Takes on pretend roles and situations 36. Makes believe with objects 37. Makes and interprets representations	**Listening and Speaking** 38. Hears and discriminates the sounds of language 39. Expresses self using words and expanded sentences 40. Understands and follows oral directions 41. Answers questions 42. Asks questions 43. Actively participates in conversations **Reading and Writing** 44. Enjoys and values reading 45. Demonstrates understanding of print concepts 46. Demonstrates knowledge of the alphabet 47. Uses emerging reading skills to make meaning from print 48. Comprehends and interprets meaning from books and other texts 49. Understands the purpose of writing 50. Writes letters and words

The objectives identify the skills and knowledge that children are expected to learn before entering kindergarten. *The Creative Curriculum Developmental Continuum for Ages 3–5* shows the sequence of developmental steps, ranging from simple to complex, that children typically demonstrate as they master a particular objective. The following list shows the sequence of steps in the Continuum for each of the language objectives. The Appendix includes a full-size version of these language objectives, to help teachers know what behavior and skills they may see in the classroom.

Language Development

Listening and Speaking

Developmental Continuum for Ages 3–5

Curriculum Objectives	Forerunners	I	II	III
38. **Hears and discriminates the sounds of language**	**Forerunners** Notices sounds in the environment *e.g., pays attention to birds singing, sirens* Joins in nursery rhymes and songs	Plays with words, sounds, and rhymes *e.g., repeats songs, rhymes, and chants; says, "Oh you Silly Willy"*	Recognizes and invents rhymes and repetitive phrases; notices words that begin the same way *e.g., makes up silly rhymes ("Bo, Bo, Biddle, Bop"); says, "My name begins the same as pop-corn and pig"*	Hears and repeats separate sounds in words; plays with sounds to create new words *e.g., claps hands 3 times when saying "Su-zan-na"; says, "Pass the bapkin [napkin]"*
39. **Expresses self using words and expanded sentences**	**Forerunners** Uses non-verbal gestures or single words to communicate *e.g., points to ball* Uses 2-word phrases *e.g., "All gone"; "Go out"*	Uses simple sentences (3–4 words) to express wants and needs *e.g., "I want the trike"*	Uses longer sentences (5–6 words) to communicate *e.g., "I want to ride the trike when we go outside"*	Uses more complex sentences to express ideas and feelings *e.g., "I hope we can go outside today because I want to ride the tricycle around the track"*
40. **Understands and follows oral directions**	**Forerunners** Associates words with actions *e.g., says "throw" when sees ball thrown; throws when hears the word* Follows oral directions when combined with gestures *e.g., "come here" accompanied with gesture*	Follows one-step directions *e.g., "Please get a tissue"*	Follows two-step directions *e.g., "When you get inside, please hang up your coat"*	Follows directions with more than two steps *e.g., follows directions to put clay in container, wipe table, and wash hands when activity is finished*

Language Development

Listening and Speaking (continued)

Curriculum Objectives	Developmental Continuum for Ages 3–5			
		I	II	III
41. **Answers questions**	**Forerunners** Answers yes/no questions with words, gestures, or signs *e.g., points to purple paint when asked what color she wants*	Answers simple questions with one or two words *e.g., when asked for name says, "Curtis"; says, "Purple and blue" when asked the colors of paint*	Answers questions with a complete thought *e.g., responds, "I took a bus to school"; "I want purple and blue paint"*	Answers questions with details *e.g., describes a family trip when asked about weekend; says, "I want purple and blue like my new shoes so I can make lots of flowers"*
42. **Asks questions**	**Forerunners** Uses facial expressions/ gestures to ask a question Uses rising intonation to ask questions *e.g., "Mama comes back?"* Uses some "wh" words (what and where) to ask questions *e.g., "What that?"*	Asks simple questions *e.g., "What's for lunch?" "Can we play outside today?"*	Asks questions to further understanding *e.g., "Where did the snow go when it melted?" "Why does that man wear a uniform?"*	Asks increasingly complex questions to further own understanding *e.g., "What happened to the water in the fish tank? Did the fish drink it?"*
43. **Actively participates in conversations**	**Forerunners** Initiates communication by smiling and/or eye contact Responds to social greetings *e.g., waves in response to "hello" or "bye-bye"*	Responds to comments and questions from others *e.g., when one child says, "I have new shoes," shows own shoes and says, "Look at my new shoes"*	Responds to others' comments in a series of exchanges *e.g., makes relevant comments during a group discussion; provides more information when message is not understood*	Initiates and/or extends conversations for at least four exchanges *e.g., while talking with a friend, asks questions about what happened, what friend did, and shares own ideas*

Language Development

Reading and Writing

Developmental Continuum for Ages 3–5

Curriculum Objectives	Forerunners	I	II	III
44. **Enjoys and values reading**	**Forerunners** Looks at books and pictures with an adult or another child Chooses and looks at books independently Completes phrases in familiar stories	Listens to stories being read e.g., asks teacher to read favorite story; repeats refrain when familiar book is read aloud	Participates in story time interactively e.g., answers questions before, during, and after read-aloud session; relates story to self; acts out familiar story with puppets	Chooses to read on own; seeks information in books; sees self as reader e.g., gives reasons for liking a book; looks for other books by favorite author; uses book on birds to identify egg found on nature walk
45. **Demonstrates understanding of print concepts**	**Forerunners** Points to print on page and says, "Read this" Recognizes logos e.g., McDonald's Recognizes book by cover	Knows that print carries the message e.g., points to printed label on shelf and says, "Cars go here"; looking at the name the teacher has written on another child's drawing, says, "Whose is this?"	Shows general knowledge of how print works e.g., runs finger over text left to right, top to bottom as he pretends to read; knows that names begin with a big letter	Knows each spoken word can be written down and read e.g., touches a written word for every spoken word in a story; looking at a menu asks, "Which word says pancakes?"
46. **Demonstrates knowledge of the alphabet**	**Forerunners** Participates in songs and fingerplays about letters Points out print in environment e.g., name on cubby, exit sign	Recognizes and identifies a few letters by name e.g., points to a cereal box and says, "That's C like in my name"	Recognizes and names many letters e.g., uses alphabet stamps and names the letters— "D, T, M"	Beginning to make letter-sound connections e.g., writes a big M and says, "This is for Mommy"
47. **Uses emerging reading skills to make meaning from print**	**Forerunners** Uses familiar logos and words to read print e.g., cereal logos, "exit" and "stop" signs Recognizes own name in print and uses it as a cue to find possessions e.g., cubby, cot, placemat	Uses illustrations to guess what the text says e.g., looking at The Three Pigs, says, "And the wolf blew down the pig's house"	Makes judgements about words and text by noticing features (other than letters or words) e.g., "That must be Christopher's name because it's so long"; "You didn't write enough words. I said, 'A Book about the Dog Biff,' and you just wrote three words"	Uses different strategies (known words, knowledge of letters and sounds, patterns in text) to make meaning from print e.g., "That word says book"; anticipates what comes next based on pattern in Brown Bear; figures out which word says banana because he knows it starts with b
48. **Comprehends and interprets meaning from books and other texts**	**Forerunners** Repeats words and actions demonstrated in books e.g., roars like a lion Relates story to self and shares information e.g., after hearing a story about snow says, "I made a snowman"	Imitates act of reading in play e.g., holds up book and pretends to read to baby doll; takes out phonebook in dramatic play area to make a phone call	Compares and predicts story events; acts out main events of a familiar story e.g., compares own feelings about baby brother to those of character; re-enacts Three Billy Goats Gruff	Retells a story including many details and draws connections between story events e.g., says, "The wolf blew the house down because it wasn't strong"; uses flannel board to retell The Very Hungry Caterpillar

Language Development

Reading and Writing (continued)

Curriculum Objectives	Developmental Continuum for Ages 3–5			
		I	II	III
49. **Understands the purpose of writing**	**Forerunners** Watches when others write Pretends to write (scribble writes)	Imitates act of writing in play e.g., pretends to write a prescription while playing clinic; scribble writes next to a picture	Understands there is a way to write that conveys meaning e.g., tells teacher, "Write this down so everyone can read it"; asks teacher, "How do I write Happy Birthday?"; says, "That's not writing, that's scribble-scrabble"	Writes to convey meaning e.g., on drawing for sick friend, writes own name; copies teacher's sign, "Do Not Disturb," to put near block pattern; makes deliberate letter choices during writing attempts
50. **Writes letters and words**	**Forerunners** Scribbles with crayons Experiments with writing tools such as markers and pencils Draws simple pictures to represent something	Uses scribble writing and letter-like forms	Writes recognizable letters, especially those in own name	Uses letters that represent sounds in writing words

Keep the sequence of steps for each objective in mind as you plan activities and experiences. Understand that children will be at different developmental levels. You will be tailoring your strategies and language as you scaffold children's learning and help them move to the next step in the sequence. The assessment information that you collect using the *Developmental Continuum* will guide you in determining each child's level.

Also recognize that children do not progress at the same rate. Some children learn new skills and behaviors quickly, while others need more time, practice, and experience before they move to the next step.

A deep understanding of children's skill development enables teachers to plan intentionally to advance children's thinking and support their language and literacy development. Teachers must provide appropriate experiences and interact skillfully with children throughout the day to support their learning. Expert teaching is key to making sure that preschoolers will have the knowledge, skills, and dispositions to succeed in kindergarten.

Creating a Literacy-Rich Physical Environment

Creating a literacy-rich environment does not mean merely covering the walls with words or placing charts from ceiling to floor. Teachers encourage literacy learning by thoughtfully planning the physical environment and including print that is meaningful to children.

For classroom literacy materials to be meaningful, they must serve a purpose. Such print materials help children communicate messages and ideas, learn new information and concepts, organize and express their thoughts, care for the classroom, and know what to do. A literacy-rich environment conveys the message that reading, writing, listening, and speaking are valuable and enjoyable.

Preschool children need to engage with literacy materials; to use them in their play; and to talk with adults about what they are doing, thinking, and feeling. Teachers must act intentionally to help children use written and spoken language throughout the day.

To create a literacy-rich environment, consider the basic principles that follow.

Organize space to promote conversations and language

Divide space into interest areas that are intimate and encourage conversation.

Create spaces for large-group discussions as well as small-group and individual work.

Encourage social interaction through the arrangement of the furnishings, e.g., two chairs at the computer or easels placed side-by-side.

Create cozy, comfortable spaces or niches to relax and read.

Define spaces and interest areas with print and pictures.

Develop a Library Area that is attractive and inviting.

Provide children access to print throughout the environment

Write children's names (using upper- and lowercase letters in conventional form) on charts, cubbies, work samples, cards.

Display a picture and word daily schedule and refer to it throughout the day.

Display the alphabet and have smaller alphabet cards available for children to handle as they write.

Display dictated signs, labels, titles for charts, posters, and other writing that serves a purpose.

Add message boards and class mailboxes for children and families to use.

Post poems, fingerplays, songs, rhymes, and recipes.

Display samples of children's writing.

Include print materials related to a study by creating experience stories, charts, labeled displays, and by providing related literature.

Remove print when it is no longer useful to children.

Enhance interest areas with literacy materials

Display books related to the interest area so that the covers are visible.

Label containers and shelves with pictures and words written conventionally with upper- and lowercase letters.

Provide reading and writing materials and tools for children to use in their play and to imitate adult literacy behaviors (e.g., paper for list-making, appointment books, phone books, pencils, markers).

Provide interesting materials to talk, read, and write about.

Add relevant posters, brochures, magazines, and newspapers.

Place sign-up sheets in interest areas or by activities that are particularly popular but can only accommodate a few children at one time.

Literacy Throughout the Day

Many young children enter school already knowing much about reading and writing. They know how to handle books; they can recognize familiar signs, labels, and logos; they know the purpose of recipes, lists, and letters; and they can recognize and write their names and those of family members. Researchers who have studied literacy experiences in these children's homes have found that literacy is a regular, integral part of the children's daily experiences. Children have many language experiences and access to reading and writing materials. They also have many opportunities to interact with supportive adults who respond to their questions, comments, and efforts and who provide experiences that help them learn to read.

In a *Creative Curriculum* classroom, teachers nourish children's literacy learning in much the same way. Opportunities for literacy learning abound, because talking, listening, reading, and writing are an integral part of the environment and every event of the day. Teachers have many conversations with children throughout the day. Children have opportunities to use and see adults use reading and writing in meaningful, functional ways from the time they arrive until they leave for the day. Here are some ways you can support language and literacy learning in your classroom. They are discussed in greater detail in later chapters.

Preparing the Environment	Interactions
Arrival	
Create an attendance chart where each child has a name card.	Have informal conversations with children and family members.
Have children and parents sign in each day.	Interact with children to facilitate language learning (e.g., talk with children, ask open-ended questions, play with children, and model literate behavior).
Create helper/job charts. Post any directions children might need for completing a job (e.g., how to care for or feed the class pet).	
Post a "Question of the Day" and have children respond in writing.	Read the "Question of the Day" with the children.
Create a message board for children and families to send and receive notes.	

Preparing the Environment	Interactions

Group Meeting

Create a picture/word daily schedule and refer to it throughout the day.

Display a chart with words to the song, story, or rhyme you are using.

Prepare name cards to use in group activities.

Have books and related props ready for story time.

Have blank chart paper and markers ready for interactive writing.

Refer to the schedule throughout day.

Sing songs; read or recite poems, rhymes, or fingerplays; and play language games.

Review the attendance chart. Explain that it shows who is at school and who is absent.

Refer to the job chart to review jobs for the day.

Have children share news about important events or experiences in their lives.

Guide discussions about study topics.

Write experience stories about study trips or visits from experts (e.g., firefighter, dentist).

Invite experts to talk with children. Have children prepare questions to ask the expert and record them on a chart.

Introduce new vocabulary as you present new props, materials, and activities.

Create class rules with the children. Record and post them, and review them when necessary.

Read and share a variety of books and other texts.

Choice Time

Create choice boards for interest areas. Children use their name cards to indicate their decisions.

Provide literacy props for children's play.

Provide abundant writing materials for children to document their learning and discoveries.

Create sign-up sheets for favorite activities.

Display intriguing pictures in interest areas to provoke conversation and writing.

Write and post rules or directions for using particular materials or equipment. Refer to them when necessary.

Post picture/word directions for routine procedures (e.g., washing hands) and call attention to them.

Interact with children to facilitate literacy learning (e.g., talk and sing with children; ask open-ended questions; play with children; retell stories; model reading and writing; and call attention to letters, words, and other features of print.)

Include a variety of books in each interest area. Read them with individuals or small groups of children. Show children how to use informational books as resources.

Offer to take dictation about children's drawings, paintings, or constructions.

Call attention to signs, labels, and other print in various interest areas. Talk about the functions of each. Involve children in creating new signs or labels needed for the areas throughout the year.

Preparing the Environment	Interactions
Small Groups	
Prepare print materials to be used in various activities, such as recipe charts, poems, name cards, blank books.	When appropriate, begin with a fingerplay to help children focus their attention.
	Read stories and share informational texts.
Have blank chart paper and markers ready for recording children's ideas.	Play language games.
Have props ready for storytelling and retelling.	Retell or reenact a familiar story
	Guide discussions about interesting topics, pictures, and objects.
Have the book(s) ready for reading aloud.	Write with the children (charts, letters, or lists).
	Make books.
	Invite children to read environmental print brought from home.
	Have children draw or write in journals.
	Integrate literacy with content area activities (e.g., label a graph, record observations during a simple experiment or cooking experience.)
Snack and Mealtime	
Write, review, and post the breakfast/lunch/snack menus.	Read the recipes and ingredient labels with the children.
Post written procedures for washing hands and cleaning dishes.	Have children prepare snack using picture/word recipes.
Post the picture/word recipe if children are to make their own snacks.	Have informal conversations with the children.
Label the food items children will use to prepare their snacks.	
Transitions	
Prepare name cards to use when dismissing children to interest areas.	Play a variety of language games.
Think in advance about appropriate songs, rhymes and chance.	Sing songs and recite rhymes, chants, or fingerplays, both to signal the beginning of the transition and to facilitate learning while children are waiting.

Preparing the Environment	Interactions
Outdoor Time	
Create inviting areas for reading and writing.	Have informal conversations with children.
Provide materials for children to record their outdoor discoveries.	Sing songs and recite rhymes or chants (e.g., while children are jumping rope or during hand play).
Provide materials for labeling plants.	
Incorporate signs from the environment (e.g., road signs, warning signs).	
Rest Time	
Offer books and writing materials (magic slates, Magna Doodles, chalkboards) for children who do not sleep.	Read a soothing story in a calm tone before the children rest.
Play soft music or recordings of environmental sounds (e.g., ocean, wind, night time sounds).	
Departure	
Prepare literacy take-home packs for children to share with their families.	Have the reporter announce the results of the "Question of the Day."
Record "What We Did Today" on an erasable board or a chart outside of the classroom so family members can discuss the day's events with their child.	Talk about the events of the day. Record the highlights on the class calendar, a chart, or in a class journal.
	Sing songs, read or recite poems, rhymes or fingerplays.
	Say something special to each child as you say goodbye.

A *Creative Curriculum* program is designed so that children associate literacy with pleasure and purpose. The attractive and functional physical design; the interesting and meaningful activities; and the support of a nurturing, competent teacher help to ensure that all children develop literacy skills through enjoyable, positive, and successful experiences.

Meeting the Needs of All Children

Early literacy development is critical for *all* children, but children come to school with vastly different levels of knowledge and understandings about language and literacy. Some have not had rich experiences at home; others come with developmental delays. Other children have specific disabilities or are English language learners. Many children have particular needs that require special consideration. There are many ways to adapt the environment, materials, and teaching strategies to meet each child's strengths and needs.

The preschool program schedule calls for a balance of large-group, small-group, and choice time activities. However, for some young children, leaving an activity in which they are deeply engaged and moving to another is unsettling and difficult. Supporting these children during transitions makes it easier for them to stop what they were doing and approach the new activity with greater ease. Once children have made the transition smoothly, teachers can prepare them for the new activity:

- Ask the children to take several deep, relaxing breaths or using warm-ups such as, *Open the cupboard, reach in, take out your listening ears, and put them on.*

- Create a picture icon board with simple directions and rules about how to attend during group time. You can review it with the children before beginning an activity and as often as necessary.

Adaptations for Children Who Are Advanced Language and Literacy Learners

A *Creative Curriculum* classroom can meet the strengths and needs of every child, including those who seem precocious because they have skills, knowledge, or abilities that are more advanced than those of their peers. A child who is already reading needs to learn new skills, as does the child who is just beginning. One of the teacher's main challenges is to match classroom experiences to each child's prior experiences and ability to learn. All children must be challenged appropriately in the early years so that they do not lose their motivation to learn.

It is important to look at the whole child and remember that a child's skills may be advanced in one area and not another. For example, a child who has exceptional verbal skills may lag in fine motor development. You may encounter a preschooler who is reading fluently but who can barely write his name. Knowing each child's unique combination of abilities will be a key factor in helping him progress in all areas.

As for all children in your class, it is important to really know the child who has advanced language and literacy skills and to provide experiences that are challenging and meaningful. Here are a few tips to remember:

- Include a selection of books appropriate to the child's reading level. Make sure the books are also appropriate for the child's level of social/emotional development.

- Continue reading aloud to the child. Interact before, during, and after the reading.

- Provide materials that will spark the child's curiosity and creativity and that will promote critical thinking skills.

- Offer books to help a child learn more about a topic that is of interest to him. (Note: This topic may not be meaningful to most children in your class.)

- Use more complex language and higher-level questions and prompts with this child.

- Avoid language activities that do not encourage the child to build on skills and concepts she has already mastered.

- Communicate with families often, to share information about what the child is doing at home and at the program.

As you work with preschoolers who have unusually high abilities or a great deal of experience, keep in mind that no single strategy will be appropriate for all. Learn what excites each child's curiosity and imagination. Finally, consider ways to encourage the child to use literacy as a way to explore many subject areas, feelings, and her own imagination.

Adaptations for Children With Disabilities

The Creative Curriculum encourages children's active involvement in literacy and play. For children with physical or cognitive limitations, this may be challenging. They may need intentional support in order to participate in many of the language and literacy experiences that other children have, such as handling a book, engaging in a conversation, or writing with a pencil and paper. Adaptations and accommodations are essential to promoting the language and literacy learning of children with disabilities. While you will find many suggestions for children with disabilities in the next chapters, the following are some general adaptations.

Environmental Supports:

- Offer alternative seating options, such as sitting on an adult's lap or next to an adult, for a child who is easily distracted.

- Use tape on the carpet or carpet squares to help children identify the boundaries of personal space.

- Provide appropriate assistive devices for the computer so all children can use the software. For children with visual impairments, make sure the software has auditory feedback.

- Place literacy-related materials where children in wheelchairs can reach them and put them away.

- Equip electronic devices, such as tape recorders and CD players, with switches that all children can use independently.

- Make sure that displayed books and other texts are accessible to all children.

Schedule and Routine Supports:

- Preview books or activities with children who need help with transitions or new experiences.

- Break tasks and activities into smaller parts and provide verbal cues as necessary.

- Encourage children to participate to the degree that they are able to do so.

- Use consistent, predictable routines to help children feel comfortable and secure. Introduce changes gradually, to encourage adaptability and flexibility.

- Create a picture board with simple directions or reminders about how to attend during group activities.

Visual Supports:

- Attach a piece of textured material to the name card of a child with visual impairments, so that he can identify it by touch.

- Include books with large print for children with visual impairments.

- Add commercial or teacher-made books with tapes for children with visual impairments.

Language Supports:

- Articulate clearly and monitor your speed so that children with language delays are better able to understand.

- Remember to repeat key directions for children with language delays.

- Make photo albums of children engaged in classroom activities and write key words or short sentences below the pictures. Children with communication delays can express their needs by pointing to the pictures.

- Use pictures and print to help children with delayed communication skills. Create picture cards with the key words of common phrases.

Sensory and Physical Supports:

- Include books that enable children to use many senses, for example, books with textures, pop-up books, and scratch-and-sniff books.

- Select books with clear, simple pictures and familiar concepts for children with developmental delays.

- Use sensory strategies, such as providing fidget and chew toys, for children who need them. (Weighted blankets and vests may be suggested by consultants.)

- Place large dots made from hot glue in the upper right-hand corner of the page. This will separate the pages, making them easier to turn for children who have difficulty.

- When making class books, use thick paper such as cover stock or cardboard, to make it easier to turn pages.

- Use Velcro or magnetic strips on attendance boards, rather than clothespins, for children who lack hand strength.

- Adapt writing tools for children with limited fine motor skills. Either purchase commercial devices or place a piece of rubber tubing over the pencil or marker to make it easier to grasp.

Adaptations for English Language Learners

If children in your classroom are English language learners, it can be very helpful for you to know the complexity and the development stages of the process. As in all areas of development, children vary in their approaches to acquiring English as well as in their rate of acquisition. Preschool children also vary in their readiness to demonstrate what they can say in their new language.

Remember that all typically developing young children have some level of language ability. Those children whose home language is not English understand a lot about language and how to use it effectively; they simply have not mastered the particulars of the English language system. They are in the process of acquiring a second language, which is encouraged more effectively when development in their first language is well supported. Helping children maintain and build their home language while promoting English fluency is especially important so that children retain their primary cultural identity, continue to stay closely attached to the customs and traditions of their families, and progress toward becoming fully bilingual (Espinosa, 2004).

The chart on the opposite page lists the stages you can expect second language learners to go through, and what you might see children do at each stage (Collier, 1995).

Stages of Learning a Second Language

Stage	What You Might See
Home language use	Children use only their home language with teachers and other children.
Non-verbal period	Children limit (or stop) the use of their home language as they realize that their words are not understood by others. This period can last from a few months to one year. Children may use gestures or pantomime to express their needs.
Early speech	Children begin using one- and two-word phrases in English and name objects. They may use groups of words such as "stop it," "fall down," or "shut up," although they may not always use them appropriately.
Conversation	Children begin to use simple sentences in English like the ones they hear in their environment. They may begin to form their own sentences using the words they have learned. Like all young children, they gradually increase the length of their sentences.
Use of "academic" language of school	Children begin to acquire English associated with specific content knowledge while they continue to develop social language.

The following are some general strategies you can use to support and facilitate children's acquisition of English as a second language.

Cultural Supports:

- Offer literacy materials that correspond to children's family experiences and their cultural and linguistic backgrounds.

- Display a few words in each family's language, beginning with simple words, such as *hello*, before using phrases.

- Incorporate children's home languages in daily classroom activities through songs, poetry, dances, rhymes, and counting.

Social/Emotional Supports:

- Establish and follow regular routines so children will feel comfortable and confident that they know when and what to do.

- Provide comfortable places where English language learners can get away from the pressures of communicating and observe until they are ready to join.

Language Supports:

- Combine nonverbal communication (e.g., gestures, intonation, and facial expressions) with your speech.

- Keep your language simple.

- Stress and repeat important words.

- Encourage English-speaking children to help English language learners.

- Talk through what you are seeing and doing (e.g., "Carlos is building a tall tower with his blocks." "I'm going to put my coat on because it is cold outside.")

- Use predictable books that allow children to join the reading by repeating key phrases.

- Frequently repeat familiar songs and rhymes with motions, so children will feel comfortable about participating and have an opportunity to practice the language.

- When possible, introduce in the home language of the children a book you are going to read aloud in English. (Multi-lingual staff members or volunteers can help if you do not speak the children's languages).

- Throughout this book we recommend asking children open-ended questions, but recognize that some open-ended questions are too difficult for beginning English language learners. Ask closed questions that children can answer by pointing to pictures or by saying one word. As children develop more English language ability, you can begin to introduce open-ended questions and support children's ability to answer by gesturing and by modeling language.

- Learn and use a few words in the children's home languages.

Literacy Supports:

- Include environmental print in the languages spoken by the children in the class.

- Color code the various languages displayed on labels and keep this coding consistent throughout the classroom (e.g., all English labels written in blue, Spanish in red).

- Provide computer software in other languages as well as English, as necessary.

- Include books, magazines, and other printed materials in languages other than English.

Family Partnership Supports:

- Recognize that multi-lingualism is a gift that families can give their children and that families who are not fluent English speakers can still promote children's language and literacy skills in their home language. Assure families that their home languages and cultures are valued.

- Let families know about the studies and activities of the children. Encourage them to talk at home about these topics in their home language, to support dual language acquisition of the concepts and related vocabulary. Provide books, vocabulary lists, and family activity suggestions.

- Send books home in advance for family members to read to their children in their home language. If the book is not available in the home language, send the English version home and ask parents to discuss the pictures in their home language. This will help the child better understand the book when you read it in English.

- Invite families to contribute food containers labeled in their home language, as well as calendars and menus to be used as play props.

These strategies help to create a supportive environment for English language learners. A carefully designed environment sets the stage for the interactions that help children begin to understand and use their new language.

Guide to Implementation

In a *Creative Curriculum* classroom, teachers promote language and literacy learning intentionally. Their understanding of how literacy develops allows them to observe and interact with children and to evaluate their learning. It also enables teachers to plan thoughtfully, choosing strategies to help children progress. This framework will help you think about the tasks involved and to plan accordingly.

Build your knowledge about early literacy development and best practices.

1. Become familiar with the components of literacy.

2. Understand literacy development and what you can do to help children progress.

3. Broaden your knowledge of early literacy and stay abreast of current research on literacy by reading professional journals, taking classes, and participating in learning teams or study groups focused on early literacy.

Establish a language and literacy-rich environment.

1. Use *The Creative Curriculum Implementation Checklist* to set up and evaluate your environment for literacy learning.

2. Create the classroom Library Area and make certain that you have included space and materials for reading, writing, listening, and retelling.

3. Include print throughout the classroom that labels objects, provides information, provides narrative descriptions, and explains classroom practices.

4. Display books throughout the classroom from a wide range of genres: predictable, narrative, concept, informational, alphabet, number, rhyming, poetry, and song books.

5. Talk continually with children about what they are doing.

6. Look for opportunities to include language and literacy in interest areas, studies, group activities, and daily routines.

7. Display the alphabet.

Inform and Involve Families

1. Encourage families to talk, listen, and read to their children. Stress the importance of reading aloud daily and having conversations about what each family member does during the day.

2. Let families know what language and literacy skills you hope children will learn and how that learning will be supported.

3. Use daily contacts with families to share information about children's literacy learning.

4. Plan family literacy sessions.
   a. Establish regular times and places for family literacy sessions.
   b. Plan topics for the year.
   c. Plan strategies for participation.
   d. Plan the use of parent activities from CreativeCurriculum.net (for subscribers) in family literacy sessions.
   e. Review other family resources and plan ways to include useful amounts of information in your sessions.

5. Keep parents informed about their children's progress.
   a. Emphasize children's strengths.
   b. Plan next steps for promoting literacy skills at home and at school.

Keep Track of Children's Progress

1. Administer a literacy screening as required by your local/state/federal program.

2. Prepare for ongoing literacy assessment.
   a. Determine what assessment tool you will be using and take the necessary steps to get started.
      1) CreativeCurriculum.net (Web-based)
      2) *The Developmental Continuum Assessment System Toolkit* (hard copy version)
   b. Create a management system for recording observations and collecting documentation.

3. Observe and document children's literacy behaviors. Collect samples of their work.

4. Evaluate children's literacy learning on the *Developmental Continuum*.

5. Use the information you learn from assessment to plan for individuals, small groups, and the whole class.

Plan for Literacy Learning Each Day

1. Large-group time
   a. Phonological awareness songs, fingerplays, rhymes
   b. Study topic discussions and planning
   c. Oral language development

2. Small-group time
   a. Phonological awareness songs, fingerplays, rhymes
   b. Reading aloud and follow-up story retelling
   c. Shared writing experience
   d. Oral language activity

3. Interest areas
   a. Add literacy props and materials
   b. Add other materials to build general knowledge

4. Routines and Transitions
   a. Repertoire of songs, rhymes, fingerplays
   b. Children's name cards
   c. Language games

inside this chapter

3

Teaching Strategies

With their understanding of the components of literacy, teachers plan ways to support children's learning with appropriate teaching strategies. The strategies described in this chapter outline six essential early literacy teaching methods appropriate for use in the preschool classroom.

Each strategy is a way of offering coherent, skills-based instruction that meets children's needs and interests. Sometimes the strategies are part of planned activities for particular times of the day. For example, a teacher might plan to read aloud as an end-of-the-day routine. At other times, teachers use the strategies more spontaneously to extend learning by interacting with children in interest areas. For example, a teacher might facilitate a conversation children are having in the Dramatic Play Area in a way that introduces more complex language and new vocabulary.

Talking, Singing, and Playing With Language

Oral language is the basis for the development of reading and writing skills. Children need many opportunities to talk, sing, and engage in playful and serious oral language experiences. Oral language activities support many components of literacy.

Teachers demonstrate that **literacy is a source of enjoyment** by creating an environment where children can takes risks safely as they experiment with language and by showing their delight in children's efforts.

Teachers promote **vocabulary and language development** when they engage children in discussions and conversations, sing songs, and recite rhymes. As they gain experience with many forms of language, children learn new words and their meanings and develop an understanding of the ways language is structured to convey meaning. Many aspects of oral language are used to read and write (e.g., choosing the appropriate words and grammar to communicate, understanding the language of others, sustaining a conversation, and discussing events in a sequence).

Children strengthen their **phonological awareness** during oral language activities. When they hear texts with repetitive language; listen to many chants, rhymes, and songs; and learn to enjoy the rhythmic patterns of language, they become more aware of the similarities and differences in the individual sounds of words. This is a step toward understanding the sound structure of language and learning to read.

Teachers promote **knowledge of print** through activities that help children understand that print is meaningful. They create experience charts with children that help them understand that personal experiences can be talked about, written about, and read about. Teachers help children learn about print by writing familiar songs, poems, rhymes, and fingerplays on charts and pointing to the words as they are sung or recited.

Once children have learned a song or rhyme, the teacher can model how the spoken words are matched to the printed words in a **book or other text**. Teachers can invite children to develop new verses and then create their own books. Placing these books in the Library Area and other interest areas allows children to practice their reading and book-handling skills.

Oral **comprehension** develops before children comprehend written language. Interacting with children, challenging them to talk about their thoughts and feelings, and asking open-ended questions to encourage their efforts are ways teachers help children build oral comprehension skills.

How to Begin

Children need opportunities to experiment with language, explore forms and meanings, and test the uses of language in different settings: social events, problem-solving situations, and everyday routines and activities. In a *Creative Curriculum* classroom, talking, singing, reciting rhymes, and playing with language are integrated throughout the program day. Children are given reasons to communicate, and they feel free to experiment with language. Teachers

- plan oral language experiences

- create an environment that encourages language use and play

Planning Oral Language Experiences

A day that is filled with enjoyable and interesting experiences encourages children to talk with others and to experiment with language. Here are three ways teachers intentionally promote children's oral language development.

Offer firsthand experiences.

Children must acquire knowledge and concepts, as well as vocabulary, in order to become skilled readers who comprehend what they read. For this reason, teachers should offer children many firsthand experiences in which they are introduced to new and interesting topics and rich vocabulary, actively explore concepts and materials, and engage in discussions to express their ideas and feelings.

Have conversations.

Conversations involve extended back-and-forth exchanges. Research shows that children who have frequent opportunities to participate in meaningful conversations with responsive adults acquire vocabulary, other language skills, and knowledge about the world, all of which contribute to early reading success. By contrast, language that is used to control children, give directions, or solicit information from children without encouraging complex thought contributes little to their literacy development (e.g., *Put this in your cubby. Eat your lunch before it gets cold. What color is this?*).

Conversations should occur at various times of the day. Some conversations are casual, such as those that typically occur during meals or when children arrive. Others are more guided, such as those that take place when an expert is invited to speak with the children about a particular topic or when you lead discussions before, during, and after reading a book aloud. Through these exchanges, whether with you individually, with a small group, or with the whole class, children learn how to communicate effectively; learn to follow conversational rules (e.g., taking turns, listening attentively, and staying on the topic); develop knowledge about the world; and gain confidence in their ability to use language.

Use songs, rhymes, and other language play activities.

Singing songs and reciting rhymes, fingerplays, chants, or tongue twisters allow children to explore language in a playful, enjoyable way. The repeated, rhythmic patterns in these language forms encourage children to experiment with language. The language refers to familiar people, animals, and objects, but new vocabulary words are also introduced. Large-group meetings are perfect settings for singing and for reciting rhymes, while small groups are more appropriate for other types of oral language activities and games.

Teachers can slow down the rate of singing and speaking for children with language delays and for English language learners. Sometimes it is helpful to make a recording of classroom favorites at a slower speed. Children can use these recordings to help them learn the words of songs, short poems, and fingerplays.

Creating an Environment That Promotes Oral Language

When the environment is filled with interesting and intriguing materials to explore, when children have a need to communicate, and when ample time and opportunity are provided, children talk. Below is a list of ways you can create an environment that encourages children to use oral language.

- Create interest areas that encourage conversations and cooperative play among children.

- Provide interesting props and materials that invite children to explore, experiment, learn new words, and use extended language. (For suggestions, see chapter 4 of this volume and the individual interest area chapters of *The Creative Curriculum for Preschool*.)

- Provide a variety of hands-on experiences that introduce children to new concepts, words, and forms of language.

- Encourage children's dramatic play because it encourages their exploration of roles, conversation, and the creative expression of ideas. Provide adequate time and materials for children to play freely and become fully engaged.

- Interact with children during choice time to encourage them to talk and share their ideas and feelings. Use open-ended questions and prompts to encourage children to expand on their ideas and experiment with language.

- Encourage children to settle conflicts with words.

- Provide story-related props that invite children to explore the language of books.

Supporting Children's Language Learning

Because each child is unique and because children have varied backgrounds, they differ in the age and rate at which they learn particular language skills. Researchers who studied these differences have concluded that the *amount* of language children experience influences vocabulary and language development the most dramatically. The implication for early childhood programs is that, to support children's language learning, teachers should offer many opportunities for children to participate in varied language experiences where they are introduced to new words, concepts, and linguistic structures. In addition, children need the direct support of teachers and other trusted adults who will listen, allow them to experiment with the uses and forms of language, and respond.

Read the following example to see how the teachers in one classroom skillfully use conversation, song, and a game to promote children's language and literacy learning. Note that the boxes on the right explain the teachers' reflections about what they are doing and noticing.

The children in Ms. Tory's and Mr. Alvarez's preschool class arrive at varied times. They routinely put their things away, check to see if they have a job for the day, then work in interest areas until it is time for the morning meeting. Ms. Tory and Mr. Alvarez freely move about the room, greeting children and family members and interacting with the children.

	(Derek and Dallas enter the classroom, talking and laughing They head toward the cubby area to hang up their jackets and backpacks.)	
Dallas:	*Not again, Derek!* (Laughs.) *That's my cubby. Here's yours.* (Points to Derek's cubby.)	
Ms. Tory:	(Stoops down and smiles at Derek.) *I think Dallas is right. Your name does have a capital D, like Dallas's name, see?* (Points to the Ds in both names.) *But your name is spelled capital* D-e-r-e-k, *and Dallas is spelled capital* D-a-l-l-a-s. (Points to each letter.) *Also remember that your picture is here to help you and to let others know that this is your cubby.*	Draws attention to letters of the alphabet. Calls attention to the similarities and differences in written words.

Ms. Tory:	(Smiles at Tasheen, who reluctantly enters the classroom with her dad, and stoops to speak to Tasheen as she unpacks her backpack.) *Welcome back. We missed having you at school these past few days. We have lots to share with you, and I bet you have lots to share with us.*	Speaks with child at child's eye level.
Tasheen:	(Smiles at Ms. Tory but doesn't speak.)	
Ms. Tory:	*I heard that you are now a big sister. Your mom and dad are so lucky to have you to help them with the new baby!*	Recognizes a smile as the child's way of communicating.
Tasheen:	(Takes a picture from her backpack and shows it to Ms. Tory.)	
Ms. Tory:	*Ahhh, I see you brought a picture of you and the new baby to share with your friends. What are you going to tell your friends about the new baby?*	Recognizes that the child is using a photo to convey a message. Asks an open-ended question to prompt a conversation.
Tasheen:	*It's a boy, and his name is Jeremiah.*	
Ms. Tory:	*He looks like he's smiling. Is he a happy baby?*	Makes a relevant comment and asks a question to keep the conversation going.
Tasheen:	*Sometimes he cries a lot, and it is really loud.*	
Ms. Tory:	*Babies do cry a lot sometimes. I wonder why.*	Wonders aloud to prompt conversation.
Tasheen:	*Dad said they can't talk, so they cry to let us know they need something.* (Tasheen and Dad smile at one another.) *Sometimes he cries because he's hungry or when he needs his diaper changed. Sometimes he just wants us to hold him.*	

Ms. Tory:	*He's not crying here. He must like it when you hold him like that.* (Points to the picture, and Tasheen smiles)	Signals that she is listening by making a relevant comment.
	I know you have lots more to tell your friends about Jeremiah. What do you need to do in order to share your picture?	Asks an open-ended question.
Tasheen:	*Put it in the Share Chair.* (Ms. Tory nods; Tasheen hugs her Dad goodbye and skips off with her picture.)	

When all the children have arrived, Ms. Tory and Mr. Alvarez move through the room to tell the children they have five more minutes to play before gathering on the rug for morning meeting.

Soft music begins to play, and the children begin putting their materials and belongings away. A few parents are still in the classroom, and they offer to help the children clean up. Mr. Alvarez overhears a conversation between Juwan and a parent.

Juwan:	*All the farm animals go in this tub. See the picture and words? That says* farm animals. (Juwan points to the picture and each word.)	Notices that child demonstrates his understanding of print.
	Then you put it on the shelf, right here. (Points to an identical picture/word label on the shelf.) *See? It says the same thing:* farm animals.	Hears child use language to give directions.
Parent:	*You read the words and looked at the pictures to know where to put the animals.*	
Juwan:	*I know.* (Juwan goes to the rug.)	
Ms. Tory:	(Sits facing the children; refers to the picture/word schedule posted on the wall behind her; points to a word and reads.) *Arrival.*	Demonstrates the purpose of print. Orients children to print.
	Let's see if everyone has arrived. (Looks at the attendance chart.) *Someone is not with us today. Who can it be?*	Asks an open-ended question to prompt children's thinking.
Children:	(Some look around, while others look at the name card on the attendance chart.)	Allows children time to investigate.
Zack:	*Malik.*	

Ms. Tory:	*That's right, Zack. Ma-lik* (Sweeps her hand under the name card.) *is not here today. I don't see Malik, and her name card is still on the side that reads* Look Who is at Home (Points to each word on the attendance chart.) *I hope Malik will be back with us tomorrow.*	Demonstrates spoken-to-written word correspondence. Demonstrates left-to-right directionality.

Ms. Tory:	(Begins singing *Clap a Friend's Name With Me*, which she had taught the children the day before. They sing to the tune of *Mary Had a Little Lamb*) *Clap a friend's name with me,* *Name with me,* *Name with me,* *Clap a friend's name with me.* *Let's try Crystal.* *Crys-tal.* (Claps each syllable in the child's name.) (They continue to sing, substituting different children's names and clapping the syllables in each.)	Uses a song to promote phonological awareness by breaking words into syllables.

Ms. Tory:	*I wrote the song on a chart so we can use it as we sing. I put a piece of Velcro in the space where one of your names will go. I think I will put Ben's name in first.* (Puts Ben's name card in the space; then sings the song for the children, this time pointing to each word as she sings.)	Demonstrates directionality. Helps children develop the concept of a word. Encourages an enjoyable interest in literacy.
Various children:	*Sing about me! Do my name!*	
Ms. Tory:	*Let's play a game to see if you can guess whom we will sing about next.* (Shows the children a brightly colored gift bag with their name cards inside. Explains that she will slowly pull a card out, revealing and naming one letter at a time, and they are to guess whose name it is.) *Are you ready?* J-	Introduces a game that will build knowledge about the alphabet.

Janelle and Juwan:	*Mine!* (Raise their hands.)	Recognizes that children are demonstrating letter knowledge.
Ms. Tory:	*Your names start with* J, *but remember to wait for the next letter.* (Continues.) *o-n-e-t-t-a.*	Supports what they know and challenges their thinking.
Jonetta:	*Mine!*	
Ms. Tory:	(Places Jonetta's name in the space and invites the children to sing the song as she points to each word. They repeat the process, inserting another child's name and singing the song.)	Demonstrates how to do the activity.

Zack:	*Will you put the chart and name cards in the Music and Movement Area so we can sing it at choice time?*	
Ms. Tory:	*We can do that, Zack! Why don't you go with Mr. Alvarez to find a good place to put the chart and name cards.* (Zack takes the bag of name cards and eagerly goes with Mr. Alvarez.)	Supports child's suggestion that will extend the learning opportunities.

Ms. Tory:	*Our meeting is almost over. Who can tell what we will do next?* (Refers to the daily schedule, pointing to the words *Choice Time.*)	Demonstrates a purpose of print. Gives the children a reason to read.
Children:	*Choice Time* (Read in unison.)	

Ms. Tory:	*To begin choice time, we will play a listening game. You will need to listen for words that have the same beginning sound as your name. If they do, you may choose an area to play. Listen carefully.*	
	If your name begins like big, ball, *and* bump, *I want you to buzz like a bumblebee to an area.* (Ben hesitates at first; then he buzzes away.)	Promotes phonological awareness by drawing children's attention to initial sounds.
	Listen again. If your name begins like the words tiny, tipsy, *and* toothbrush, *I want you to tiptoe to an interest area.* (Continues until all the children are dismissed.)	

You will find other examples of ways teachers interact with children to support language learning, in chapter 4.

Tips to Share With Families

- Have conversations about what you are doing together and what you notice. Offer interesting observations that invite your child to respond.

- Encourage friends and other family members to use your child's home language during family activities.

- Sing, march, dance, and make up songs in the language you are most comfortable speaking.

- Teach your child songs that you sang growing up. (Don't worry if you can't carry a tune.)

- Teach your child nursery rhymes.

- Make up silly rhymes and sayings.

- Make up rhymes involving your child's name.

- Think aloud about what you are doing so your child learns the language that describes everyday experiences.

- Use new words when you talk with your child.

- Describe what you experience and ask questions that encourage your child to talk with you.

- Try to keep conversations going back and forth at least five times. Asking your child for more information is often a good way to keep a conversation going.

- Accept your child's way of speaking, while modeling conversational skills and standard language.

- Look for your child's non-verbal attempts to communicate, and model language that she might use to express her ideas and feelings.

- When you ask your child a question, give him plenty of time to think about what you are asking and to respond.

Reading Aloud

While many activities contribute to children's literacy development, none is more powerful than reading aloud. Research indicates the value of reading aloud to support each of the components of literacy development.

For most children, being read to is an emotionally satisfying experience. The intimacy and warmth children associate with sharing books with adults helps to promote **literacy as a source of enjoyment**. This association leads children to explore books, practice reading behaviors, and later read successfully for their own information and pleasure.

Reading aloud is a primary way to enrich children's **vocabulary and language**. As children listen to story books, informational books, and poetry, they hear words that are new, interesting, and more rare than words they hear in conversations. Reading to children also introduces book language, language that is usually more formal, complex, and abstract than language heard in everyday conversation.

The language in many children's books focuses attention on the sounds of words, promoting **phonological awareness**. Reading stories with rhyme and alliteration help children become sensitive to the similarities and differences in the individual sounds in words. Books that contain repeated and varied language patterns highlight and segment the sounds of words while others encourage children to experiment with language.

Reading aloud helps children to gain **knowledge of print**. Children learn that print conveys meaning. Children develop understandings about the correspondence and differences between spoken and written languages, and they learn about directionality (that English is read from left to right and top to bottom) when they see the teacher sweeping her fingers under the text as she reads. They observe book-handling skills, such as how to hold a book upright and turn the pages in order.

Reading aloud helps children to understand that **letters** can be grouped together to form **words** and that words have meaning. Alphabet books typically introduce a letter along with pictures of objects with names that start with the sound represented by the letter. This helps children recognize and name the letters of the alphabet and introduces them to letter-sound associations. Picture concept books also contribute to children's understanding of individual words, because each page usually pictures an object identified by a single printed word.

The language of **books** is different from the language of conversations. By hearing books read aloud, children learn how to listen to and understand the language of stories and informational texts. They develop a sense of story, that stories have a setting, characters, a theme, a plot, and a resolution. When they hear books read aloud by adults who read fluently, change their voice for different speakers, and use inflection to aid comprehension, children develop understandings about how ideas and feelings are communicated through written language.

Interactions between adults and children before, during, and after a text is read aloud help children develop **comprehension** skills. When teachers invite children to make predictions, prompt them to supply words or phrases, ask and answer questions, offer information, and relate the text to real-life experiences, they help children process the meaning of the language they are hearing.

How to Begin

Read aloud several times daily, to meet the needs of all children, including those who are English language learners and those who have had few previous experiences with books.

Successful story reading and book sharing involve more than selecting a book from the shelf and reading it aloud. Like other activities and experiences offered to preschool children, reading aloud requires planning. Teachers must

- choose good books to read aloud

- plan for small groups and individuals, as well as for the large group

- establish regular times for reading aloud

- judge the appropriate amount of time to allow

- create a physical space where children will be comfortable

Choosing Good Books
Know your children's interests, cultural backgrounds, and life experiences so you can select books that will be meaningful to the children.

Characteristics of a Good Book to Read Aloud

- The adult reader likes it.

- The topic is already or likely to be of interest to the children.

- It is a good match for the children's developmental levels (e.g., for young preschool children, the book has lots of rhymes and repetition; for older preschool children, the story has suspense, plot twists, dialogue, and engaging characters).

- It relates to the children's experiences and interests.

- A familiar—and favorite—author wrote it.

- The story and illustrations are relevant to children's families and cultures.

- The story and illustrations introduce new family and cultural experiences.

- It is a well-loved favorite that children like hearing again and again.

- New information and ideas are presented through text and pictures.

For further guidance on the types of books to choose for your classroom, see pages 356–358 of *The Creative Curriculum for Preschool*. As you decide the appropriateness of a book, consider these questions:

- How long will it take to read? Can the children pay attention for that length of time?

- Will any concepts or ideas be unfamiliar to the children? How can I explain them?

- Do the illustrations have tiny details or hidden surprises to point out to the children?

- How can I make sound effects (e.g., animal noises or sirens) and gestures part of the reading?

- How can I vary my voice to dramatize the different characters?

- What props (e.g., hats or musical instruments) would enhance the reading?

- How can I invite the children to participate? Can they say rhymes, join in with the last word of repetitive phrases, predict what might happen next, or answer questions?

Planning for Groups and Individuals

In most preschool classrooms, teachers tend to share books with large groups of children rather than with small groups or an individual child. While sharing books with the whole class is often an appropriate activity, large-group interaction must be limited so that it does not interrupt the flow of the narrative. To give them more opportunities to respond, children should regularly be offered opportunities to listen to stories and informational books in small-group settings and individually with an adult. Children's literacy learning and motivation to read are affected more by the interaction that occurs between adults and children during the reading than by the actual reading of the book.

Some research shows that children who hear stories in small-group settings show stronger comprehension skills than children who hear stories read to them individually. One-on-one readings lead to more comprehension than large group readings. Children who hear stories read in a small group or one-on-one generate more comments and questions than children in a whole class setting (Morrow 1987, 1988; Morrow & Smith, 1990).

Establishing Regular Times to Read Aloud

Young children thrive when they have consistent daily routines, so establish regular times for reading to them. In a *Creative Curriculum* classroom, teachers read to children at least twice a day. You may choose to start or end the day with a book, and you may read to children after choice time or before nap time. Of course you can still look for other opportunities to read, such as during snack time or outdoors, while maintaining your regularly scheduled reading times.

Many teachers find it helpful to plan routines that help define reading aloud periods. These might include singing a specific song, reciting a rhyme, or wearing a special hat or apron to signal to children that reading aloud time is about to begin. Once children are gathered, teachers help children get ready to listen and respond by reviewing expectations for behavior during reading. Story and book reading time is interactive and usually ends with a follow-up fingerplay or movement activity or a discussion that helps children make a personal connection to the story.

Judging How Much Time to Allow

Especially at the beginning of the year, not all of the children in your class will be equally ready for group reading. Consider how long particular books take to read and whether the children can pay attention for those lengths of time. Some children will have had few previous experiences with books and are not accustomed to listening to books read aloud, while others may become restless or distracted even if they are experienced. You can plan for these children by scheduling short read aloud times and by using books that have bold illustrations and simple, predictable, or repetitive text. Other strategies include making sure that distractions are minimized during this time, asking an assistant or volunteer to sit close to these children to help them focus on the book, or making plans to share books with these children in smaller groups or individually in the Library Area. As children become accustomed to reading routines, you will be able to share books that are longer and have richer, more complex text.

Creating Special Places for Reading

If reading is to be an enjoyable experience for children, you will need to create a space where they can sit comfortably and be near enough to you to hear the book and see the pictures clearly. The Library Area is the ideal location for reading aloud if it is an attractive area equipped with soft furnishings, beautiful picture books, and props that invite lively interactions with books. If the Library Area is not large enough to accommodate all of the children, use the space where you typically hold group meetings and reserve the Library Area for small-group reading or sharing a book with one child. Wherever you choose, remember that the space should be one that children come to recognize as a special place for sharing books with friends.

Effective Ways to Read Aloud

Reading aloud well is not a skill that comes easily for all teachers, but it is one that can be developed over time. Try these strategies:

Practice reading the book before you read it aloud to children, so that you become very familiar with the language, characters, and plot.
Write questions and reminders on Post-it notes, then stick them on the appropriate pages so you will know how and when to prompt the children's thinking.

Start the reading by giving children a reason to listen to the book.
The first step in reading aloud is to gain the children's attention and help them focus on the book. You might read the title, author, and illustrator; look at the cover and discuss what the book might be about; and suggest things for which the children can look and listen.

Here are more suggestions for introducing a book:

- Explain how the story is related to familiar feelings or a recent experience.

- Share an object that is an important part of the story.

- Relate a new book to a familiar one.

- Explain how the book is related to what the children are studying.

While reading, use strategies that hold the children's attention and that provide information about books and print.

Start to read as soon as the children are seated comfortably and you have their attention. Here are some tips for reading aloud:

- Hold the book to one side so the children can see the pictures.

- Use your voice and facial expressions to make the characters and their experiences come alive.

- Change or define words to help the children understand the story.

- Stop to talk about the pictures, answer questions, discuss what might happen next, and think about what the characters might be feeling.

- Answer questions related directly to the book; save other questions for later.

- Run your finger under the text.

- Pause at the end of sentences.

- Invite children to join in with repeated and predictable words, phrases, and rhymes.

- Discuss interesting words and ask what the children think they mean.

- Repeat words that rhyme or have sounds like those found in other words the children know.

After reading, discuss various aspects of the story or invite children to participate in follow-up activities.

Here are a few suggestions:

- Ask the children to react to or share their opinions of the story.

- Briefly summarize the story (characters, setting, theme, plot, and resolution).

- Continue to help the children make connections between the story events or characters and their own lives.

- Discuss or clarify new words introduced in the story.

- Encourage the children to respond to the story through drawing, writing, constructing, or retelling.

- Explain that the book will be placed in the Library Area or another interest area and encourage the children to explore it more.

Ms. Tory is a preschool teacher who is skilled at sharing books with her class. In the example that follows you will see how she shares *Jennie's Hat* by Ezra Jack Keats. The comments on the right explain how Ms. Tory uses the read aloud strategies and prompts suggested in the "Interactive Story Reading" chart found on page 140.

It is choice time, and the children are engaged in various activities throughout the room. Ms. Tory picks up the xylophone and begins to play a soft melody. Looking up from their play, the children see Ms. Tory making her way toward the rocking chair in the Library Area. The children begin putting away their materials, then eagerly join Ms. Tory, one by one, as she sits holding a large round gold box in her lap. Mr. Alvarez helps children who are still cleaning up and then they too, join the other children on the rug. Ms. Tory makes sure everyone is comfortable and comments on how well the children cleaned up. Mr. Alvarez joins the group, and Ms. Tory begins story time.

> Transitions children to story time by using the xylophone as a signal. Makes sure everyone is comfortable and relaxed before beginning story time.

Ms. Tory:	*Today I have a story for you about a girl who gets a gift that disappoints her a little. Does anyone know what I mean by disappointed?*
Dallas:	*Sad.*

> Introduces new vocabulary before reading the story.

Setsuko:	*Yeah, sad because you think you're going to get something and then you don't get it.*	
Ms. Tory:	*Have you ever been disappointed?* (Children offer examples of disappointments.) *Show me how your face looks when you are disappointed.*	Helps children connect the story with prior experiences.
Ms. Tory:	*The gift the girl was waiting for was something you wear on your head. Can anyone guess what that might be?*	Encourages predictions. Provides a way for children to participate.
Various children:	*A scarf! A cap! A hat! A visor! A football helmet!*	
Ms. Tory:	*Those are all ideas of things someone might wear on his or her head. Why would someone need or want to wear something on her head?*	Asks an open-ended question. Promotes logical thinking.
Sonya:	*My grandma wears a scarf on her head so her hair won't blow everywhere.*	
Leo:	*My Dad wears a cap to keep the sun out of his eyes.*	
Crystal:	*Yeah, My Mom wears a visor to keep the sun out, too.*	
Dallas:	*And football players wear helmets so their heads won't get hurt when they get tackled! You have to wear a helmet if you play football. It's a rule!*	
Ms. Tory:	*Those things help to protect us—from sun, getting hurt, or getting our hair all messed up.*	Acknowledges the children's contributions to the discussion.

Ms. Tory holds up the box and asks the children to think to themselves about which of the items they mentioned is most likely to be in the box. She asks them to listen while she gently shakes the box.

Plans a way to capture the children's interest and gathers all necessary props (hat and hat box).

Ms. Tory:	*Do you think this could be a football helmet?*	Encourages reasoning skills.
Setsuko:	*No. The box isn't big enough.*	

Dallas:	*And we would hear a clunking sound.*
Ms. Tory:	*How about a scarf?*
Sonya:	*No. A scarf doesn't need a box. My grandma keeps her scarves folded in a drawer in her dresser.*

Ms. Tory slowly cracks open the lid of the box to reveal a small section of the brim of a straw hat.

Leo:	*I think it's a cap, because I saw that piece that hangs over your face.*	
Ms. Tory:	*You mean you saw the brim? A cap does have a brim, but so do a visor and a hat. Let's take a look at what's in the box.*	Introduces new vocabulary.
	(Ms. Tory takes the hat out of the box, briefly talks about it, then places it on top of her head.) *It's not a football helmet, a scarf, or a cap. But, it does have a brim, as Leo thought.*	Helps children verify their predictions.

Ms. Tory:	*The title of this story is* Jennie's Hat, *and the author's name is Ezra Jack Keats.* (Ms. Tory holds up the book and runs her fingers underneath the words as she reads.)	Uses book language such as *title* and *author*.
	(She points to the cover picture of the girl with the basket on her head and leads a discussion about who the girl might be and why she has a basket on her head.)	Demonstrates that print is read from left to right.
		Draws children's attention to the illustration to help children make predictions and discuss their ideas.
	(She shows the first several pages of the story and asks the children to describe what they see and predict what they think will happen.)	Takes children on a picture walk through the book to demonstrate how pictures can be used as clues to predict and confirm what the story is about.
	(She returns to the beginning of the book and reads the first few pages about Jennie's disappointment in her new hat.)	She notices that children listen attentively to see if their predictions are correct.
Tyrone:	*She didn't like her hat!*	

Ms. Tory:	*Jennie was disappointed in her hat. Have you ever cried because you were disappointed?*	Helps the children make connections to the story.
Ms. Tory:	(Continues to read.) *"She put on a straw basket to see what sort of hat it would make. Then she drew pictures. 'HAT-CHOO!,' she sneezed. 'Bless you, dear,' called her mother, 'and what are you doing?' 'I'm drawing a hat-erpillar—I mean a caterpillar,' answered Jennie.'"*	
	Have you ever heard anyone sneeze like that? (Children shake their heads, no.) *What do you think a hat-erpillar is?*	Asks *who, what, when, where, why,* and *how* questions.
Dallas:	(Children sit quietly. Then Dallas points to the picture on the page and responds.) *Not a hat-erpillar, a caterpillar! See, there is the picture of the caterpillar!*	
Ms. Tory:	*Why do you think Jennie called it a hat-erpillar?* (Children offer a variety of responses. Ms. Tory continues reading and asking questions.)	Draws children's attention to initial consonant sounds by repeating a nonsense word.
Ms. Tory:	(Continues reading.)	
Carlos:	*The birds are following Jennie.*	
Ms. Tory:	*Hmm, I wonder why?* (Pauses.)	Uses open-ended comments to encourage thinking.
Ms. Tory:	(Reads text about the birds that swooped down, flapping and fluttering around Jennie's new hat. She makes swooping movements with her arms and flaps her hands as she does so. Ms. Tory invites the children to join her making flapping, fluttering, and swooping motions.)	Uses movement to illustrate new vocabulary words and to spark interest in the story. Involves the children in physical activity. Asks *wh-* questions. Encourages children to talk about the story.
	Why were the birds following Jennie?	
Children:	*To put things on her hat!*	
Crystal:	*Jennie is happy now! But she wasn't at first, when she just had that plain hat.*	
Dallas:	*The birds were Jennie's friends.*	

Setsuko:	*Jennie's hat is beautiful now!*	
Ms. Tory:	(Finishes the story.) *And that's the end of the story.*	Uses book language, e.g., *The end.*
Sonya:	*Why did her mom wrap up her hat?*	
Ms. Tory:	*Well, what did the story say?* (Ms. Tory points to the last sentence and reads it again.) *"It would be saved and looked at and remembered for a long, long time."*	Responds to a child's question and promotes comprehension skills by asking children to recall details from the story.
	Did you enjoy the story? What did you like best?	Asks children to critique the story and explain their opinions.
	I'll put Jennie's Hat *in the Library Area, along with this hat.* (Takes the hat off of her head.) *You may read it on your own or with a friend.*	Showcases the book after reading.

For a more thorough discussion of strategies related to interactive story readings with groups of children and individual children, see chapter 4.

Tips to Share With Families

- Surround your child with books. Help your child get a library card, because borrowing books from the library is free! Take your child to the library for story time. Books from bookstores can be expensive, but you can get inexpensive books at garage and yard sales, thrift shops, and library book sales.

- Choose books that both you and your child enjoy. Tell her how much you enjoy looking at books together. Reread favorite books.

- Let your child choose which books to read. Letting your child read what interests him is one way for reading to be meaningful and enjoyable.

- Choose books in your home language if that is what you speak best.

- If you are not comfortable reading aloud, or if you do not know English and would like your child to hear stories in English, you may borrow books with accompanying audiocassettes from the library. There are also computer programs that highlight words on the screen as a voice speaks. Children can choose to hear the story and play related games in English, French, German, or Spanish.

- If you are not comfortable reading aloud, choose wordless books where the story is told through pictures.

- Find a comfortable space and make your book-sharing time special.

- Use gestures and facial and vocal expression as you read.

- Talk about what is happening in the story and, when possible, how the story relates to your child's life.

- Ask your child questions and give him time to respond. Discuss what happens in the story and point out details of the illustrations. Ask questions such as, *What do you think will happen next?* or, *Why is she doing that?*

- Let your child ask questions. Stop and answer, even if it interrupts the story.

- Occasionally run your fingers under the words as you read. Point out how words are read from left to right and from top to bottom. Explain that words are separated by spaces.

- Take books with you in the car, or on the bus or subway.

- Let your child tell you the story or take a turn "reading" the book to you.

Storytelling

Storytelling, one of the oldest art forms, is a common form of entertainment and a way cultures pass their beliefs, values, and traditions from one generation to the next. It helps children learn social skills, such as how to relate to and get along with others. Oral storytelling supports children's literacy learning, knowledge and understanding of the world, and social/emotional well-being.

Storytelling encourages children's emotional involvement with literature. When a story is well-told, interactive, and fun, children view **literacy as a source of enjoyment**. They are filled with the wonder and excitement of stories and are motivated to become storytellers, as well as listeners and readers.

Storytelling helps children build **vocabulary and language** skills by showing them that speech carries messages. Through storytelling, children gain experience with a broad range of language: new vocabulary words, unfamiliar expressions, rhymes, dialogue, and the structure of extended narrative. Storytelling also teaches children that they can communicate their thoughts, ideas, and feelings not only with words, but with body language, gestures, and facial expressions. Adult storytelling encourages children to act out and retell stories, which promotes their oral language and cognitive development.

Many stories use rhymes, tongue twisters, and other forms of word play. When children hear patterns repeated again and again by the storyteller, and when they actively participate in the storytelling or retell these stories on their own, they gain **phonological awareness**.

As children hear many stories, they develop understandings about story structure that contribute to their understanding of **books**. They learn that the setting, characters, and theme of a story are introduced in the beginning of a story. They also learn that storytellers recount key events (middle) and end the story by stating a moral or with another conclusion (ending). Storytelling introduces children to various types of narrative, such as folktales, fairy tales, and fables, and it enhances children's later reading skills by inspiring them to read stories they have heard. It also supports their ability to communicate their own experiences. Telling a simple story is a skill essential for children's later independent writing; children who are able to compose a story to tell are more likely able to dictate or write a story.

Certain storytelling strategies contribute to children's understanding and **knowledge of print**. For example, using a story clothesline (on which pictures of the major events of the story are clipped to the clothesline, from the children's left to the children's right) helps children understand the left-to-right progression that is used in text.

Listening to oral stories enhances children's **comprehension**. In order to find meaning, they must focus on the description of the setting, the characters and their problems, and the sequence of story events. The interactions that occur between the storyteller and the listener before, during, and after the telling of a story are key to greater comprehension.

How to Begin

Storytelling is possible for everyone. It requires no equipment, only the story and the imaginations of the storyteller and listeners. It is sometimes more challenging than reading because you do not have the language and illustrations of a book to support your narration, but storytelling can be learned. These ideas will help you get started:

- Think of yourself as a storyteller.

- Select appropriate stories.

- Prepare for storytelling experiences.

Thinking of Yourself as a Storyteller

Think about a time when you used a phrase such as *Once I... or Remember when...?* as you began to recount an experience that was important to you. You were introducing a story. As human beings, we have a natural desire to express ourselves, share our life stories with others, and hear their stories. Even very young children eagerly tell their families, teachers, and friends about the latest events and experiences in their lives.

Selecting Appropriate Stories

Like reading aloud, storytelling requires planning. By knowing the needs, interests, and abilities of the children in your class, you will be able to select appropriate stories, modify their length and the pace at which they are told, and determine ways for children actively to participate.

Finding stories that are well-suited to the age and interests of the children in your class is important. There are many kinds of stories to choose from, such as folktales, fairy tales, tall tales, and trickster stories. With young children, you may wish to begin with a folktale that has simple story elements.

Recall the stories that captured your attention as a young child and identify the characteristics that made them appealing to you. It is likely that they had one or more of the following qualities:

- **a simple plot** (an easy to follow sequence of events), e.g., *The Enormous Turnip* by Kathy Parkinson

- **repetitive words or phrases**, e.g., *The Gingerbread Boy* by Paul Galdone

- **predictable or cumulative storylines**, e.g., *I Know an Old Lady Who Swallowed a Fly* by Simms Taback

- **strong or interesting characters**, e.g., *The Three Billy Goats Gruff* illustrated by Ellen Appleby

- **interesting, entertaining, or humorous situations** e.g., *Anansi and the Moss-Covered Rock* by Eric A. Kimmel

- **action or suspense**, e.g., *Where the Wild Things Are* by Maurice Sendak

- **an exciting or satisfying conclusion**, e.g., *Henny Penny* by Paul Galdone

- a **clear message or moral**, e.g., *The Little Red Hen* by Lucinda McQueen or *The Tortoise and the Hare* by Aesop

Your enthusiasm for a story can be contagious. The stories that are meaningful to you will likely become the children's favorites, and they will attempt to retell them on their own.

Preparing for Storytelling

Oral storytelling requires interaction between the teller and listeners. When children listen to stories without the use of a book, they must use their imaginations differently from when illustrations are provided. As a storyteller, you must think about ways to capture and hold the children's attention. Your childhood memories of listening to stories can be helpful. Think of your feelings during the telling of a story, the storyteller's portrayal of the characters, or the ways in which the storyteller involved you in the telling. Keep in mind that the storytelling experience will be more valuable for the children if the story and the storyteller are engaging.

Once you have chosen a story, spend time with it. It may take a number of tellings to find an effective way to tell it to children. The following tips will help you prepare for storytelling.

Think about the details of the story characters.
Develop a clear image of the characters and use many and varied words to describe each one. Think about how the characters might speak, sound, move, and act. Practice portraying the characters.

Develop a strong beginning.
Begin the story with an opening phrase such as *Once upon a time...* or *Long, long ago, in a land far away...* to signal to the children that they are leaving reality and entering the world of make-believe. As you begin, establish the mood of the story and introduce the characters, setting, and theme. Stimulate the children's senses by describing sights, sounds, tastes, and smells in detail.

Learn the story.
Most traditional stories are plot-driven, that is, they are based upon a particular sequence of events. If you understand the plot, you can tell the story simply by recounting what happens in your own words; it is not necessary to memorize the words as someone else has told it. After you have learned the plot, let your imagination work. Picture each event in your mind and think about the language—the descriptive words and phrases—the children will understand. Then tell the story out loud to yourself in your own words. Decide when to lower your voice, when to pause for effect, and when to speak faster. Create different versions of the story and practice telling it to different listeners. Telling slightly different versions of a story is part of a long oral tradition. Of course, if the telling is enlivened by repetitive lines or phrases, you will want to use them.

Develop an ending.
Tales traditionally end with a sentence that lets the children know the story is over and that brings them back to reality. Some familiar endings include, *That's a true story!* and, *They all lived happily ever after.*

Telling Stories With Children

Before storytelling, make sure that classroom distractions are minimized, that the area is comfortable enough for children to relax, and that they can be near you. Place any props you are using where you can reach them easily.

The following chart provides an example of how two teachers, Ms. Tory and Mr. Alvarez, captured their children's attention with an oral story. The children had recently been to a petting farm where they handled and fed many animals. They seemed to be especially interested in the goats, so Ms. Tory thought it was a perfect time to tell the Norwegian folktale *The Three Billy Goats Gruff*. The notes on the right explain the teachers' thinking about why they are saying and doing these things.

Ms. Tory places a globe, a toy troll, and a tone block in the Library Area. Then she invites the children to join her for a story.

> Collects the props and materials in advance.

Ms. Tory:	*Today Mr. Alvarez and I are going to tell you a story. Since I won't be reading the story from a book and showing you the pictures, you will have to listen carefully to imagine what is happening in the story. Is everyone comfortable and ready to listen and think?* (Children nod their heads, yes.)

> Prepares the children for listening and makes sure they are comfortable.

The story is an old Norwegian folktale called The Three Billy Goats Gruff. *A folktale is a story that people have told over and over and over again. In fact, this story has been told so many times we really aren't sure who the author is.*

> Introduces the story and gives a little background information about the type of story, its author, and its source.

When I was a little girl, my dad used to tell me stories that his dad told him. Now I tell the same stories to my son. Do any of your parents or grandparents tell you stories from long ago that someone else told them?

> Fosters children's understanding by drawing on their personal experiences.
>
> Asks for personal contributions.

Carlos:	*My great grandmother tells me stories about when she was a little girl in Mexico, before she came to America.*

Ms. Tory:	*Well, this story was first told in another country called Norway. Norway is far, far away, even farther away than Mexico. See? Here is where we live, and here is Norway.* (She uses a globe to show the children where Norway is in relation to their homes. Children comment on how far away Norway seems to be. Ms. Tory settles the children and then continues.)

> Gives background information about the story's origin.
>
> Makes a connection between the setting of the story and where the children live.

Does anyone know what a billy goat is?

> Asks a question that will help children learn about the main characters.

Susie:	*A goat. Like the ones we saw at the farm.*
Ms. Tory:	*It is a goat. But what do you think a **billy** goat is?*

Juwan:	*I have a friend named Billy.*
Ms. Tory:	*Is your friend a boy?* (Juwan nods his head, yes.) *That might give you a hint.* (Ms. Tory pauses and waits for a child to respond. She continues.) *Even though some girls are named Billie, a billy goat is a male, or boy, goat. So this is a story about three boy goats. Let's begin.*

Explains or defines unfamiliar words to build children's vocabulary and understanding.

Allows time for children to answer and proceeds when they do not.

Ms. Tory:	*Once upon a time, in a land far away, there lived three billy goats. And the last name of all three billy goats was Gruff.*

Opens the story with a statement that lets children know that they are entering an imaginary world.

Ms. Tory:	*The youngest billy goat Gruff was very, very small. He had two little horns just starting to show on the top of his head and he spoke in a soft voice.* (Each time Ms. Tory introduces a new character, she changes the pitch of her voice and uses her hands to show the size of the goats and its horns.)

Uses her voice and gestures to help children imagine the characters.

The second billy goat Gruff was a middle-sized goat. He had horns, too, and he had a few whiskers on his chin.

The last and oldest was great big billy goat Gruff. He was HUGE! He had long, pointed horns, almost like spears; big hooves; and a beard. He made his two brothers feel safe because he was so big and strong.

Ben:	*My brother Broderick is strong!*
Ms. Tory:	*Does anyone remember what billy goats like to eat?*
Zach:	*Grass and seeds.*
Carlos:	*And sometimes old shoes and stuff like that!*

Asks a question to help children connect to the story.

Ms. Tory:	*Well, these billy goats loved to eat sweet, green, juicy grass more than anything else. One day when they were grazing on grass near their home, one of them noticed a lush hillside not too far away. The grass looked green and tasty, and, when the breeze blew, the goats could smell its sweet smell. They just had to have it, so they decided to go up to the hillside to get some of the grass.*
	But…(Ms. Tory pauses and looks in the children's eyes.) *there was a problem. You see, to get to the other hillside, the billy goats had to cross a bridge. Now the bridge wasn't the problem, but what lived under the bridge was a BIG problem.*
	What do you think lived under the bridge?
Children:	*A monster!*

Ms. Tory:	(Ms. Tory lowers her voice, moves a little closer to the children, and speaks slowly and deliberately.) *Under the bridge lived a TROLL.* (Ms. Tory takes out a toy troll and shows it to the children.) *This is a toy troll. But the troll that lived under the bridge was BIG and UGLY and VERY, VERY MEAN!*
	His eyes were as big as saucers, so he could spot a goat a mile away. And his nose was as long as a poker, which meant he could smell a goat a mile away (Mr. Alvarez stands nearby and makes gestures to indicate the size and nature of the troll.)
Kate:	*He would scare me! He's so big and mean and ugly!*
Ben:	*Yeah! I bet he gets the billy goats when they cross the bridge. Huh, Ms. Tory?*

Side notes:

Makes eye contact with the children and maintains it throughout the telling. This helps to hold the children's attention and provides information about whether and how storytelling strategies should be modified.

Uses her voice to emphasize story details.

Uses simple, natural gestures.

Encourages children to comment during the storytelling.

Ms. Tory:	*Well, the first billy goat to cross the bridge was the small billy goat Gruff. He went trip-trap, trip-trap, trip-trap over the bridge.* (Ms. Tory uses the tone block to make faint, fast, trotting hoof sounds.)	Uses props, as appropriate, to enhance storytelling.
	About that time the troll roars in the meanest, loudest voice you've ever heard.	
Mr. Alvarez:	*Who's that tripping over my bridge?* (Clenches his fist and uses a deep, roaring voice.)	Uses movement and a dramatic voice.
Ms. Tory:	(Responds in a quivering, high-pitched voice.) *It is I, the tiniest billy goat Gruff. I'm going to the hillside to make myself fat.*	
Mr. Alvarez:	*I'm coming to gobble you up!*	
Ms. Tory:	(Again in a tiny, pleading voice.) *Oh, no! Please don't take me. I'm much too little. Wait for my brother, the middle-size billy goat Gruff. He's much bigger and meatier than I am.*	
Mr. Alvarez:	*Very well. Be off with you!*	
Susie:	*That billy goat tricked you!* (Points to Mr. Alvarez.)	
Mr. Alvarez:	*You're right. I may need some help!* (Invites children to participate.) *Let me hear you say, in your meanest troll voices, "Now I'm coming to gobble you up!"* (Children respond.)	Involves children in the telling.

The story continues with Ms. Tory playing the part of each billy goat and Mr. Alvarez playing the troll. To represent the difference in the size and strength of each goat, she plays the tone block more and more slowly, loudly, and deliberately, and she alters the pitch, tone, and volume of her voice.

Ms. Tory:	Pretty soon, all three billy goats were on the hillside eating that sweet, juicy, green grass. They ate so much that they got really, really fat and they could hardly make it home. In fact, they are probably still fat. And so—snip, snap, snout—this tale's told out.	Concludes the story with a sentence that will signal the end of the story and the return to reality.
	What did you think about that story?	Asks an open-ended question.
Children:	It was good! That big billy goat wasn't afraid of the troll.	
	At first I was scared! But I'm not now.	
Ms. Tory:	It can be a little scary. Do you think that story really happened or do you think it was make-believe?	Acknowledges child's feeling and asks a question to help children distinguish between real and make-believe.
Carlos:	Make-believe, because goats don't really talk.	
Ben:	And there is no such thing as a troll.	

Ms. Tory affirms their responses and continues the discussion. She asks the children if they would like to hear the story again. She and Mr. Alvarez make plans to create puppets and a backdrop to use next time. After that, they will invite the children to retell the story using the props, and they will add the props to the Library Area for the children to use at choice time.

Ms. Tory is a skilled storyteller, so she used minimal props to tell the story. However, it is appropriate to use props, or visual aids, with young children as long as they do not distract children from listening to the story. A few simple props can be useful in holding young children's attention during storytelling, and placing them in the Library Area encourages children to tell and retell stories on their own. A discussion of various storytelling props and techniques can be found in the section "Story Retelling."

Tips to Share With Families

- Make up stories with your child as the main character.

- Tell stories about when you and other family members were children.

- Tell stories about your child when he or she was younger.

- Tell stories where the main character does what your child did that day. The main character does not have to be a child.

- Invite family members to share stories about their life experiences.

- Use familiar storytelling phrases, such as, *Once upon a time…, They lived happily ever after, In a far-away land…,* and *The end.*

- Change your voice to portray different characters.

- Involve your child by having him add sound effects or motions.

- Involve your child by encouraging her to repeat a refrain or supply a missing word.

- Take turns telling parts of the story.

- Use props, such as an old hat, puppets, household items (e.g., a pot for a helmet, a piece of fabric for a cape).

- Laugh and have fun.

Story Retelling

Reading aloud and telling stories are effective strategies in promoting children's literacy learning. However, what happens before, during, and after these experiences is also important in children's literacy development. Research confirms that story retelling, when children recount in their own words a story they have heard or read, is one of the most effective strategies for developing children's comprehension and their understanding of story structure. Retelling activities support the development of many other components of literacy as well.

Retelling activities enable children to experience **literacy as a source of enjoyment**. Positive experiences make it more likely that children will choose to engage with books and other literacy activities during choice time.

Oral retellings provide opportunities for children to increase their **vocabulary and language** as they experiment to confirm their understanding of new words and expressions. As children assume the roles of the characters in the story, they use dialogue from the story and inflect their voices. Oral retelling can help improve English language learners' facility with English. Retelling is particularly effective for children who have had few literacy experiences, because these children are more likely to engage in active literacy experiences than in those that require them to listen more passively.

Many stories for young children are told with rhyming words or phrases. Others focus children's attention on the separate sounds of language and encourage children to experiment with the sounds. When children have opportunities to retell stories with these features and repeat particular words or phrases, they gain **phonological awareness**.

Retelling helps children understand **books** by giving them experience with story structure. Children learn to introduce the story with its setting, characters, theme, and initial events (beginning); to give an organized, sequential account of the story's plot (middle); and to offer a resolution (ending).

Retelling is not simply recalling events or facts from a story. Retelling requires that children think through the story and organize the details of the characters, setting, and plot. In doing so, they develop understandings about story structure (develop **comprehension**). Retelling also requires them to infer and interpret how characters feel, speak, and act.

How to Begin

Retelling skills must be taught. Children need guidance, support, and lots of practice. These suggestions will help you to begin:

- Select appropriate stories and model ways to retell them.

- Use props for oral retellings.

Selecting Appropriate Stories and Modeling Ways to Retell Them

Choose stories you have already read to the children and that have simple plots (e.g., *The Mitten* by *Alvin Tresselt*), familiar characters (e.g., *The Three Little Pigs* by Paul Galdone), repetitive phrases (*Do You Want to Be My Friend?* by Eric Carle) or familiar sequences (*The Very Hungry Caterpillar* by Eric Carle). The predictability of simple texts helps children succeed in their early attempts at retelling.

Children benefit from listening as you retell stories. Always be sure to include a clear beginning, middle, and ending, and relate the same sequence of events as the version you read earlier. Explain to the children that storytellers must tell the story in a way that even listeners who never heard it before will understand. They must include all of the information that the audience needs to know and organize it so that it makes sense. As you model story retelling, explain how you decide what to tell. Demonstrate the use of various props. Discuss and model what the characters say and sound like.

Using Props for Oral Retellings

Props are visual prompts for young children. They provide concrete references for story details, help children to organize their thoughts, and suggest to children what to do or say. Some props (e.g., puppets, costumes) help children to play the parts of the characters.

Provide object props.

Collect toys or other materials to represent particular characters or events in a story. For example, for the story *Jump, Frog, Jump!* by Robert Kalan, you might use a toy fly, frog, fish, snake, turtle, net, and basket. A piece of blue felt or fabric could represent the pond in which the story is set. As you tell the story, place the appropriate object on the pond.

Make clothesline story props.

Create pictures to represent important story events and characters. Hang a clothesline in a section of the Library Area that is out of the line of traffic. Place a basket of clothespins close by. As you retell the story, clip the appropriate picture to the clothesline, in sequence from the children's left to the children's right. (See the activity "Clothesline Storytelling," in chapter 5).

Offer felt, magnetic, or Velcro props.

Create pictures that represent the important events of a story on felt, fabric, or sturdy card stock (colored and laminated for durability). Fasten self-stick Velcro or a magnetic strip to the back of each picture. Retell the story by putting the pictures on a felt or magnetic board in the order they are mentioned in the story. You can create individual felt story boxes by lining the inside of a pizza box with felt. Accompanying story pieces can be made and stored inside each box. When children are ready to retell a story, they simply open the box, remove the pieces, and retell the story, using the lid as a felt board. Likewise, cookie sheets can serve as magnetic story boards.

Use costumes and dramatic play props.

Dramatic story enactments are particularly effective with young children because they love to dress up and pretend. As they work together to enact a story, children explore the roles of various characters. Set the stage by providing simple costumes (e.g., old clothing, large pieces of fabric, uniforms, hats or headbands, masks) and props to help children get into character. Create the setting by drawing a simple scene on a sheet or large cardboard box. Explain to the children that you will read a story and then they will act it out by pretending to be the characters. Ask them to pay special attention to what the characters say and do and how they express their feelings. After reading, lead a discussion about the story and invite children to volunteer for each part. Provide support by serving as the narrator and prompting children when necessary. Once children know the process, they are able to do it on their own or with minimal support.

Collect puppets.

Puppets are especially useful for retelling stories that have repetitive dialogue, such as *Chicken Little, The Little Red Hen*, and *The Three Billy Goats Gruff*. Timid children often feel more secure when they may use puppets in retellings. After selecting a story, decide which type of puppet (e.g., hand, stick, finger, or body) to use and assemble a collection to represent the story characters. Although commercial puppets are available for purchase, puppets can be made out of almost anything (e.g., oven mitts, wooden spoons, cardboard tubes, paper plates, or hair curlers) and children enjoy the diversity. Next, prepare children for the retelling, following the same procedures described above in "Costumes and dramatic play props" (reading, discussing the characters, and prompting when necessary).

Supporting Children's Story Retelling

Retelling activities can involve the whole class, a small group, or an individual child. After modeling the retelling of a familiar story, give children a variety of opportunities to retell the story. Each way involves a different level of support. For example, you may work individually with a child, encouraging him to retell a portion of the story (the beginning or ending) while you retell the rest. You can engage the whole class in retelling a story using clothesline props or another technique, or you can work with a small group of children to reenact a story while you narrate.

Young children usually need a lot of support during early retelling experiences. You can assist them by offering open-ended prompts. For example, to help children get started, you might say, *Tell us whom the story is about*, or ask, *Where did the story happen?* To help children who have difficulty recalling the events, you might ask, *What happened next?* To prompt children to extend their description of a character you might say, *Tell me more about this character*. Prompts such as these help children understand that all parts of a story are important when it is being retold.

Teachers help children develop and refine their retelling skills by creating a special place in the classroom where children can retell stories they have heard during story time. In a *Creative Curriculum* classroom, teachers designate a portion of the Library Area specifically for retelling stories. Books and related props are stored there and used by children during choice time.

In the example that follows, Ms. Tory models and guides a group of children in retelling *Jennie's Hat* by Ezra Jack Keats (Puffin Books, 2003), one of the children's favorite books. The notes on the right explain the teacher's thinking about what she is saying and doing.

Ms. Tory places the following props on a shelf in the Library Area: a hat box with a straw hat inside, a basket, a lamp shade, a flower pot, a TV antenna, a shiny pot, and a hat covered with flowers. She places other props in a basket, including artificial flowers, plastic eggs, greeting cards, a paper fan, colored leaves, and an artificial bird's nest. She gathers a small group of children together at story time.

> Plans in advance to have ready the props she needs.
>
> Provides object props to use as visual prompts.

Ms. Tory: *Children, today I would like you to help me tell one of your favorite stories, from the book* Jennie's Hat. *Do you remember the story?*

> Involves the children in discussing the story before the retelling.

Derek:	Yeah. It's about a girl who gets a hat and she doesn't like it.	
Crystal:	In the end she likes it.	
Sonya:	Yeah, because the birds put all kinds of things on it.	
Leo:	Like flowers and leaves and eggs and sticks.	
Ms. Tory:	You remember a lot about the story. Let's start at the beginning of the story and think about everything that happened.	Acknowledges the children's responses.
Ms. Tory:	Once there was a girl named Jennie. She was waiting for a present from her favorite aunt. She was sure her aunt was sending her a big, beautiful hat covered with lots of flowers.	Introduces the story setting and characters.
	The present finally came, and Jennie was very excited. But when she opened the box... (Ms. Tory pauses and opens the hat box to take out the plain straw hat.) there was only a plain hat, just like this one. Jennie was so disappointed.	Introduces the story theme. Uses props to help in recalling the story.
	Do you remember what Jennie's mom said?	Prompts children to recall story details.
Crystal:	She said she thought it was a nice hat. But Jennie still didn't think so.	
Ms. Tory:	That's right. Do you remember what Jennie did next? (She pauses and points toward the props on the shelf.)	Recalls and prompts children to recall the plot episodes.
Derek:	She tried to use a bunch of other things for hats.	
Ms. Tory:	Yes, first she tried on a basket, then a lampshade, a flower pot, a TV antenna, and a shiny pot. (Ms. Tory puts each on her head.) None of these would do.	Uses a prop for each key story detail.

Ms. Tory:	(Glances at her watch.) *Just about that time, Jennie noticed that it was time to feed the birds. She got some bread crumbs, went to the park, and began scattering the crumbs.* (Pretends to throw crumbs on the ground.) *What happened then?*	Acts out the story details to focus children's attention.
		Asks a question to give children an opportunity to be part of the retelling.
Children:	*The birds came fluttering all around, and they hopped on Jennie's head, and they ate up all the food.*	
Ms. Tory:	*Jennie had so much fun at the park that she forgot about her hat until she started to walk home. She wished that her hat was just a little fancier.*	
	The next day Jennie got up and peeped out of the window. Do you remember what she saw?	Asks a question that will help to move the storyline forward.
Leo:	*A lot of ladies wearing hats with flowers.*	
Crystal:	*And a lot of ladies at her church had flower hats. But Jennie just had her plain hat.*	
Ms. Tory:	*You're right. Jennie had to wear her plain hat to church. However, when Jennie and her parents were leaving the church,…*(Ms. Tory pauses)	Prompts children to recall the resolution.
Sonya and Leo:	*The birds came. They brought lots of stuff to put on Jennie's hat.*	
Ms. Tory:	*Like what?*	
Crystal:	*Lots of flowers and eggs.* (Ms. Tory puts the flowers and eggs on the hat.)	Prompts children to recall details.
Ms. Tory:	(Shows the children the box of props and adds each prop to the hat as it is named.)	Uses props as visual prompts.
Derek:	*Leaves.*	
Sonya:	*Cards and valentines.*	
Leo:	*A fan and a bird's nest.*	

Ms. Tory:	At last, Jennie had a beautiful hat! She waved to the birds and said, "Thank you!" (Children wave.)	Prompts children to recall the ending of the story.
	Do you remember how the story ended?	
Derek:	Yes. Jennie thought her hat was so beautiful that she and her mom wrapped the hat.	
Ms. Tory:	She wrapped it up so it could be saved and looked at for a long, long time.	Accepts the detail the child contributed and adds additional information.
Ms. Tory:	Thank you for helping me to retell the story. You remembered all the things that happened.	
Ms. Tory:	I'm going to put these things (motions to hat, flowers, etc.) in the Library Area for you to use to retell the story on your own.	Encourages independent retelling.

Tips to Share With Families

- Use stuffed animals, toys, and other household items as props to retell stories.

- Act out stories that you have read with or told to your child, with both of you assuming roles.

- Encourage your child to tell the story while looking at the pictures in a book.

- Allow your child to tell the story in his or her own words.

- Retell stories with your child, taking turns to tell different parts.

- Give prompts freely when your child needs assistance in telling a story; e.g, if you are retelling *The Mitten*, ask, *What happened after he lost the mitten?*

Writing

When given opportunities, children experiment with writing and explore different ways to convey messages in print. Research confirms that reading and writing develop together as interactive and interrelated processes. Writing is an essential part of a preschool literacy program and supports the development of several components of literacy. Although teachers demonstrate letter formation, the main focus in preschool is writing as a communication tool rather than handwriting instruction.

Young children enjoy the process of writing, the social relationships they develop during the process, and the sense of accomplishment they feel as they use writing to express themselves (**literacy as a source of enjoyment**).

Children increase their **vocabulary and oral language** skills as they read and as they talk about their early writing and drawing. As they realize that what they think and say can be written down, their oral language becomes the basis of what they write.

Writing with children helps them to understand the sound structure of words (**phonological awareness**). For example, a child may become aware of syllables if a teacher, while writing Leo's name, says *Leeeeee* (while writing *L-e*) and *oooooo* (while writing *o*). When writing a word, the teacher calls attention to each phoneme by saying the sound aloud as she writes the letter(s). Once children become aware that words are a sequence of sounds represented by letters, they begin to try to sequence letters in a conventional way.

Writing helps children develop their **knowledge of print**. As teachers model writing and talk about their purpose, thinking, and actions while writing, children learn that print conveys meaning and that what they say can be written and then read. As adults model writing, children learn left-to-right directionality, spoken-to-written word correspondence, the concept of word, spacing, punctuation, and capitalization. By offering children opportunities to create a variety of texts (e.g., stories, lists, letters, cards, recipes) through interactive writing, they learn that print is organized differently for different purposes.

As teachers talk with children about print while they model writing, children learn about **letters and words**. They learn specific letter names, become aware of letter features, and how letters are formed (the line segments used to form each letter and the direction and sequence in which the segments are written). Children also learn that letters represent one or more sounds, that letters are grouped together to represent words, and that words have meaning.

The writing process helps promote children's understanding of **books**. As children attempt to compose their own stories by dictating or writing them on their own, they develop and refine their sense of story. When children respond to a variety of literature by producing their own, they learn about the features and structure of each. For example, when children create their own alphabet books, they learn that alphabet books typically introduce one letter per page, with pictures of objects whose names begin with the sound (phoneme) represented by the letter.

How to Begin

Both teacher-initiated and child-initiated writing experiences should be a part of daily life in the classroom. Teachers must

- consider the characteristics, needs, and interests of their children

- plan for a variety of writing experiences

- provide materials and opportunities for children to write on their own

Considering Children's Characteristics, Needs, and Interests

In any class, children are at different stages of development in their awareness of print and the purposes of writing. Children demonstrate their knowledge and understanding of written language through their own writing, dictation, and comments. Teachers can use the *Developmental Continuum* to guide their observations and to reflect on what children are doing. They then plan experiences and interact with children in ways that help children develop understandings about written language.

Support can take many forms: responding to children's writing (regardless of the format) as attempts to communicate, modeling the mechanics of writing (e.g., demonstrating letter formation), answering children's questions, offering information, and, when appropriate, asking questions that will help children think about written language.

Planning Writing Experiences

In a *Creative Curriculum* classroom, teachers engage children in learning about and producing many kinds of written language. Meaningful writing experiences are included in various events of the day so that children learn how written language is used to meet their needs. Some of these experiences are teacher-initiated and directed; others are child-initiated and offer children opportunities to explore writing on their own.

Write names.

When teachers plan activities that require children to recognize and write their names, they help children learn that written language can be used to express identity and show ownership. In a *Creative Curriculum* classroom, teachers give children reasons to write their names, such as signing their names on

- attendance sheets upon arrival each day (see page 83 of *The Creative Curriculum for Preschool*)

- drawings, stories, greeting cards, letters, and other work products

- sign-up sheets for a popular activity

- "question of the day" charts

To help children learn to write their names, provide name cards written conventionally with upper- and lowercase letters. Children's ability to write their names develops over time, depending upon their level of motor control, knowledge of letters as discrete units, and awareness of the distinguishing features of letters. Many children's first attempts at name writing are likely to be single shapes or lines and contain no letters at all. As children practice writing and become more aware of print, they begin including letter-like symbols and letters in their signatures.

Make lists.

When teachers involve children in making lists, children learn that written language can be used to satisfy needs and desires (e.g., to recall information or to have a turn with a new toy). List-making is an effective strategy because it is a brief activity and each child may contribute more than once. Class lists are useful to document

- things to do to prepare for a special event

- things children saw on a neighborhood walk or a study trip

- supplies needed for making snacks

- children wanting a turn with a new toy

- favorite things (foods, places to go, colors)

- characters in a story

Write cards, letters, and notes.

These writing experiences show children that written language enables them to communicate with others. Children can

- create greeting cards for family members and friends on various occasions

- write thank-you notes or letters to classroom volunteers, guest speakers, and the sponsor of a class field trip

- participate in a pen pal program with another preschool class and write letters to one another

- use a message board or post office in the classroom and write letters to each other

Write instructions.

When teachers write instructions, children learn that written language can be used to tell others what or how to do something. Teachers can

- involve the children in making signs, labels, or notices for the classroom (e.g., *Do not touch, Please flush, Exit, Please be quiet*)

- involve the children in making class rules, write them down, post them, and review them regularly

- create simple rebus (picture and word) recipes

Record information.

When teachers create various written documents, children learn that written language is used to communicate information. Teachers can

- make a telephone and address book with the children in your class (remember to ask for parental permission) and refer children to it during play; place note pads and pencils nearby to encourage children to write messages

- invite children to help make written announcements or invitations for special events, such as a family breakfast or a class art show

- create a picture dictionary or word wall of common words for children to refer to when they are writing independently

- create a log for children to record their observations, such as changes in a tadpole or the growth of sprouting beans

- chart children's experiences during a class trip or special school event

Take dictation and create journals.

When teachers take dictation and offer opportunities for independent journal writing, children learn that written language is a way to express their personal thoughts, ideas, feelings, and opinions. Teachers can

- encourage children to dictate captions (words or sentences) or stories about a drawing, painting, or photo

- record children's thoughts about daily classroom events, experiences related to the latest topic of study, exciting outdoor discoveries, or information learned from a visiting expert on a chart, on the class calendar, or in a class journal

- give each child a personal journal in which to draw, dictate, or write about a self-selected topic

Write in response to literature.

Offering children opportunities to respond to literature in writing helps them to understand that written language is a tool to express themselves creatively. Teachers can

- have children create and dictate the narrative for a story published as a wordless book and record their language on Post-it notes

- invite children to draw and write about a character who appears in a series of books (e.g., *Curious George*)

- have children create experience stories and record them on a chart

- have children create and dictate stories for a chart or book, using predictable books as a model

- use other types of books (e.g., informational books, alphabet books), poems, rhymes, songs, and chants to encourage children's expressive language development

Providing Materials and Opportunities for Children to Write

Children first notice print in real-life settings where writing is used for meaningful purposes. For many children, print is not part of everyday experiences, so they do not understand it as a useful tool. Preschool teachers must offer meaningful opportunities for children to write, through teacher-directed activities such as those described in the previous section.

Teachers also need to make provisions for child-initiated writing. Children need time, opportunities, and materials to explore writing on their own. They need to try the ideas about writing they have formed through their observations of and interactions with others.

In a *Creative Curriculum* classroom, the Library Area is the primary place where children explore writing by creating cards, drawing, dictating, writing stories, and making books. On pages 359–360 of *The Creative Curriculum for Preschool*, you will find an extensive list of writing materials to include in the Library Area.

A second area where reading and writing props are important is the Dramatic Play Area. Through dramatic play, children explore real-world situations in which reading and writing are useful. As children explore adult roles in their play, they imitate writing behavior in order to understand its purpose and conventions. For example, in a pretend doctor's office, the child assuming the role of the doctor is likely to write on patient charts or scribble prescriptions, while the receptionist might sign patients in or keep an appointment book.

Writing is not limited to just the Library and Dramatic Play Areas. Teachers encourage children to explore reading and writing in all interest areas by placing paper, writing tools, and other print props alongside toys, games, and play props. By providing literacy materials in all interest areas, children have opportunities to explore print in their own way, deciding when, what, and how to write. For more ideas and information on incorporating literacy in interest areas, see chapters 4 and 5 of this volume and the interest area chapters of *The Creative Curriculum for Preschool*.

Writing should also be integrated with content activities for math, science, social studies, the arts, and technology. With each topic of study, materials can be added and experiences planned to encourage writing and reading (e.g., books and book-making, experience charts, graphs, and journal writing).

Supporting Children's Writing

Materials alone are not enough. Teachers must thoughtfully and intentionally model and interact with children to promote their literacy learning. One of the most powerful strategies teachers use to help children learn about written language is to talk about it when they write, themselves. When teachers describe their thoughts and actions as they write, children learn about the functions and conventions of print (e.g., letter names, letter features, how letters are formed, letter-sound associations, spacing, punctuation, directionality, etc.). Children come to understand that letters can be grouped together to form words, that words have meaning, and that words are ordered to record sentences.

The chart that follows shows how one teacher, Mr. Alvarez, used writing during a large group meeting to introduce many literacy skills and concepts. The notes on the right indicate the teachers' reflections about what they are doing.

The children sit on the rug, facing Ms. Tory for their morning meeting.

Ms. Tory:	*Our morning meeting is almost over. Who can tell what we will do next?* (The children recite in unison as Ms. Tory points to the words Choice Time.)	Shows the importance of functional print.
	Before you go to your interest areas, Mr. Alvarez is going to share some new things with you. (Mr. Alvarez takes Ms. Tory's place in front of the children.)	
Mr. Alvarez:	*I have three new things to share with you today. Let me make a short list of them on this chart paper so I won't forget what they are.*	Demonstrates and talks about the meaningful purpose of print.
	The first thing we need to discuss is a new toy for the Sand and Water Area. It's a pump, so I'll write the word pump. *Let's see, I'll start here* (points to the left side of the paper and names each letter as he writes) *p-u-m-p,* pump.	Demonstrates left-to-right directionality. Calls attention to letters and demonstrates how they are formed.
	The second thing we need to talk about is the snack for the day. Since I'm writing a list, I'll write snack underneath pump: *s-n-a-c-k.*	Talks about the format of a list.
Shawn:	*That's my name!*	
Setsuko and Sonya:	*And mine!*	
Mr. Alvarez:	*Your names do begin with an* s, *but there is one difference. Let's see if anyone can tell the difference.* (He says each child's name aloud; then writes it on the chart.)	Acknowledges the children's responses and challenges them to think further about the information.
Jonetta:	*It's bigger!*	

Mr. Alvarez:	*You are watching closely, Jonetta. Their names begin with a capital, or uppercase S, and the word* snack *begins with a lowercase* s. *The letters are formed the same way, but they are different sizes. See?* (Mr. Alvarez writes *Ss* so the children can see the difference.)	Calls attention to the features and forms of letters.
Setsuko:	*I have both.*	
Mr. Alvarez:	*You certainly do, Setsuko. A capital S at the beginning of your name and a lowercase s in the middle of your name.* (Mr. Alvarez draws a line under each *Ss* as he speaks.)	Confirms Setsuko's observation.
	The third thing I would like to share is the set of pictures from our trip to the apple orchard. Let's see. What should I write?	Involves the children in generating language.
Malik:	*How about pictures?*	
Mr. Alvarez:	*What do the rest of you think?* (The children nod their heads, yes.) *Pictures.* (Mr. Alvarez repeats the word as he writes it on the chart.) *Hey,* pictures *and* pump *start with the same letter,* p.	Draws children's attention to a particular letter and letter sound.
	(Mr. Alvarez returns to the top of the list and reads *pump*.) *Have you ever seen a pump before? Can you guess what it does?* (He takes the pump from a nearby box and explains that a pump is a tool that people use to help move water from one place to another. He has prepared a tub of water so he can demonstrate how it works. The children ask several questions and take turns pumping the handle. Mr. Alvarez records their questions on chart paper and repeats their words as he writes.)	Plans a way to introduce a new toy.
		Links new vocabulary word to prior knowledge.
		Demonstrates speech-to-word correspondence.
		Involves the children in a physical activity.
		Shows he values the children's questions by writing them on the chart.
Mr. Alvarez:	*You've asked some very interesting questions, and I bet you'll discover some of the answers when you work with the pump in the Sand and Water Area. I've written your questions on the chart so we can come back and talk more about them at our next meeting.*	Talks about the purposes of print.

Mr. Alvarez:	*We need to create a pegboard label for the pump so you will know where to put it when you are finished using it.* (Mr. Alvarez has cut a picture of the pump from a catalog and glued it on card stock. Together they create a label. He talks as he writes.) p-u-m-p.	Prepares the materials he needs in advance.
	(He reads the word slowly, sweeping his hand under the word.) *Does anyone notice anything special about the word* pump?	Calls attention to how print works and promotes knowledge of the alphabet.
Alexa:	*It has two of the same letter.*	
Mr. Alvarez:	*That's right, Alexa. Iit has two* ps, *one at the beginning of the word and one at the end. Listen and you'll hear the sound that the letter* p *makes.* (He reads the word slowly again to call attention to the /p/ sounds in the word.) *I'll put this label on the pegboard in the Sand and Water Area, along with the pump. Be sure to try it when you work there today.*	Calls attention to the features of words. Calls attention to the sounds represented by letters.
	I'll cross out the word pump *now, because we have talked about it.*	
Mr. Alvarez and children:	(Mr. Alvarez looks at the list again, then takes the snack menu out of the box. He holds it so all the children can see.) *Today's snack is Trail Mix. You will have an opportunity to make your own trail mix in the Cooking Area.*	
	Let's look at the recipe and read the list of ingredients. (He holds up a picture/word recipe made with labels from familiar food products. He sweeps his hand under the words.) *Cheerios, pretzels, raisins, almonds.* (The children call the almonds *nuts.* He explains that almonds are one type of nut and points out the word *Almonds* on the package. He continues to read the directions with the children and tells them that the recipe will be posted for them to follow.)	Introduces new vocabulary words.

Mr. Alvarez:	*Who remembers what to do if you want to prepare snack but the Cooking Area is too crowded?*	Talks about the purpose of print. Provides children with a meaningful reason to write.
Zack:	*Write your name on the snack sign-up sheet.*	
Mr. Alvarez:	*Zack, will you show everyone the sign-up sheet?* (Zack shows the children the new sign-up sheet for the day, and Mr. Alvarez reminds them that the sign-up sheet helps to make sure that everyone has a turn to make snack. He reminds them to cross their names off of the list when they have finished preparing snack and to let the next person on the list know it is her turn. *Let me cross snack off our list.* (He draws a line through the word.) *Do you remember the third thing we need to talk about?* (He points to the word pictures on the list.)	Helps children to see the speaking, writing, and reading connection.
All children:	*Pictures!* (Mr. Alvarez takes a photo album out of the box and shows a few pictures to the children.)	
Mr. Alvarez:	*I'm going to put these in the Library Area for you to look at. I'll be visiting the Area today so you can dictate a few sentences about the pictures. That way, your families will be able to read about all the things that happened on our trip to the apple orchard.* (Puts a line through the word pictures.) *That's the last thing on our list. I think it's time for you to choose the Area in which you want to play.*	Talks about the purpose of print.

Tips to Share With Families

- Prepare your child's small muscles for writing by offering materials that strengthen them, such as playdough, clothespins, beads and string, Legos.

- Tell your child what you are doing when you write, e.g., *I'm making a shopping list so I can remember what to get at the store.*

- Have a box or another place where your child can keep writing and drawing supplies.

- When your child tells you stories, write them down and read them back.

- Encourage your child to write greeting cards and letters to family members.

- Encourage your child to make signs for her play.

- Write simple notes to your child.

- Help your child recognize his name and show him how to write it.

- Together, make words with magnetic or other toy letters.

- Bring writing supplies when you travel, such as paper and pencils, a Magna Doodle, or a magic slate.

- Outdoors, write letters in dirt or sand by using sticks or fingers, or use chalk on the sidewalk.

Playing: Children's Work

Children explore and construct understandings about the world through their play. Teachers support children's literacy learning by incorporating reading and writing materials into children's play so they can experiment with them. The key components of literacy are promoted through play and the social interactions that occur within the context of play.

When play is self-initiated, self-directed, open-ended, creative, and relatively risk-free, children enjoy learning. When reading and writing are incorporated in their play, children begin to understand **literacy as a source of enjoyment**.

As children play in interest areas and interact with adults and peers, they have opportunities for **vocabulary and language development**. They learn the names of props, ask and answer questions, exchange ideas, and explain what they are doing. In socio-dramatic play, they must communicate with others and negotiate roles and events. They also recreate real-life experiences and use increasingly sophisticated language as they act out various roles.

By using literacy materials in their play, children explore their **knowledge of print**. They attempt to imitate what they have seen adults and older children doing when they read and write. Children use written language to communicate for different purposes during their play (e.g., making signs and labels for constructions, greeting cards for friends and family, and signing their names on waiting lists to use equipment).

Children learn about **letters and words** as they manipulate alphabet materials, play matching letter games, and write. When print materials, such as labeled picture cards, are coupled with alphabet manipulatives, children can explore how letters are put together to form words.

Play is essential to building children's **comprehension** skills. Through play, children gain background knowledge and actually experience the meaning of language they will encounter in print. Firsthand experiences enable children to link new information with what they already know, thereby constructing understanding of what they hear and read.

During play, children have opportunities to see, handle, and create various kinds of **books and other texts**. Labels and signs are used to organize materials in every interest area; menus and recipes are found in the Cooking and Dramatic Play Areas; charts, graphs, and photos with descriptions that record children's learning are displayed; written directions for routine procedures are posted so children can manage independently (e.g., clean-up, hand-washing, and tooth-brushing procedures). As children read and listen to books, retell stories, and talk about their experiences, their sense of story structure is enhanced.

How to Begin

In a *Creative Curriculum* classroom, the environment is arranged carefully. Teachers

- plan the physical environment to support literacy learning

- include literacy materials for meaningful reading and writing experiences

Planning the Environment

The physical environment of a *Creative Curriculum* classroom is arranged in clearly defined interest areas that are equipped with props and materials that facilitate children's play. These small, intimate spaces encourage children's social interaction and use of language. The interest areas are organized using labels, signs, lists, and charts so that children know what to do and so that they learn important literacy skills. Teachers stock these areas with interesting props and an abundant supply of reading, writing, and oral language materials. They make sure that there is adequate space for children to work, that the areas are clean and well lit, and that the materials are stored so children can reach them easily.

Research confirms that children learn about language as they observe and interact with others in social situations. When teachers provide opportunities for children to play with peers in literacy-rich settings, children learn collaboratively about reading and writing. They help each other figure out the meaning of print (e.g., "That says *love*."), coach one another in literacy-related tasks (e.g., "This is how you make a *T*."), and help each other understand literacy-related roles (e.g., "The doctor writes the prescriptions, not the patient.").

Selecting Materials Thoughtfully

The Library Area is the hub of literacy learning in a *Creative Curriculum* classroom and usually the place where most of the literacy materials are stored. However, literacy materials are included in all interest areas. Teachers carefully select materials that reflect the interests, backgrounds, and real-life experiences of the children, so that literacy learning is meaningful for them. For example, including writing materials, informational books, posters, and charts about the growth cycle of frogs in the Discovery Area, along with an aquarium with tadpoles, encourages interested children to use literacy as a learning tool. Meaningful experiences enable children to understand purposes for literacy skills, and they are able to explore reading and writing at their own pace and in their own way. For more ideas about how literacy learning is supported in interest areas, see chapter 4.

Supporting Children's Play

The interactions between teachers and children during play are critical to children's language and literacy development. Teachers need to observe children's play carefully, to determine the most appropriate level and type of support to offer. When adults become too involved or controlling, children lose interest and stop playing.

When teachers understand the components of literacy, they can interact with children deliberately to encourage them to explore literacy in ways that they might not try on their own. Consider this example:

> *A teacher noticed that the children in the Dramatic Play Area have many pretend phone conversations. To promote children's awareness that print has meaning and can be used to communicate with others, the teacher added paper and pencils to the area. She then pretended to have a phone conversation and to take an important message for one of the children. Then she read the message to the child.*

Teachers' enthusiasm about children's early attempts to read and write also influence children's view of themselves as readers and writers. By respecting children's efforts—however conventional or unconventional they might be—teachers can help children to feel confident and competent, and to know that the classroom is a place where they can experiment safely with oral and written language.

Teachers assume various roles during play in order to support children's literacy learning. These roles include being an observer, facilitator, player, and leader.

Observer

Sometimes children are deeply involved in play, and the teacher only needs to observe, offer encouragement through a smile or nod of the head, or validate a child's effort.

Malik: (Has a doll in her lap, the phone receiver to her ear, and is writing on a note pad.) *Give her one spoonful of medicine before she goes to bed and one when she wakes up. OK, I'll bring her to see you tomorrow. Thank you, Doctor.*

Ms. Tory: (Looks at the pad on which Malik wrote.) *I see you wrote down what the doctor said. Good thing you were able to talk to him on the phone. Doctors can be so busy at times.*

Faciltator

As a facilitator, the teacher does not participate in play but supports children by providing props and materials or helping children arrange an area for a particular kind of play. The following conversations took place between Crystal, Ben, and Dallas and their teacher, Mr. Alvarez, as they set up a restaurant in the Dramatic Play Area.

Ben:	(Looks at Mr. Alvarez.) *We need a sign or paper that tells people what they can buy at the restaurant.*
Mr. Alvarez:	*A sign?*
Ben:	*Yeah, so people will know what kind of food we have and how much it costs.*
Mr. Alvarez:	*Oh, yes, you will need menus.* (Mr. Alvarez hands Ben menus from a familiar local restaurant.)
Mr. Alvarez:	*This is a nice place you have here. What is the name of your restaurant? I want to tell all of my friends about it.*
Crystal:	*We don't have a name yet.*
Mr. Alvarez:	*Well, when you decide on the name, let me know. I will be happy to help you make a sign and hang it up so everyone will know about your restaurant.*
Mr. Alvarez:	*Here are some pads so the waiter or waitress can write the customers' orders.*
Dallas:	*I'm going to be the waiter!*

Player

As a player, the teacher participates in children's play at their invitation. Assuming a role or character, the teacher extends children's play through dialogue or literacy activities related to the play theme. This encourages children to assume roles and to talk about what they are doing. In the scenario below, the children have positioned chairs in rows of two to simulate a bus. Kate is seated in the driver's seat while Setsuko, Sonya, and Carlos are pretending to be passengers.

Kate:	*Ms. Tory, do you want to go on a bus trip?*
Ms. Tory:	*I would love to.*
Kate:	(Holds out her hand.) *Where's your ticket?*
Ms. Tory:	*I didn't know I need a ticket. Where do I get one?*

Carlos:	*You have to buy one. I'll get you a ticket.* (Carlos gets off the bus and goes to a nearby table. Ms. Tory follows him.)
Ms. Tory:	(Acts in character.) *Excuse me. Is this where I get a bus ticket?*
Carlos:	*Yes. How many do you want?*
Ms. Tory:	*Just one.*
Carlos:	*Here you go.* (Carlos scribbles on a piece of paper and hands it to Ms. Tory.)
Ms. Tory:	*How much do I owe you?*
Carlos:	*Fifty dollars.*
Ms. Tory:	*Fifty dollars! That's a lot of money! Let me see if I have enough.* (She pretends to search her pockets.)
Ms. Tory:	*Hmm. I'm all out of cash. Will you take a check?*
Carlos:	*I guess so.*
Ms. Tory:	(Ms. Tory reaches for a blank piece of paper and thinks aloud as she writes.) *Kate's Bus Company. Fifty dollars. Mrs. Tory.*
Ms. Tory:	(Hands the paper to Carlos.) *Here you go.*
Carlos:	*OK. Let's go.* (Carlos returns to his seat on the bus.)
Ms. Tory:	(Gives the ticket to Kate, sits in a chair, and continues the role of bus passenger.)

Leader

As a leader, the teacher directs aspects of children's play, not by controlling the play, but by intentionally introducing new ideas. In the following example, a spring holiday is approaching and the children in an oceanside community have been talking about going to the beach. Mr. Alvarez is in the Dramatic Play Area with Crystal and Juwan. They are pretending that they are going to the beach, and they have asked him to pretend that he is their Dad. Sonya is also in the Dramatic Play Area, but she is not initially involved in Crystal's and Juwan's play. Notice how Mr. Alvarez skillfully introduces literacy into the children's play.

Juwan:	*We need to go to the store to buy food and stuff for our trip.*
Mr. Alvarez:	*You're right. Before we go, we need to make a list. You know how I forget things.*
Crystal:	*OK. Hand me that paper, and I'll start the list. Let's see... We're gonna need snacks and suntan lotion, beach towels, and a hat to keep the sun out of our eyes.*
Sonya:	*Hi. What are you doing?*
Crystal:	*Making a list so we can remember what to get at the store. We're going on a trip to the beach.*
Sonya:	*Who's going?*
Crystal:	*Me and Dad* (motions to Mr. Alvarez) *and Juwan.*
Sonya:	*Who's gonna keep your baby brother?* (Points to the doll in the high chair.)
Crystal:	*Hmmm.* (Puts finger to chin as though she is thinking.) *You mean while we go to the store or to the beach?*
Sonya:	*To the store. Want me to keep him?*
Crystal:	*Yeah! We might be gone a while, and he might get fussy.* (Picks up keys and looks at Mr. Alvarez) *Let's go, Dad. Juwan come on. Sonya is gonna keep the baby.*
Mr. Alvarez:	*We can't go until we give her instructions for taking care of the baby, especially since he has been a little fussy. Here.* (He hands Crystal a memo pad.)
Crystal:	(Talks as she writes.) *Give him a bottle in 20 minutes. Rock him and then put him in his crib. He likes for you to sing* You Are My Sunshine. *That is his favorite song.*

While four roles have been described, it does not mean that the teacher assumes only one role exclusively when interacting with children. Often the teacher assumes multiple roles during a play episode, according to the needs of the children.

Incorporating literacy in children's play allows them to construct understandings about literacy experiences they have in other contexts. It is also a way to provide developmentally appropriate instruction.

Tips to Share With Families

- Do things together that you both enjoy (e.g., taking a walk, baking cookies, swimming) and talk about what you notice and what you are doing, thinking, and feeling.

- Encourage your child's dramatic (pretend) play by asking questions and sometimes assuming a role. ("Are you making cookies for me? I like chocolate chip ones." "I'd like to take a trip on your airplane. Where are you going?")

- Collect empty food containers, grocery bags, paper and pencils to make shopping lists, and make some play money, to encourage your child to pretend that he is going to the grocery store.

- Offer old clothes, hats, suitcases, plastic dishes, empty food containers, and writing materials, so your child can play house. Make office supplies available as well.

- Provide writing materials for your child to use as she plays.

- Offer your child different kinds of art materials and talk about how they can be used.

- Give your child a chance to talk about what he is doing and thinking as he plays.

Studies: Using Literacy to Learn

The Creative Curriculum for Preschool (pp. 190–198) encourages the use of studies as a way of building content knowledge and helping children develop process skills. A study is an in-depth investigation of a topic worth learning more about. As children work on studies, they find the answers to their questions. They practice and apply literacy skills in meaningful ways, in order to learn information about the topic.

Beginning the Study

To illustrate how children use literacy to learn, consider the study that evolved in Ms. Tory's and Mr. Alvarez's class:

> *It was spring, and the children began to notice changes outside. While outdoors, they began picking wildflowers and wild onions. They brought them back to the classroom and used them in a variety of ways. They arranged them in vases to display in the Dramatic Play Area and glued them on the covers of folded card stock to create greeting cards. Some children blew the dandelions and watched to see where the seeds landed. At group time, the teachers talked with the children about the flowers and asked them to describe the different ways they used them. They also recalled seeing flowers in other places. As their interest continued to grow, Ms. Tory and Mr. Alvarez decided that a study of flowers would offer many opportunities for the children to learn content.*

The teachers then created a web of big ideas to identify the content children could learn. They started by brainstorming words that relate to flowers. In addition to helping them identify the content, this also enabled them to record important vocabulary words that could be taught.

Once they had generated a long list of words on Post-its, they grouped the words into categories on a piece of chart paper. They drew a circle around each group and labeled it. The labels identified the big ideas of the topic.

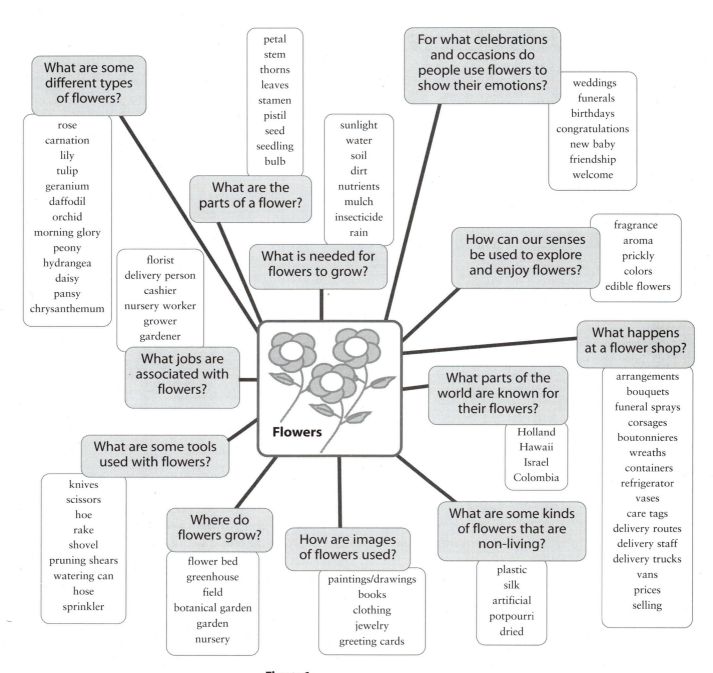

What are some different types of flowers?

rose
carnation
lily
tulip
geranium
daffodil
orchid
morning glory
peony
hydrangea
daisy
pansy
chrysanthemum

What are the parts of a flower?

petal
stem
thorns
leaves
stamen
pistil
seed
seedling
bulb

For what celebrations and occasions do people use flowers to show their emotions?

weddings
funerals
birthdays
congratulations
new baby
friendship
welcome

What is needed for flowers to grow?

sunlight
water
soil
dirt
nutrients
mulch
insecticide
rain

How can our senses be used to explore and enjoy flowers?

fragrance
aroma
prickly
colors
edible flowers

What jobs are associated with flowers?

florist
delivery person
cashier
nursery worker
grower
gardener

What happens at a flower shop?

arrangements
bouquets
funeral sprays
corsages
boutonnieres
wreaths
containers
refrigerator
vases
care tags
delivery routes
delivery staff
delivery trucks
vans
prices
selling

What are some tools used with flowers?

knives
scissors
hoe
rake
shovel
pruning shears
watering can
hose
sprinkler

What parts of the world are known for their flowers?

Holland
Hawaii
Israel
Colombia

Where do flowers grow?

flower bed
greenhouse
field
botanical garden
garden
nursery

How are images of flowers used?

paintings/drawings
books
clothing
jewelry
greeting cards

What are some kinds of flowers that are non-living?

plastic
silk
artificial
potpourri
dried

Flowers

Figure 1

They reviewed the information found in chapter 3 of *The Creative Curriculum for Preschool*, to see how their web addressed the key science and social studies components and skills. Both teachers considered how children could use literacy and math skills to learn content. They also discussed how this topic relates to the standards required for their program.

Mr. Alvarez and Ms. Tory thought of the many ways that they could address literacy, math, science, social studies, the arts, and technology through the study of flowers.

A good study begins with what children know and then leads them beyond their everyday experiences. Ms. Tory led a discussion about the children's flowers to find out what they already knew. Ms. Tory asked, *I wonder how all the wild flowers grew all of a sudden, like magic?* The children offered ideas, which Ms. Tory recorded on a chart.

During their discussions at group time, Ms. Tory kept a list of the children's questions.

> ### What We Want to Know About Flowers
>
> *Why do they die?*
>
> *Where do they come from?*
>
> *How big can flowers grow?*
>
> *How can a little seed turn into a flower?*
>
> *If you cut a flower, will it keep growing?*

She continued to add to the list each day as the children wondered aloud. This list of questions became the heart of their study. The experiences that Ms. Tory and Ms. Alvarez offered and encouraged were designed to help the children find answers to these questions. Ms. Tory wrote a note to families to let them know about the flower study and ways they might participate.

Investigating the Topic

Ms. Tory and Mr. Alvarez first thought of all the possible experiences that could help the children find answers to their questions and to gain deeper understandings about flowers. The following were some of their ideas for incorporating literacy skills.

Flower Experiences	Ways to Use Literacy Skills
Site visit to a flower shop (or nursery or garden)	Help children formulate questions for the florist and practice asking them before the visit. Provide clipboards for children to write or draw observation notes. Read informational books about flower shops and flowers before the visit. Take photos of environmental print at the flower shop or nursery and display them. Collect samples from the florist of printed materials, e.g., care tags, flyers, advertisements. Compose a thank-you note with the children and address the envelope. Write an experience story after the site visit.
Plant flowers	Explore with children the letters and words on seed packets; create matching games. Read and follow directions for planting seeds with the children; make a book with seed packets. Create a chart of job responsibilities for caring for the flowers. Keep journals to document observations of growing flowers. Look at books and catalogues with pictures of flowers from around the world. Read books about flowers, such as *The Tiny Seed* (Eric Carle), *The Dandelion Seed* (Joseph P. Anthony), *Gardening Tools* (Inez Snyder), *Bumble Bee, Bumble Bee, Do You Know Me?: A Garden Guessing Game* (Anne Rockwell), *Planting a Rainbow* (Lois Ehlert).
Flower arranging	Help children write letters to their families, asking for flowers from their yards. Look at magazines, flyers, books, and florist Web sites to see flower arrangements. Learn new vocabulary words, such as *oasis, container, vase, arrangement, bouquet, corsage*. Learn the names of the flowers in the children's arrangements, such as *roses, daisies, daffodils*. Learn descriptive words and record them on a chart, such as *violet, fragrant, thorny*. Write enclosure cards for the flower arrangements. Discuss the occasions and celebrations for which people use flowers. Make up rhymes or poems to deliver with flowers (e.g., *Roses are red, violets are blue, sugar is sweet, and so are you*); draw children's attention to the rhyming words. Make a book with magazine pictures of bouquets, corsages, boutonnieres, bud vases, sprays.
Create a flower shop in the Dramatic Play Area	Refer to the photos taken on the site visit to the florist; create signs with the children. Write a list of what to include in the flower shop on chart paper. Create advertisements, brochures, enclosure cards, care tags; identification labels. Create a poster identifying the types of flowers for sale. Complete order forms for flower arrangements; add a map and instructions for delivery.
Conduct experiments with flowers	Place white carnations in containers with colored water; make a chart of the children's predictions about what will happen; discuss results. Experiment with flowering plants (light/no light; water/no water; plant food/no plant food); write predictions and findings.

There were far too many experiences to be completed in a week. Learning takes time. Ms. Alvarez and Mr. Tory used the Weekly Planning Form (see *The Creative Curriculum for Preschool*, pages 526–527) to record the materials they needed and to identify what they hoped to accomplish each week. They adjusted their plans on the basis of their observations of children engaged in the study.

Over the next few weeks, the teachers guided children through various investigations and activities to help them find the answers to their questions. They used open-ended questions to help children plan, predict, and solve problems. Examples of the types of questions and prompts they used to build knowledge and encourage language development include:

- *I wonder why the tall flower topples over when you put it in the short vase. What can you do so it won't fall over?*

- *What do you think would happen if we didn't water the geranium?*

- *How do you think the florist gets the flowers that are in the cooler?*

- *How do you think this tiny sunflower seed grows to be so tall?*

Ms. Tory and Mr. Alvarez displayed the children's documentation of their study.

Concluding the Study

To bring closure to their study of flowers, the children planned a flower show for their families and other visitors. The children created invitations, welcome banners, and programs. They worked in groups to create floral arrangements. They followed recipes to prepare snacks and juice. When the guests arrived, each group told about their arrangement, the types of flowers they used, and the process of creating it. The guests were given a tour of the flower garden they had planted. After the celebration was over, the children delivered their arrangements to residents in a nearby nursing home.

As you can see, this study of flowers uses literacy in ways that are meaningful and relevant to children. The study helps children understand purposes for reading, writing, listening, and speaking, and it helps them practice literacy skills.

inside this chapter

Literacy Learning in Interest Areas

4

Children in a *Creative Curriculum* classroom spend a significant part of each day in child-initiated play in interest areas thoughtfully designed by teachers. When each interest area is organized with literacy in mind, children's time is well spent and literacy learning is maximized. This chapter describes how to make each interest area a valuable place for literacy learning and shows how teachers interact with children in ways that promote each component of literacy. While the Library Area is the place where the most significant number of books and materials is located, each area of the classroom must become a place where children's literacy skill development is promoted in a purposeful, integrated way.

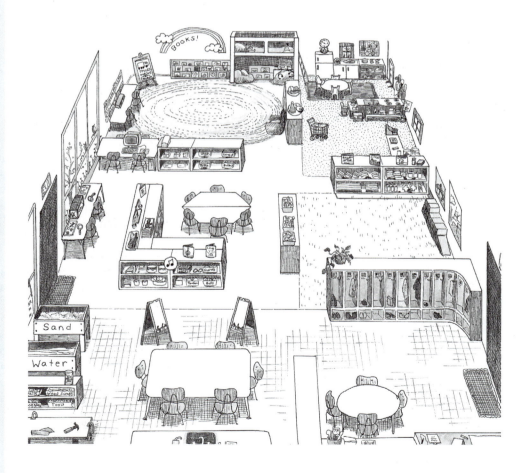

The Library Area as the Hub of Literacy Learning

The Library Area is the resource area for many materials and the place where concentrated literacy learning often occurs. An effective Library Area helps children develop the motivation and skills necessary to read and write. As they hear stories read aloud every day, look through books on their own, listen to story tapes, retell familiar stories, and make up their own stories, they also have many opportunities to grow in all areas of development.

Creating an Effective Library Area

The Library Area should include places for looking at books, listening to recordings, writing, retelling familiar stories, and perhaps using a computer. When arranged attractively and stocked thoughtfully with materials, the Library Area can be one of the most popular places in the classroom. Consider the books, tapes, writing materials, and storytelling props that are most appropriate and appealing for the children in your classroom. Organize and display the materials so that children will be drawn to them and will be able to use them easily.

Selecting Books

As with all materials, keep the ages and interests of the children in mind when you select books. In general, younger preschoolers like books with a simple, predictable plot about familiar experiences; colorful, bold illustrations that are clear and detailed; and rich language (rhymes, nonsense words, and repetition). Older preschoolers have a longer attention span and can follow more complicated plots. They appreciate humor and fantasy and are beginning to enjoy stories about faraway places.

Instead of displaying all of your books at one time, put out a manageable number of books and rotate them regularly. That way, the children will notice new books and will be excited by old favorites they haven't seen for a while. As new interests emerge, add relevant books. Select books that

- relate to the interests and life experiences of children and that will help them develop understandings about the world

- are predictable and allow children to participate by chanting or supplying words and phrases

- enrich children's language development

- help children gain knowledge of the alphabet and phonological awareness

- represent a variety of genres

- reflect diversity and promote inclusion

For children whose home language is not English, provide books written in their primary languages. This practice sends the message to children and their families that each home language is honored and respected.

For a more thorough discussion of each of these books features, see pages 356–358 of *The Creative Curriculum for Preschool*.

Materials for Story Retelling

After children have heard a story several times and have seen the story retold using props, they will want to retell it independently. In the Library Area, include materials that encourage children to tell and retell stories, such as flannel boards and puppets. For more guidance about books and props for story retelling, see chapter 3, pages 102–103.

Materials for Listening

Include tapes of familiar stories so children can practice following a story in a book, turning the pages at the appropriate time and matching the narrative with the pictures. If possible, the Library Area should include a few small cassette players and a variety of tapes (or CD players and CDs) for children to select. Headphones allow children to listen without disturbing others.

The same general guidelines for selecting books apply to selecting story tapes. The best tapes are short, lively, unbiased in content, and well narrated by both men and women. In selecting story tapes, begin with stories that are familiar to the children or that accompany books you have in the classroom. You can make tapes, yourself, recording books that the children particularly love. As you record the story, include sound effects or other cues to let children know when to turn the page while reading with the tape. Pause occasionally while recording the story, to encourage the children to supply a word or phrase. Invite family members and community volunteers to make tapes for the children as well.

Materials for Writing

A place for writing offers children opportunities to write for different purposes, such as creating greeting cards or writing messages to friends. The Library Area should include a table and chairs as well as a shelf for storing an assortment of writing materials. At a minimum, include

- alphabet strips
- name cards
- a variety of paper, envelopes, and stationery
- a variety of writing tools (pencils, markers, crayons)
- stencils and letter stamps
- bookbinding supplies

For a complete list of materials, see the chart on page 360 of *The Creative Curriculum for Preschool*.

Observing and Responding to Children

Some children have had many experiences with books at home and come to school with early reading and writing skills. Others have had little experience with language and literacy. Teachers can guide children's learning when they know what specific reading and writing skills children are acquiring.

Skills for Engaging with Books

Learning to read is a complex process that involves developing many skills. Look for and encourage children's skills as they progress to reading and writing.

Listening for understanding. Listening and reading are closely related. As children listen to stories, they learn the meaning of new words. They try to make sense of these words by connecting them to their own experiences. Later, when children begin reading, they have an easier time recognizing words when they know their meanings. Listening to stories improves children's understanding of grammar and the structure of language. These skills help pave the way for figuring out what makes sense in the text.

Exploring books. Imitating adults and older children, young children like to play at reading. Even though children may not actually be reading, they explore many reading-like behaviors. They hold the book correctly and turn the pages appropriately. Children also want to have books read to them, frequently asking for the same picture book again and again at one sitting. Adults often tire of rereading the same story, long before the children. Children enjoy repetition because they love to anticipate what happens next and feel powerful knowing the answer. Repetition supports the development of children's understanding of story structure and their efforts to learn the conventions of print.

Understanding how stories work. Children gradually recognize that stories have a beginning, middle, and end. They use pictures as cues to remember the details of their favorite stories and to confirm their growing understanding of print concepts. You might hear children use story language such as, "Once upon a time...," or, "...and that's the end of our story." After hearing a story repeatedly, children call on their comprehension and verbal skills to retell the story.

Understanding the function and value of print. Readers understand why and how print is used. From meaningful print throughout the classroom, such as a menu, a daily schedule, or a name on a cubby, children learn that print provides information. Children use books as a source of information, as when they want to locate a picture of a bug they found on the playground or a truck they saw passing on the street.

Recognizing that written words are symbols. When children are first introduced to books, they follow the story through the pictures. With multiple experiences and adult guidance, they gradually learn that printed words function differently from pictures and that words are symbols that stand for ideas and feelings.

Connecting written symbols with sounds. As children explore the sounds and rhythms of language, they begin to understand that spoken words are made of individual sounds that are represented by the letters of the alphabet. When they listen to the story of the duck named Ping, a child may say, "That starts the same way as my name!"

Matching words with the printed text. You may see children run their fingers along the text or point to individual words as a book is being read. They may begin matching spoken with printed words by pointing. These behaviors indicate that they are beginning to understand the concept of a word, although they may not necessarily read words correctly.

Recognizing printed words. Children who have learned this skill take an active interest in the text and are curious about finding words they know on the page. They may ask questions such as, "What does this say?" or "Where does it say that?" Children develop a sight vocabulary. They notice words from favorite books or commercial products and excitedly point them out in less familiar books and in the environment.

Developmental Steps in Writing

Long before children come to school, they have seen writing displayed and used in their environment. When children have opportunities to write in the context of everyday activities, they learn many important literacy skills, such as understandings about print conventions, functions of print, and phonological awareness.

The Creative Curriculum Developmental Continuum for Ages 3–5 maps the stages of writing in objective 50, "Writes letters and words." The following is additional information about each of the steps, to use as a guide to analyzing children's writing.

Forerunner: Scribbling. Young children love to use pencils, pens, crayons, and other writing tools to imitate adult writing. These early attempts at writing mark the first developmental stage. Although writing at this stage looks more like scribbling than anything else, it follows a definite form. In the child's mind, beginning attempts at writing are quite different from beginning attempts at drawing. The illustration at the right shows how a child organized scribbles horizontally on the page.

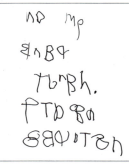

Step I: Scribble Writing and Letter-Like Forms. In the second stage of writing development, scribbles are gradually transformed into separate marks. Many times, a recognizable letter will emerge from a row of small marks. The first letter of a child's name is usually one of the first to be written. With practice, children begin to write recognizable letters that begin to outnumber unconventional marks.

Step II: Writes Recognizable Letters. In this stage, the child writes recognizable letters. Sometimes a child will fill a whole page with one letter. Sometimes every letter he knows will be written randomly on a page. Usually the first letters to be written are the ones that are most important to a child: those in his own name. In the illustration at the right, a child wrote a shopping list of five items and read it to the teacher: eggs, ice cream, cherries, potato chips, and bubble gum. As you can see, she writes many letters, but has not yet begun to associate each letter with its corresponding sound.

Step III: Uses Letters That Represent Sounds in Words. By the end of the preschool years and early in kindergarten, children's writing generally shows increased organization. Children learn that letters are not just placed randomly on the page. Often they will write rows and rows of letters, sometimes in alphabetical order. Next, children attempt to write words by writing the sounds they think they hear. For example, in the illustration at the right, a child drew a picture of a brontosaurus and wrote, "Brtsrs." When children spell this way, they are grasping the concept that a word is made up of a series of sounds that are recorded in a particular order. This is an important skill in learning to read.

Responding to Each Child

Because the Library Area offers so many opportunities for learning, visit the area, observe, and talk with children when they are working there. An appropriate starting point for your observations is to look for the reading and writing behaviors described earlier. In observing a child's use of the Library Area, notice if the child

- shows a preference for certain topics or books and often connects them to personal experiences

- talks about the story, pretends to read it, and identifies words in the text

- handles a book appropriately and, in English, follows print from left to right, top to bottom, and front to back

- retells stories in his own words or by using props

- writes or scribbles messages to communicate meaning

Your observations can be used to plan specific activities to extend each child's learning and growth. For further guidance, review the Observation, Reflection, and Response chart on page 369 of *The Creative Curriculum for Preschool*.

Interacting With Children in the Library Area

Teachers are role models for young children. If you show children how much you enjoy books, and if they see you writing often and for a purpose, children will want to imitate you. The Library Area is a place where you can spend time sharing books, retelling stories, listening to tapes, and writing with individuals and small groups of children.

Reading Books With Small Groups and Individual Children

The Library Area is ideal for sharing books with small groups of children. The intimate setting enables you to interact with children positively and enhance their language and literacy learning. The following chart shows the kinds of questions you might ask and comments you might make.

Interactive Story Reading

Kind of Question or Comment	Example
Completion—Omit a word at the end of a sentence and let the children fill it in.	"Run, run, as fast as you can. You can't catch me. I'm the Gingerbread _____!"
Open-Ended—Ask the children a question that will encourage them to think of several different answers.	"What do you think the Gingerbread Man is doing in this picture?" "I wonder why the Gingerbread Man wanted to run away. What do you think?" "How would you feel if you were a Gingerbread Man?"
Who, What, When, Where, Why, and How—Ask the children these kinds of questions about the narrative and the pictures.	"What did the baker use to make the Gingerbread Man?" "What did the little old man say when the Gingerbread Man ran away?" "Where did the fox want the Gingerbread Man to go?" "Why do you think the fox wanted the Gingerbread Man to ride on his head across the river?" "How did the fox trick the Gingerbread Man?"
Connections—Help the children see how the story relates to their own experiences.	"Have you ever eaten gingerbread?" "Did anyone ever try to trick you?"

There will also be times when you or another adult will read a book to just one child. On these occasions, you can focus on specific skills with that child. Here are some strategies you can use.

Before reading:
Have the child sit comfortably beside you or in your lap.

> **Note a child's preferences:** *This must be your favorite book. You've picked it out every morning this week. Tell me what you like best about it.*

> **Look at and discuss the book's cover:** *The title of this book is... I wonder what the story is about.*

> **Take a "picture walk"** with the child by talking about the illustrations in the story and asking the child to predict what will happen: *I wonder why the insects are hiding in the grass in that picture.*

During reading:

Reinforce child's correct handling of books: *I can see from the careful way you are turning the pages that you really know how to take care of our books.*

Encourage the child to think critically: *What would you do if you were Andrew? Why do you think Peter's mother said, "No"?*

Help the child think of and express new ideas and solutions: *That glue on her shoes really slowed her down, didn't it? What else would you do?*

Encourage the child to anticipate the storyline as you read: *What do you think will happen next?*

Explore feelings: *Have you ever felt like Francis? I bet you know just how Ira felt about sleeping at a friend's house. Have you ever stayed overnight at a friend's house?*

Relate what is happening in the story to the child's own life: *The little boy in this story has a new baby brother, just like you do, Tasheen.*

Encourage the child to point to words: *Can you find where it says* dog? *It starts like your name, Derek.*

After reading:

Discuss the completed story with the child: *What did you like about this story? Who was your favorite character?*

Encourage the child to retell or act out the story: *Would you like to use flannel board pieces to tell the story?*

Retelling Stories With Children

Children also try to retell stories they know or make up new stories. You may assume one of many roles during these retellings:

- **Narrator**—You narrate the story as they act it out.

- **Player**—You assume a role in the story at the children's request.

- **Resource Person**—You assist in finding props.

- **Observer**—You observe the action as children retell the story using props they have chosen independently.

Carefully follow the lead of the children during their retelling and determine when children need additional support. For further information on retelling stories, see chapter 3, pages 101–107.

Listening to Tapes With Children

Take the time to join one or two children in listening to a taped story. For some children, you may need to turn the pages of the book to keep pace with the recorded voice. Other children may be able to do this on their own.

Some children may be reluctant to select a tape on their own, or they may be unsure about how to operate the tape recorder. Sometimes the assistance of another child is all that's needed. Once children learn to operate the equipment, they can listen to tapes independently.

Promoting Children's Writing

Keep writing tools and paper readily available. Show an interest in writing and in what children do. Try these approaches.

> **Model writing and explain your purpose:** *I need to write a note to the director to remind her that we have a study trip next week.*
>
> **Comment on the child's work:** *I see you've been busy writing. Will you read to me what you wrote?*
>
> **Describe what you see:** *You made a whole row of As and then a row of Ms.*
>
> **Help a child use the equipment:** *Let me help you find a way to put the caps on the markers.*
>
> **Ask questions or make statements that help a child solve a problem:** *Do you want to know how to write Alexa's name? I wonder if we can find her name on something in the classroom.*

A teacher's genuine interest and involvement in the Library Area helps to reinforce children's growing interest in writing and reading.

Special Challenges in the Library Area

Children who have fine motor difficulties in manipulating small items, and children who have trouble attending to and processing language, may not seem to be particularly interested in Library Area activities. The following suggestions can help children with special challenges participate actively in the Library Area with their peers and develop language and literacy skills.

Chapter 5, *Literacy Activities*, suggests activities for the Library Area.

If a child...	Try these strategies...
Shows variable attention during listening and reading activities	Encourage the child's involvement in stories with hands-on experiences. For example, adapt pop-up or flap books by cutting off the flaps, laminating them for durability, then re-attaching them to the book with Velcro. The child can interact with the book by pulling each item off, or putting it on, during the reading of the story. Use related props with every story, so that the child has something to hold and manipulate (e.g., a spider ring for the *Itsy-Bitsy Spider* book). Use books that repeat phrases frequently, to encourage the child's learning and engagement. Encourage the child to be the lead storyteller, to encourage her attention and participation.
Has difficulty hearing, understanding, or seeing books read orally	Have the child sit close to you. Speak slowly to allow time for processing, and repeat text as necessary. Use exaggerated facial expressions, vocal tones, and non-verbal gestures. Encourage the use of a magnifying glass, binoculars, or "third eye" magnifying lens for a child with vision problems. Use peer reading buddies to provide individualized support to the child while looking at books.
Has language delays or is an English language learner	Use simple gestures and point to specific characters or details in illustrations, to improve the child's comprehension. Using American sign language for basic words in a story, rhyme, or song also supports language development. Adapt vocabulary, sentence, and text length to the child's level of understanding. Use teacher-made or commercial books that present songs that are sung in the classroom and books that have photographs of particular interest to the child.
Has trouble holding and manipulating reading materials	Use adaptive equipment such as book trays or holders. Use peer buddies as page turners. Attach Velcro tabs on page edges to make page turning easier for children with fine motor difficulties.
Avoids writing	Include large writing tools in many interest areas. Encourage the child who is interested in playing with magnetic letters and numbers to trace around them and to make words with them.
Has difficulty holding and manipulating writing tools and materials	Use adaptive equipment to encourage writing, such as pencil grips, very large crayons, and Velcro hand or wrist straps to hold writing tools. Consult with an assistive technology professional for the latest tools available to support children with fine and visual motor problems.

Literacy in the Block Area

Blocks are a powerful tool for representing stories and reenacting real events, for sparking conversations, for communicating and negotiating ideas, and for inspiring writing. Take advantage of children's love of block play to develop important literacy skills.

Examples of What a Child May Do…	Examples of Related Curriculum Objectives	Examples of How This Relates to Literacy
Build a fire truck with blocks	36. Makes believe with objects	Understands that the block structure is a symbol for a real object, an important step in understanding that letters symbolize sounds and words are symbols for ideas and feelings
Use a plank to create a drawbridge and talk about how it goes up and down	39. Expresses self using words and expanded sentences	Uses specialized vocabulary to communicate complex ideas
Build a skyscraper with a friend and figure out how to keep it from falling	23. Approaches problems flexibly 39. Expresses self using words and expanded sentences	Uses language to communicate, negotiate, and predict
Write a sign that reads "Don't knock my building down"	49. Understands the purpose of writing	Uses writing to communicate meaning
Match blocks with shape labels when returning them to the shelf	27. Classifies objects	Matches shapes, which relates to matching and discriminating letters and words
Place blocks on top of one another carefully	19. Controls small muscles in hands 20. Coordinates eye-hand movement	Develops important pre-writing skills such as eye-hand coordination, visual perception, and small muscle control

Adding literacy-related props to the Block Area not only stimulates the development of language and literacy skills, but it also inspires children to build more creatively. Children's books placed in the Block Area can spark children's creativity and serve as a resource for building ideas.

materials

- [ ] books and pictures about construction, buildings, workers, tools, construction and emergency vehicles, architecture, repairs, roads, bridges
- [ ] blueprints
- [ ] advertisements for construction materials and tools
- [ ] floor plans
- [ ] graph paper
- [ ] memo pads
- [ ] newspapers
- [ ] repair manuals
- [ ] traffic signs
- [ ] logos from local businesses

book suggestions

Alphabet City (Stephen Johnson)

Alphabet Under Construction (Denise Fleming)

As the Crow Flies: A First Book of Maps (Gail Hartman)

Bridges Are to Cross (Philemon Sturges)

Bruno the Carpenter (Lars Klinting)

Building a House (Byron Barton)

Cars and Trucks and Things That Go (Richard Scarry)

City Signs (Zoran Milich)

Freight Train (Donald Crews)

Get to Work, Trucks (Don Carter)

The House in the Meadow (Shutta Crum)

How a House Is Built (Gail Gibbons)

I Read Signs (Tana Hoban)

Inside Freight Train (Donald Crews)

Me on the Map (Joan Sweeny)

Mike Mulligan and His Steam Shovel (Virginia Lee Burton)

New Road! (Gail Gibbons)

Using Blocks to Teach Literacy Skills

The developmental stages of block play will help you to think about how to incorporate literacy skills in the Block Area (see *The Creative Curriculum for Preschool*, pages 256–259). You may have a child in your class who is at Stage I: Carrying Blocks. This child is exploring the physical properties of blocks and what she can and cannot do with them. Your interactions with this child might involve talking about how heavy or how long a block is. Your conversations with a child who is at Stage IV, Building Elaborate Constructions, might be entirely different. This child might use blocks to build a castle, a fire truck, or a city and engage in socio-dramatic play about the construction. You might offer additional literacy materials such as paper for signs or books about the topic. The key is first to observe the block play and match your interactions to the child's stage of development.

Here are examples of what you might say as children use the materials.

Unit Blocks

This is a really interesting construction. Will you tell me about it?

Would you like to make a Do not knock down *sign to keep your building safe?*

I noticed that your tower keeps falling when you build it on the carpet square. I wonder why that happens.

You know, this skyscraper you built today is even taller than the one you built yesterday. How did you make it so tall?

This road you made curves just like a letter S.

You made a house out of wood and a house out of bricks for the Three Little Pigs. What could you use for the third house? Let me know when you're ready to act out the story. I'd love to watch it.

Let's match these blocks to the shapes on the shelf while we clean up.

I see you're making a bridge. How is your bridge like the one in this book?

Hollow Blocks

You made the top of your castle just like the one in the book. You put one block standing up; then you left a space; then you stood another block up. I wonder why castles were built like that.

You made a drive-through window for the bank just like the one where your mother works. Would you like to make a sign for your bank to let everyone know that it is open for business?

Block Accessories (vehicles, animals, people)

Have you ever seen a front-loader? What do you think it is used for?

Would you like to make a license plate for this car? Here's a piece of paper you can use to write the letters and numbers for it.

I have a driver's license that shows I know how to operate a car and follow the rules of the road. Would you like to make your own driver's license with words about you and your picture on it?

I see you've made a zoo. Have you ever been to the zoo? Zoo is an easy word to spell: z-o-o. It almost sounds like boo! *Would you like to make a zoo sign over your entrance?*

You placed all the dolls in the bed you made out of blocks. Do you think they would enjoy hearing you read them a bedtime story?

Do you remember what the Little Engine said? "I think I can! I think I can!"

Loose Parts (PVC pipes, cardboard tubes and boxes, rain gutters, newspaper rolls)

You're using the box just as they did in the story. First the children used the box as a cave. Let me think. How else did they use the box? How will you use the box?

That piece of pipe curves just like the letter J. I know some friends in our class whose names begin with J. Do you?

The house you're building is enormous. Tell me all about it.

Signs

I see you're making a stop sign so the cars won't crash. Stop begins the same way as your name: Stephen/stop.

It looks like you're making a neighborhood like ours. Do you want to cut this grocery store name from the newspaper and make a sign for your store?

Observing Children's Progress

While children are engaged in block play, look for these indications of literacy development:

- using language to communicate their ideas

- talking with their peers and adults about their constructions

- describing what they are doing with the blocks

- controlling the small muscles in their hands and wrists as they carefully stack blocks

- describing size, shape, and position

- using words learned in a different context

- matching shapes when they return blocks to the shelves

- writing signs for their constructions

Chapter 5, *Literacy Activities*, suggests activities for the Block Area.

Literacy in the Dramatic Play Area

Children's language and literacy skills grow when their dramatic play experiences encourage the use of rich, expressive language and when they explore reading and writing as they play. Dramatic play allows children to use literacy in a meaningful way as they reenact real-life situations. They write phone messages, read to dolls, and have conversations about being adults. As they play, children experience being readers and writers.

Examples of What a Child May Do…	Examples of Related Curriculum Objectives	Examples of How This Relates to Literacy
Pretend that the pot is a drum	36. Makes believe with objects	Uses symbols in dramatic play, which prepares the child to use other symbols, e.g., letters as symbols that represent sounds in words; words as symbols for ideas and feelings
Talk about the print on the empty food containers	47. Uses emerging reading skills to make meaning from print	Makes connections between written language and spoken language
Button, buckle, snap, and zip dress-up and doll clothes	19. Controls small muscles in hands	Develops hand strength and coordination, which are needed to use writing tools
Talk on a play telephone with a friend	43. Actively participates in conversations	Learns to take turns in conversations, which is a communication skill
Write a shopping list	49. Understands the purpose of writing	Explores the power of the printed word and how to use it to communicate
Place a stack of baseball caps on his head and say, "Caps for sale! Caps for sale! Fifty cents a cap!"	48. Comprehends and interprets meaning from books and other texts	Recalls the events of a story that was read aloud

Think about the materials you can add to the Dramatic Play Area to further language and literacy development. When selecting books for the Dramatic Play Area, choose titles that enhance children's thematic play, such as house, office, and restaurant play. Also consider the individual needs of the children in your class. Books can help children deal with significant events such as a new baby, a death in the family, or moving to a new neighborhood. The chart that follows offers helpful suggestions for this interest area.

materials

- [ ] blank address books
- [ ] books and magazines
- [ ] calendars, date books, appointment books
- [ ] clipboards
- [ ] empty food containers
- [ ] maps
- [ ] menus, recipe cards, and cookbooks
- [ ] message boards
- [ ] newspapers
- [ ] notepads
- [ ] old checkbooks
- [ ] typewriter or computer keyboard
- [ ] pencils, pens, markers
- [ ] photo albums
- [ ] price lists
- [ ] receipt books
- [ ] signs
- [ ] stationery, greeting cards, and envelopes
- [ ] telephone book

book suggestions

Amazing Grace (Mary Hoffman)

Friends at School (Rochelle Bunnett, Matt Brown)

Go Away, Big Green Monster (Ed Emberly)

Going to the Dentist (Fred Rogers, Jim Judkis)

Going to the Doctor (Anne Civardi)

Goodnight Moon (Margaret Wise Brown)

Guess How Much I Love You (Sam McBratney)

Hats, Hats, Hats (Ann Morris)

How Do Dinosaurs Get Well Soon? (Jane Yolen)

How Do Dinosaurs Say Goodnight? (Jane Yolen)

Jesse Bear, What Will You Wear? (Nancy White Carlstrom)

Let's Talk About It: Adoption (Fred Rogers, Jim Judkis)

Let's Talk About It: Extraordinary Friends (Fred Rogers, Jim Judkis)

Lilly's Purple Plastic Purse (Keven Henkes)

Making Friends (Fred Rogers, Jim Judkis)

Mama, Do You Love Me? (Barbara M. Joosse)

Manners (Aliki)

Miss Spider's Tea Party (David Kirk)

"More, More, More," Said the Baby (Vera Williams)

My First Day at Preschool (Edwina Riddell)

The Napping House (Audrey Wood)

New Baby (Fred Rogers, Jim Judkis)

The Paper Bag Princess (Robert Munsch)

Peter's Chair (Ezra Jack Keats)

Talk, Baby! (Harriet Ziefert)

Tell Me Again About the Night I Was Born (Jamie Lee Curtis)

What Is Your Language? (Debra Leventhal)

When a Pet Dies (Fred Rogers, Jim Judkis)

Where's Spot? (Eric Hill)

William's Doll (Charlotte Zolotow)

◖ Literacy Props for Dramatic Play Settings

Bank—checkbooks, credit cards, deposit slips, signs (e.g., *Open/Closed, Do not enter, Next window, Thank you, Today is _____*)

Camping—blank books for nature journals, field guides, brochures, first aid manual or poster, maps, outdoor camping magazines, signs (e.g., *Camping site, Do not feed the bears, First aid, No swimming, Picnic area, Please put out the campfire*)

Garage—car manuals, repair guides, books about cars and trucks, auto store or car dealership advertisements, signs (e.g., *Gas, Keys, Parking, Pay here, Tire sale, Waiting area, Do not enter*)

Dentist/Doctor's Office—appointment books and cards, books about dentists, teeth, oral hygiene, eye charts, file folders, magazines, signs (e.g., *Please be seated, Smile!, The dentist/doctor is in/out*)

Fast Food Restaurant—coupons, tray liners, order pads, food containers, Braille menus, nutrition charts, newspaper ads, books about food, logos on uniforms, signs (e.g., *Drive through, Open/Closed, Order here, Pay here, Trash, Thank you, Come again*)

Florist—books and magazines about flowers and plants, price list, seed and flower arrangement catalogs, enclosure cards, care tags, order forms, newspaper ads, signs (e.g., flower names, *Today's special, Cash and carry*)

Grocery Store—coupons, newspaper inserts, receipts, grocery lists, food containers, signs (e.g., areas of the store, *Recycle your bags, Today's specials, Pay here, Checkout*)

Police Station—books about police officers and safety, clipboards, folders, driver's licenses (expired or teacher-made), parking tickets, badges, street maps, signs (e.g., traffic signs, *Dial 911, Driver's licenses, Lost and found, Parking tickets*)

Post Office—envelopes; stationery; stamps, rubber stamps and ink pads; greeting cards; address labels; postcards; books about mail, letters, mail carriers, and the post office; signs (e.g., *Local mail, Special delivery, Air mail, Zip codes, Next window, Stamps, U.S. mail*)

Shoe Store—catalogs, shoe boxes, shoe ads, order forms, receipts, signs (e.g., *Sizes 1-2, Checkout, Women, Men, Children, Open/Closed, Big sale today*)

Veterinarian—books about pets, animal care, identification tags, breed and pet care posters, pet care brochures, appointment book and cards, signs (e.g., *Pet supplies, Quiet please—sick pets, Wait here*)

Using Dramatic Play to Teach Literacy Skills

In the Dramatic Play Area, teachers observe children's play and consider ways to help them discover a need for reading and writing. By talking with children to suggest additional roles and play scenarios that involve the use of reading and writing, and by providing literacy materials that children can use in their play, you promote the development of skills.

Dress-Up Clothes

Where are you going with your briefcase? Do you need another pencil to write with at your office?

You look like you're getting ready to do some work in those overalls. What will you work on? What kind of tools do you need?

Are you on your way to put out a fire? Here's a map to help you find the office building.

The design on your shirt is very interesting. I see a reddish stripe here…That color is called burgundy, *and it's right next to a beige stripe. Where else do you see colors like these in our classroom?*

Food Containers (Environmental Print)

What kinds of cereal do you have in your store today? How can you tell what is inside the box?

I see some words on these containers that begin the same way as your name begins. Can you find them?

Would you like to look in our box of coupons to see what we should buy at the store? The coupons help you save money.

So, you want to bake some cookies? Here's some paper and pencil to make your shopping list. What ingredients do you need to buy?

Telephone, Telephone Book, Address Book, and Message Board

Hello! My name is Mr. Alvarez. What's your name? How are you today? I've been thinking about taking a trip to the city. What do you think I will see when I get there?

Would you like to call Tasheen? Let's look for her name in our class telephone book. Let's see. What letter does her name begin with? We need to turn to the T pages.

Are you talking to the doctor about your sick baby? Why don't you write what he tells you to do on the pad, so you can remember?

Dolls and Stuffed Animals

Your baby is fussy today. Maybe, if you rock him and read him a story, he will calm down.

I see you are pretending to be Goldilocks. Would you like me to help you gather some things to help you act out the story?

Doctor's Office Play

Doctor, my baby is sick. Will you write a prescription for some medicine so she can get better?

Let's check your eyes so we know whether you are seeing correctly. Can you read the letters on our chart?

I need to make an appointment for next week. Will you write my name in the doctor's appointment book?

Observing Children's Progress

When you observe children engaged in dramatic play, look for these indications of literacy development:

- pretending to read or retelling a story to a doll, a stuffed animal, or another child

- recognizing letters, especially those in their own names and on food containers

- returning materials to the proper location on the shelf, using picture and word labels or matching silhouettes

- attempting to write a list or message

- recognizing a name in a class phone or address book

- conversing with friends and adults in a series of exchanges and talking about topics that do not involve only the here-and-now

- using fine motor skills to button, buckle, zip, snap, and tie

- using new vocabulary to converse

- using symbols in play

- using invented or developmental spelling that indicates a beginning understanding of sound-symbol relationships

Chapter 5, *Literacy Activities*, suggests activities for the Dramatic Play Area.

Literacy in the Toys and Games Area

In the Toys and Games Area, children are surrounded by letters and words. They use words to describe how they are putting together a puzzle or sorting a collection of objects. They talk about objects as they play, comparing size, shape, and color. While using beads, pegboards, puzzles, dominoes, and collectibles, they develop reading skills such as left-to-right progression, visual discrimination, and matching similar objects. As they use magnetic letters and alphabet blocks, children explore letters, then arrange and rearrange them to form words. As they play with letter and word materials, they construct important understandings about written language.

Examples of What a Child May Do...	Examples of Related Curriculum Objectives	Examples of How This Relates to Literacy
Work a simple jigsaw puzzle	20. Coordinates eye-hand movement 23. Approaches problems flexibly	Analyzes puzzle pieces, which later helps the child to determine the distinguishing features of letters and words (visual discrimination; figure/ground perception)
String beads	19. Controls small muscles in hands	Builds fine motor skills that are important for holding and controlling writing tools and handling print materials
Play with magnetic letters	46. Demonstrates knowledge of the alphabet	Begins to understand how letters are used to form words
Participate in a game of alphabet bingo	46. Demonstrates knowledge of the alphabet	Matches and recognizes letters
Sew a lacing card	20. Coordinates eye-hand movement	Develops eye-hand coordination that is important for writing
Describe a rocket built with Legos	39. Expresses self using words and expanded sentences	Engages in conversation and uses descriptive language

Listed here are some specific literacy-related materials and books for the Toys and Games Area. Just as books in your home are not confined to one room, books in a *Creative Curriculum* classroom are placed throughout each interest area.

materials

- ☐ alphabet bingo
- ☐ alphabet blocks
- ☐ alphabet puzzles
- ☐ basic vocabulary pictures and games
- ☐ environmental print puzzles
- ☐ labeled picture cards
- ☐ letter sorting and matching games
- ☐ magnetic letters
- ☐ matching games
- ☐ name games
- ☐ rhyming picture games
- ☐ sequence cards
- ☐ sorting and classification materials

book suggestions

Alexander and the Wind-Up Mouse (Leo Lionni)

Can You See What I See?: Picture Puzzles to Search and Solve (Walter Wick)

Chicka Chicka Boom Boom (Bill Martin and John Archambault)

I Spy (Walter Wick)

Look Alikes Jr. (Joan Steiner)

Max's Toys: A Counting Book (Rosemary Wells)

Olivia and the Missing Toy (Ian Falconer)

Using Toys and Games to Teach Literacy Skills

As you interact with children in the Toys and Games Area, your conversations can help them learn important literacy skills. When you talk with children, first encourage them to describe what they are doing. Observe how they are playing with the materials and talk with them about what you see.

Magnetic Letters

What letters do you need for your name?

How is this letter like this one?

Can you find a letter like this one somewhere else in the classroom?

Environmental Print Puzzles, Lotto Games, Concentration Games

Have you ever seen this word before? Tell me about it.

Someone in our class has a name that begins the same way as the word soup. *Who is that?*

Some of these words from food containers start the same way: Juicy Juice, Blue Bonnet, Fiddle Faddle, Peter Pan. *I wonder what would happen if we changed some of the first letters. (Play with one example:* Peter Pan, Meter Man, Deter Dan. *Then encourage the child to try other letter substitutions.)*

Sequence Cards

Would you like to make up a story about these pictures? What do you think happened first? What happened next? How will you end your story?

Have you ever seen (done) this before? Tell me about it.

Name Games (name puzzles, memory games, matching names with photos)

May I read your name? Juwan. *(Read slowly, sweeping your finger under the name.)*

I see two letters in your name that are the same. Can you find them?

Sonya, your name begins the same way as sun, seed, sit, *and* six. *Can you think of any more words that begin the same way?*

The names of some children in our class are very short, like Ben. *Other names are very long, like* Setsuko. *Do you think your name is a short name or a long name?*

Construction Toys (Legos, Unifix cubes, K'nex, Tinker Toy)

Tell me about what you are building. Would you like to make a sign for it?

Have you ever seen a _____ like this before? Tell me about it.

What do you think would happen if you_____?

I wonder how you could make this move.

Toys Featuring Storybook or Nursery Rhyme Characters

Do you remember the story of _____ (e.g., Curious George)? Tell me about it.

Hey, Diddle Diddle, the cat and the fiddle. Diddle and fiddle rhyme! Do you see any other puzzle pieces that have rhyming words (e.g., moon/spoon)?

Observing Children's Progress

As you observe children playing with toys and games, look for these indications of literacy development:

- recognizing their names in name games

- recognizing and talking about letters and creating words as they use alphabet manipulatives

- matching letters or numbers while playing Bingo

- using their fine motor skills to grasp and manipulate small toys, beads, and other small objects

- talking about pictures on games and puzzles

- conversing with each other, solving problems and negotiating the rules of games

- recognizing environmental print

- talking about print on the toys and games, e.g., a puzzle with street signs or words

Chapter 5, *Literacy Activities*, suggests activities for the Toys and Games Area.

Literacy in the Art Area

Art experiences provide ideal opportunities to develop language and literacy skills. Children want to talk about their creations and to hear the ideas of others, thus motivating them to develop expressive and receptive language. They can learn many new words, such as *bright*, *dull*, *shiny*, *gooey*, *messy*, *sticky*, *pound*, and *roll*. Through art, children express the stories that are in their minds, as well as other ideas and feelings.

Examples of What a Child May Do...	Examples of Related Curriculum Objectives	Examples of How This Relates to Literacy
Paint strokes and shapes	20. Coordinates eye-hand movement	Practices basic strokes and shapes that make up all letters of the alphabet
Draw and color with pencils, crayons, and markers	21. Uses tools for writing and drawing	Refines fine motor skills necessary for writing
Pound and shape clay	19. Controls small muscles in hands	Strengthens small hand muscles and builds stamina for writing
Sponge paint a patterned border	30. Recognizes patterns and can repeat them	Develops the ability to detect patterns in letters and words
Draw a picture of a storybook character	48. Comprehends and interprets meaning from books and other texts	Develops the ability to comprehend and recall story details
Follow directions to use glue properly	40. Understands and follows oral directions	Develops listening comprehension skills

Stock the Art Area with additional literacy-related materials so children have the opportunity to handle and use printed materials in a variety of ways. This encourages curiosity about the letters and words on the materials, and it enables children to use print in their artwork, to copy print, or just to observe other children as they use print. By including books related to art in the area, children begin to think in more complex ways about their own representations. The following chart offers suggestions.

materials

- ☐ alphabet cookie cutters
- ☐ alphabet rubber stamps
- ☐ alphabet sponges
- ☐ brochures and pamphlets
- ☐ chalkboards and colored chalk
- ☐ colored pens and pencils
- ☐ greeting cards
- ☐ magazines and newspapers
- ☐ titled posters of famous artwork
- ☐ pre-made blank books to illustrate
- ☐ Wikki Sticks

book suggestions

The Art Lesson (Tomie dePaola)

Babar's Museum of Art (Laurent De Brunhoff)

Harold and the Purple Crayon (Crockett Johnson)

I Spy: An Alphabet in Art (Lucy Micklethwait)

Legend of the Indian Paintbrush (Tomie dePaola)

Little Blue and Little Yellow (Leo Lionni)

Matthew's Dream (Leo Leonni)

Mouse Paint (Ellen Stoll Walsh)

Museum ABCs (Metropolitan Museum of Art)

My Crayons Talk (Patricia Hubbard)

When Pigasso Met Mootisse (Nina Laden)

Books With Illustrations That Inspire the Use of Specific Art Techniques

Pictures give children a chance to see the world in many different ways. Illustrations in children's picture books can inspire children to experiment with different media and techniques. After sharing one of these stories with the class, place it in the Art Area, along with the appropriate materials, so children can recreate a page or scene from the book. They might also want to use the illustrator's technique to create an original book.

Collage	*The Very Hungry Caterpillar* (Eric Carle)
Water color	*Sand Castle* (Shannon Brenda Yee)
Charcoal	*Marshmallow* (Clare Turlay Newberry)
Pastels/chalk	*Gilberto and the Wind* (Marie Hall Ets)
Block printing	*Millions of Cats* (Wanda Gag)
Color mixing	*Mouse Paint* (Ellen Stoll Walsh)
Crayons	*Harold and the Purple Crayon* (Crockett Johnson)
Black ink on white paper	*Where the Sidewalk Ends* (Shel Silverstein)
Painting on cloth	*Tar Beach* (Faith Ringgold)

Using Art Materials to Teach Literacy Skills

Introduce literacy in the Art Area carefully and informally so as not to interrupt the children's creative processes. Look for the right moment to engage children in conversation. As you interact, observe what they are doing with the art materials and think about incorporating literacy learning in a way that will enhance their art experience.

Paint

You mixed yellow and blue to make green, just like in our story of Little Blue and Little Yellow. *What could you mix together to make purple?*

You painted many circles on your page, Olivia. They are just like the letter O *that begins your name.*

How does that fingerpaint feel? Can you write your name in it?

How should we paint for the backdrop for our Little Red Hen show? Let's look in the book for some ideas.

Clay and Art Doughs

You rolled your clay like a snake. Can you make a letter S with your clay?

Would you like to sing our song about clay while we work?

> *Pounding, pushing, poking, pulling*
> *Playing with clay is fun!*
> *Squeezing, squishing, smashing, shaping*
> *Now we're almost done.*

You've worked so hard to create your clay dog. Here's a card for you to write the word dog, *so we can put it on our display shelf. Don't forget to add your name, because you are the sculptor.*

Print-Making

You carved the letter B *into the Styrofoam meat tray and made a print of it. What do you notice about the printed B? You're right: it came out backwards! What do you think will happen if you make a rubbing of it?*

Your grandmother will enjoy this card you made. Would you like to write a note to her on the inside?

Woodworking

I wonder why they call this tool a C-clamp?... a T-square?

Let's look at our safety rules on this sign before we begin sawing.

Collage

You've worked hard to organize all of our beautiful junk for our collage-making. Let's label the containers so we'll know what's inside. I'll write Shiny Things *on this label. What other labels do we need to write?*

Leo Lionni made his illustrations in Swimmy *by cutting tissue paper shapes and gluing them, just as you're doing.*

3-D Constructions

Would you like to make popsicle stick puppets so we can act out today's story? What characters do we need to make?

How can this cardboard tube be used in the machine you're building?

Markers, Crayons, Colored Pencils

Tell me about your picture. Would you like me to write your story so we can share it with others?

Your rubbings help me guess how your objects might feel. This one looks like it might be bumpy, and this one looks like it might be scratchy.

◀ Observing Children's Progress

As children explore in the Art Area, look for these indications of literacy development:

- controlling the small muscles of their hands while coloring, cutting, and drawing

- drawing or painting basic shapes and strokes

- noticing the letters and words on magazines, newspapers, art materials, and labels

- talking about letter shapes in their creations, such as an *S* made with a clay coil or a *Z* made with paint

- representing story characters or scenes in their artwork

- writing their names on their artwork

- listening and following directions for using art materials

- using words and expanded sentences to describe what they are doing

- conversing with friends or adults about their artwork

Chapter 5, *Literacy Activities*, suggests activities for the Art Area.

Literacy in the Discovery Area

In the Discovery Area, children use literacy skills to help learn about the world around them. While engaged in scientific discoveries, they learn new words, ask and answer questions, make predictions, and explain why and how. To represent what they have learned, they may begin to write words in journals, on charts, and in stories. In the Discovery Area, children learn to use informational books as a resource to find answers to their questions.

Examples of What a Child May Do...	Examples of Related Curriculum Objectives	Examples of How This Relates to Literacy
Take care of the class pet	22. Observes objects and events with curiosity	Learns new vocabulary and acquires background knowledge
Sort a collection of leaves	27. Classifies objects	Uses visual discrimination skills that are important for noticing similarities and differences in letters and words
Use a screwdriver to take apart an old toaster	19. Controls small muscles in hands	Builds small hand muscles that are important for writing
Plant seeds in a cup and label it with the seed packet	45. Demonstrates understanding of print concepts	Uses print to label objects in a functional way
Follow directions on how to mix Oobleck	40. Understands and follows oral directions	Develops listening comprehension skills, e.g., sequencing
Look in a book to find the name of an insect	48. Comprehends and interprets meaning from books and other texts	Understands that books are resources for finding information

The chart that follows lists materials that you may add to the Discovery Area to enhance scientific thinking and literacy learning. Books are also suggested for this area.

materials

- ☐ clipboards
- ☐ graph paper
- ☐ index cards, note pads
- ☐ journals
- ☐ nature magazines
- ☐ pencils, pens, markers, crayons
- ☐ pet care books and posters
- ☐ plant care instructions
- ☐ plant and animal identification cards
- ☐ seed catalogs and packets

book suggestions

Picture Books

The Carrot Seed (Ruth Kraus)
Changes, Changes (Pat Hutchins)
The Grouchy Ladybug (Eric Carle)
A House for Hermit Crab (Eric Carle)
Mickey's Magnet (Ruth Kraus)
Parts (Tedd Arnold)
Rainbow Fish (Marcus Pfister)
Round Trip (Ann Jonas)
The Salamander Room (Ann Mazer)
The Snail's Spell (Joanne Ryder)
The Snowy Day (Ezra Jack Keats)
Two Bad Ants (Chris Van Allsburg)
The Very Busy Spider (Eric Carle)
The Very Hungry Caterpillar (Eric Carle)
The Very Quiet Cricket (Eric Carle)

Informational/Non-Fiction

Bugs! Bugs! Bugs! (Bob Barner)
A Color of His Own (Leo Lionni)
Diary of a Wombat (Jackie French)
Diary of a Worm (Doreen Cronin)
The Magic School Bus Inside a Beehive (Joanna Cole)
Me and My Amazing Body (Joan Sweeney)
Me and My Senses (Joan Sweeney)
My First Body Book (Christopher Rice)
My Visit to the Aquarium (Aliki)
Watch Them Grow (Linda Martin)
The Way Things Work (David Macaulay)
What Do You Do With a Tail Like This? (Steve Jenkins & Robin Page)

Alphabet Books

African Animals ABC (Sarah Schuette)
The Alphabet Tree (Leo Lionni)
Animalia (Graeme Base)
The Butterfly Alphabet (Kjell Sandved)
Eating the Alphabet (Lois Ehlert)
An Edible Alphabet (Bonnie Christenson)
The Flower Alphabet Book (Jerry Pallotta)
The Icky Bug Alphabet Book (Jerry Pallotta)
Old Black Fly (Jim Aylesworth)
The Yucky Reptile Alphabet Book (Jerry Pallotta)

Using Discovery Materials to Teach Literacy Skills

Your interactions with children in the Discovery Area can promote language and literacy skills and encourage more complex scientific thinking.

Animals

How can we let other children know to be careful to keep their fingers out of the rabbit cage?

Do you have any ideas about how a spider spins a web? This book shows us many different kinds of spider webs.

How do you think our new baby chicks will change? We can take a picture of the chicks each day and write how they change.

Will you write your name on the chart after you have fed the fish?

Plants, Seeds, and Flowers

I notice that our plant seems to be dying. Let's make a list of all the things that might be wrong so we can solve the problem.

Would you like to make a leaf book? You can glue your leaves on the paper, and we'll write the name of the tree underneath. If we don't know the name of the tree, we'll look it up in a book.

I see you are making a beautiful arrangement of flowers for your mother. You used many wildflowers. Here's a card so you can write a note to her.

The directions on this seed packet say that we should only plant the seeds about an inch deep.

Nature Materials and Collections (shells, rocks, leaves)

How has this leaf changed from when it was on a tree?

Which kinds of rocks do you like best: rough or smooth; gray, brown, or white; flat or round?

I wonder what kind of animal lived in this shell. How can we find out?

Can you form your name with the twigs?

Your rock is just like the one in Sylvester and the Magic Pebble. *What do you think would happen if you made a wish when you hold it?*

Physical Science Materials (magnets, discovery bottles, gears, pulleys, balls, mirrors)

Do you have an idea about how I can use these materials to move this marble in different ways?

Write your name or a letter on this card and hold it up to a mirror. What do you notice?

Your horseshoe magnet is just like the one in Mickey's Magnet. *What do you think it will pick up? Let's write what you predict.*

Sensory Table or Sensory Tubs

Tell me how the gak feels. I'll write down all the words you use to describe it: cold, slimy, gooey, creepy, squishy. *Maybe later we can make up a poem using those words.*

I wonder why some of the rocks stayed in the colander after you sifted the soil.

Thanks for helping shuck the corn. Have you ever said, "Aw, shucks"? It's the same word, but it means something different.

I see that you have written an S in the shaving cream, Sarah. It's the first letter of your name and sounds like this: /s/. Do you know any other words that begin with the /s/ sound?

Take-Aparts

Tell me how you think this clock worked.

Have you found the ON/OFF switch yet? What other words are important on this old radio?

Before you take this apart, would you like to draw what's inside? I'll help you label the parts so you can have a diagram to look at later.

Observing Children's Progress

As children explore in the Discovery Area, look for these indications of literacy development:

- looking in books for more information

- recording their predictions and findings

- describing what they are doing and why

- asking and answering questions

- using new vocabulary

- conversing with their peers and adults about their discoveries

- connecting what they are learning to prior experiences

- using their fine motor skills when using tweezers, tongs, or other tools

Chapter 5, *Literacy Activities*, suggests activities for the Discovery Area.

Literacy in the Sand and Water Area

Sand and water play gives children many opportunities to develop language and literacy skills. New vocabulary, such as *gritty*, *grainy*, *coarse*, *fine*, *sieve*, *colander*, *texture*, *empty*, *full*, *pour*, *trickle*, *sprinkle*, *dripping*, *mold*, and *measure*, can be easily incorporated into conversations about sand and water. Children develop expressive and receptive language by participating in conversations with playmates and adults during their play. Children often become quite talkative at the sand and water table as they exchange ideas, ask and answer questions, and create scenarios or retell stories with the materials.

Examples of What a Child May Do...	Examples of Related Curriculum Objectives	Examples of How This Relates to Literacy
Pour water carefully from one container to another	19. Controls small muscles in hands	Controls hand movements, which is necessary for writing
Use a finger to write a name in the sand	50. Writes letters and words	Uses touch, which is important for kinesthetic learners
Work with a friend to figure out how to move water through a moat	23. Approaches problems flexibly	Uses language to communicate ideas and solve problems
Make pretend birthday cakes out of wet sand	36. Makes believe with objects	Engages in symbolic play, which precedes the use of letters as symbols for sounds
Pour sand into a sieve and hold it up as the sand trickles through	22. Observes objects and events with curiosity	Learns the meaning of new words, such as *sift*, *sieve*, *trickle*

Literacy-related props will enhance your Sand and Water Area. While hands-on, active involvement is the primary experience in this area, there are also many children's books to inspire play.

materials

- ☐ alphabet cookie cutters or sand molds
- ☐ vinyl bathtub books
- ☐ chart with recipe for sand pies
- ☐ ice cubes with small plastic letters frozen inside
- ☐ laminated name cards, words, or letters
- ☐ list of rules generated by the children about sand and water play
- ☐ local business logos attached to popsicle sticks or drinking straws
- ☐ posters of sand castles and boats
- ☐ prediction charts: *What Will Happen?*
- ☐ signs printed with permanent markers on Styrofoam meat trays
- ☐ sink-or-float sorting charts
- ☐ sponge or foam letters
- ☐ storybook characters (laminated or plastic) and related props (twigs for trees, Legos, plastic houses, vehicles)
- ☐ street or traffic signs

book suggestions

At the Beach (Ann Rockwell)

Beach Day (Karen Roosa)

Better Not Get Wet, Jesse Bear (Nancy White Carlstrom)

Bubble, Bubble (Mercer Mayer)

Curious George Goes to the Beach (H. A. Rey)

In the Middle of the Puddle (Mike Thaler)

In the Sand (Kate Burns)

Let's Try It Out in the Water (Seymour Simon)

On My Beach There Are Many Pebbles (Leo Lionni)

The Quicksand Book (Tomie dePaola)

Sally Goes to the Beach (Stephen Huneck)

Sand (Ellen Prager)

The Sand Castle (Brenda Shannon Yee and Thea Kliros)

Sandcastle (Mick Inkpen)

Sea, Sand and Me! (Patricia Hubbell)

Splish, Splash (Stephen M. Scott)

A Swim Through the Sea (Kristin Joy Pratt)

Using Sand and Water to Teach Literacy Skills

After creating a literacy-rich Sand and Water Area, ask meaningful open-ended questions to help children express their thoughts verbally and to develop literacy skills.

Sand and Sand Props

Which letters can you write in the sand?

How does the sand feel?

Tell me about what you are building.

You're making a street just like the streets in our neighborhood. What signs would you like to add?

All your dump trucks are going in the same direction. Which sign could you add to let others know that there is only one way to travel?

You molded the sand into a letter M. *Do you have any friends whose names begin with the letter* M?

Here are some props to retell Goldilocks and the Three Bears *in the sand. Do you remember how the story goes? What happened first?*

You made a funny word with your letters. You wrote BATNIP: *B-A-T-N-I-P. Do you think there is such a thing as a batnip? I see a little word I know in* batnip: BAT. *Can you find it?*

The sand you packed in the bucket feels cool and damp. Now that you have it in the bucket, what will you do next?

This sand is hard and sticks to the bucket. I wonder why.

Water and Water Props

You're adding Lego people to the boat, one at a time. That is just like today's story, Who Sank the Boat? *I wonder how many Lego people can fit on the boat before it sinks?*

Can you find a way to arrange these sponge letters to spell your name?

I wonder why some things sink and some things float? Would you like to make a prediction about which things sink or float? Here are cards with the words sink *and* float. *You can use them to label the toys you sort.*

When you finish at the water table, I'll help you look in a book to find a picture of a boat just like this one. Then we'll know what to call it.

Have you ever been to the beach (or river, lake, swimming pool)? Tell me about it. I'll write what you say to share with others at group time.

You made your tugboat push this other boat. It's called a barge. What kinds of things is your barge carrying? Where is it going?

Observing Children's Progress

As children explore in the Sand and Water Area, look for these indications of literacy development:

- using language to solve problems and communicate their ideas

- understanding and using new words

- representing ideas through symbolic play

- using fine motor skills to sift, pour, build, and squeeze

- talking about and recognizing print found on props

- connecting sand and water play to prior knowledge

- engaging in conversations about what they are doing

- using print in sand and water play

Chapter 5, *Literacy Activities*, suggests activities for the Sand and Water Area.

Literacy in the Music and Movement Area

Music and movement activities can play an important role in language and literacy development. Songs can be used to promote an awareness of sounds and ways to experiment with language. Children can be encouraged to attend to the features of sounds, such as pitch (high/low), volume (loud/soft), and rate (fast/slow). They can make up new words to songs, learn new vocabulary, and hear and create rhythms. The repetition in songs parallels repetitive phrases in predictable books. As children read a picture book that uses a familiar song as the text, they sing and begin to recognize words on the page.

Movement activities encourage children to follow directions and practice other language skills. With their bodies, they demonstrate comprehension of directions, songs, and stories, and they express the ways that music and language make them feel. They practice the large muscle skills that usually develop before the small muscle skills necessary for writing.

Examples of What a Child May Do…	Examples of Related Curriculum Objectives	Examples of How This Relates to Literacy
Make up a birthday song	39. Expresses self using words and expanded sentences	Expresses thoughts and feelings verbally
Make up silly, nonsense words to a familiar song	38. Hears and discriminates the sounds of language	Develops phonological awareness, isolating words and manipulating sounds
Hop, skip, and jump to music	14. Demonstrates basic locomotor skills	Develops the large motor skills that usually precede the small motor skills necessary for writing
Tap rhythm sticks to songs	38. Hears and discriminates the sounds of language	Isolates words and syllables in a song
Sing a song about a boa constrictor or a kookaburra	39. Expresses self using words and expanded sentences	Learns new words in a fun, meaningful way
Dance with a scarf, letting it flow from one side of his body to the other	14. Demonstrates basic locomotor skills	Makes movements that cross the midline of the body, thus involving both sides of the brain in ways that are important for reading and writing
Sing *Down by the Bay* while turning the book pages	45. Demonstrates understanding of print concepts	Follows print from left to right, top to bottom, and front to back; uses picture cues to comprehend the story; may recognize words in print

Books and music go together easily. You can support children's literacy development in the Music and Movement Area by adding print or other materials that focus on reading, writing, listening, and oral language skills. Songs are an important tool for encouraging phonological awareness. Some songs help children focus on one aspect of language, such as rhyming. Others help children focus on other aspects, such as alliteration and phoneme manipulation.

materials

☐ alphabet songs on tape or CDs

☐ color-coded music cards to use with xylophones, tone bells, or melody bells

☐ posters of musical instruments

☐ rebus (picture) movement cards

☐ song charts and cards

☐ songs for following oral directions (*Hokey Pokey* or *Looby Loo*)

☐ taped listening activities

book suggestions

Songs That Promote Phonological Awareness

The Ants Go Marching

Apples and Bananas

Baby Bumblebee

Down by the Bay

Eensy-Weensy Spider

Hokey Pokey

John Jacob Jingleheimer Schmidt

My Bonny Lies Over the Ocean

The Name Game

Polly Wolly Doodle

A Sailor Went to Sea, Sea, Sea

Someone's in the Kitchen (Fe, Fi, Fiddley-I-O)

Willoughby, Wallaby Woo

Books About Music and Movement

Angelina Ballerina (Helen Craig)

The Bat Boy and His Violin (Gavin Curtis)

Ben's Trumpet (Rachel Isadora)

Best-Loved Children's Songs from Japan (Yoko Imoto)

Cada Nino: Every Child: A Bilingual Songbook for Kids (Tish Hinojosa and Lucia Angela Perez)

Charlie Parker Played Bebop (Chris Raschka)

book suggestions (continued)

Books About Music and Movement, *continued*

Getting to Know You!: Rodgers and Hammerstein Favorites (Richard Rodgers)

How Sweet the Sound: African-American Songs for Children (Wade and Cheryl Hudson)

Hush!: A Thai Lullaby (Minfong Ho)

Max Finds Two Sticks (Brian Pickney)

M Is for Music (Kathleen Krull)

Music, Music for Everyone (Vera B. Williams)

Philadelphia Chicken: A Too Illogical, Zoological Musical Review (Sandra Boynton and Michael Ford)

Rap a Tap Tap: Here's Bojangles – Think of That (Leo Dillon and Diane Dillon)

Song and Dance Man (Karen Ackerman)

Take Me Out of the Bathtub and Other Silly Dilly Songs (Allen Katz)

Tessa's Tip-Tapping Toes (Carolyn Crimi)

A Tisket, A Tasket (Ella Fitzgerald)

What a Wonderful World (Ashley Bryan)

Willie (Virginia Kroll)

Song Storybooks

A-Hunting We Will Go! (Stephen Kellogg)

Baby Beluga (Raffi)

Do Your Ears Hang Low?: A Love Story (Caroline Jayne Church)

Down by the Bay (Raffi)

Inch by Inch: The Garden Song (David Mallet)

Just the Two of Us (Will Smith)

Mary Had a Little Lamb (Mary Ann Hoberman)

Mary Wore Her Red Dress and Henry Wore His Green Sneakers (Merle Peek)

Miss Mary Mack (Mary Ann Hoberman)

There Once Was a Man Named Michael Finnegan (Mary Ann Hoberman)

There Was an Old Lady Who Swallowed a Fly (Simm Taback)

Today is Monday (Eric Carle)

Using Music and Movement to Teach Literacy Skills

As children engage in spontaneous music and movement activities, try not to interrupt them. Time your interactions so that they encourage children to experiment in new ways and to develop important language and literacy skills.

Singing and Songs in Print (song charts, cards, and books)

> *Each time you hear a word that rhymes with* late, *clap your hands.*

> *What do you think a* ____ *(e.g., water spout, tuffet, dell) is?*

> *I see you're listening to the song called_____ (e.g.,* On Top of Spaghetti*). What happens in the song?*

> *Where do you begin when you are reading the song on this chart?*

> *The first letter in your name is M. Here is an M on the song chart. How many more Ms can you find on this chart?*

> *Can you make up some silly words for this song?*

> *Can you sing the ABC song to a different tune? How about to the tune of* Mary Had a Little Lamb?

Movement Props and Experiences

> *This music is slow, and you're taking slow steps like a turtle. Now the music is fast! How will you move to it?*

> *Can you move your scarf around in a circle like the letter O? How about like a letter S?*

> *Move your streamer high up in the air when I hold this card that reads,* Up. *Hold it low to the ground when I raise the card that reads,* Down. *The arrows on the card will give you a hint.*

> *Can you make a gigantic motion when you hear the loud sounds in this song?*

> *Wave your wand each time you hear the /b/ sound in the song.*

Musical Instruments

Which song would you like to sing very, very slowly? Which song would you like to sing quickly?

When you hit the drum hard, it made a loud sound. What will happen when you hit it softly?

Can you tap the sticks to your name?

How should we play this tambourine to show that we are happy? ... sad? ... mad? ... scared?

Can you copy the pattern I make with the rhythm sticks? Can you tap a pattern for me to copy?

Each time you see a colored note on this card, ring the bell that is the same color. Would you like to try to read and play this song?

Which song would you play if you were Abiyoyo from today's story?

How can we use the instruments to make sounds effects as we retell our story?

Observing Children's Progress

As children explore in the Music and Movement Area, look for these indications of literacy development:

- making up new words to songs

- detecting patterns in songs and rhythmic movements

- following the words on a song chart, from top to bottom and left to right

- demonstrating listening comprehension by using appropriate motions in songs and movement activities

- following directions during movement activities

- using language to describe their motions

- including singing and movement as they retell stories

- talking about the story line of a song

- hearing and moving to a beat

Chapter 5, *Literacy Activities*, suggests activities for the Music and Movement Area.

Literacy in the Cooking Area

Cooking activities provide many opportunities to enhance literacy learning. Children can find a favorite recipe in a cookbook, create a shopping list, locate newspaper coupons, read product labels, and follow instructions for preparing food. They learn the names of foods, as well as words to describe how they taste. They also learn the names of various cooking tools and processes. Cooking is a way for children to use all of their senses as they learn to read and write.

Examples of What a Child May Do...	Examples of Related Curriculum Objectives	Examples of How This Relates to Literacy
Follow the steps on a picture and word (rebus) recipe	45. Demonstrates understanding of print concepts	Understands that print has a purpose; tracks print from left to right and top to bottom; develops sequencing concepts
Identify the correct ingredient by recognizing print on the packaging	47. Uses emerging reading skills to make meaning from print	Learns the meaning of particular symbols
Grate, chop, stir, knead, pound, cut, pour, measure, peel	19. Controls small muscles in hands	Strengthens and controls the small muscles necessary for writing
Find newspaper coupons for a shopping trip	48. Comprehends and interprets meaning from books and other texts	Learns about forms of print other than books, such as coupons
Use descriptive words (e.g., yummy, sweet, bitter, sour, salty, crunchy)	39. Expresses self using words and expanded sentences	Expands vocabulary
Follow safety directions	40. Understands and follows oral directions	Builds listening comprehension skills
Write a shopping list	49. Understands the purpose of writing	Understands that written language assists memory

The following chart contains literacy-related materials to add to your Cooking Area. You will also find children's storybooks and cookbooks that are related to food and cooking.

materials

- alphabet cookie cutters
- blank recipe cards
- calendar for recording snack helpers
- cookbooks
- coupons
- environmental print on containers of ingredients used in recipes
- graphs and charts, for example,

  Did you like the soup? Yes/No
  How many of each fruit did we use in our salad?
  Healthy Foods/Not Healthy Foods

- grocery store circulars
- labels for utensils and ingredients
- letter molds
- menus
- nutritional charts
- paper
- picture and word (rebus) recipe cards
- recipe charts
- writing tools

book suggestions

Storybooks

Bear Wants More (Karma Wilson)

Bread and Jam for Frances (Russell Hoban)

Bread, Bread, Bread (Ann Morris)

Cloudy with a Chance of Meatballs (Judi Barrett)

Corn is Maize: A Gift from the Indians (Aliki)

Dim Sum for Everyone (Grace Lin)

Eating the Alphabet (Lois Ehlert)

Everybody Cooks Rice (Nora Dooley)

Growing Colors (Bruce McMillan)

Growing Vegetable Soup (Lois Ehlert)

How Are You Peeling? (Saxon Freymann and Joost Elffers)

The Hungry Thing (Jan Spepian)

I Know an Old Lady Who Swallowed a Pie (Alison Jackson)

Magda's Tortillas (Becky Chavarria-Chairez)

Matzah Ball Soup (Joan Rothenberg)

In My Momma's Kitchen (Jerdene Nolen)

More Spaghetti, I Say! (Rita Golden Gelman)

Pancakes for Breakfast (Tomie dePaola)

Pickles to Pittsburg (Ron Barrett)

Strega Nona (Tomie dePaola)

Today is Monday (Eric Carle)

Tony's Bread (Tomie dePaola)

The Tortilla Factory (Gary Paulsen)

The Very Hungry Caterpillar (Eric Carle)

Who Took the Cookie from the Cookie Jar? (Bonnie Philemon and Lass Sturges)

Children's Cookbooks

Betty Crocker Kids Cook! (Betty Crocker Editors)

Blue Moon Soup (Gary Goss)

Children's Quick and Easy Cookbook (Angela Wilkes)

Cooking with Herbs: The Vegetarian Dragon (Julie Bass)

Delicious Dishes: Creole Cooking for Children (Berthe Amos)

Kids Cooking: A Very Slightly Messy Manual (Klutz Press)

Kids First Cookbook (American Cancer Society)

The Kids Multicultural Cookbook: Food and Fun Around the World (Deanna F. Cook)

Mother Goose Cookbook: Rhymes and Recipes for the Very Young (Marianna Mayer)

Once Upon a Recipe: Favorite Tales, Food and FUNtivities (Judy Edelman)

Pretend Soup and Other Real Recipes for Preschoolers and Up (Mollie Katzen)

The following chart suggests a few cooking activities related to children's stories.

Green Eggs and Ham (Dr. Seuss)	Add green food coloring or chopped spinach to scrambled eggs
Blueberries for Sal (Robert McCloskey)	Make blueberry jam
The Little Mouse, The Red Ripe Strawberry and *THE BIG HUNGRY BEAR* (Don Wood and Audrey Wood)	Clean and slice strawberries
The Little Red Hen (Paul Galdone)	Bake bread
Miss Spider's Tea Party (David Kirk)	Make and compare solar tea and brewed tea
Eating the Alphabet (Lois Ehlert)	Make fruit kabobs
Strega Nona (Tomie dePaola)	Cook pasta
Harold and the Purple Crayon (Crockett Johnson)	Make purple cows (ice cream and grape juice)
How Many Bugs in a Box? (David A. Carter)	Prepare ants on a log (celery sticks, cream cheese, and raisins)
Chicka Chicka Boom Boom (Bill Martin and John Archambault)	Prepare a coconut

Using Cooking to Teach Literacy Skills

You can teach literacy skills in the Cooking Area as you interact with children. Talk about different ingredients, food preparation steps, the changes that occur as foods cook, and children's favorite part: tasting.

Cooking Ingredients

I wonder why some bananas are green and some are yellow.

How are these two cheeses alike? How are they different?

From where does milk come? How does it get to the store?

Have you ever heard of the word beverage? *What do you think it means?*

Zucchini starts with the letter Z. *Do you know any other words that begin with* Z?

Strega Nona had a magic pasta pot. What made her pot so magical? What would happen if our pasta pot were magical?

Little Miss Muffet ate some curds and whey. What do you think they are?

Let's make a list of all the things you can put butter on.

I hear two little words in pancake. *Listen:* pan...cake.

Examine the melons we have today. How do they feel when you touch them? What colors are they on the outside? Can you guess what color they will be on the inside? Let's cut them open and find out.

Recipe Cards, Cookbooks, Recipe Charts

Let's read the recipe before we begin cooking. We want to make sure we have all the ingredients before we start.

This recipe asks us to bring the soup to a boil and then simmer it. How will we do that?

Here are some picture and word cards of how to make a peanut butter sandwich. Let's put them in the right order. What happens first? What happens next? Now we can follow the steps to make our sandwiches.

The directions for making the cake are right here on the box. Let's read them to see what we should do.

Would you like to create your own recipe? Tell it to me, and I'll write it down. If you like, you can draw a picture of your dish, and we'll add it to our class cookbook.

When you see an uppercase T *on a recipe, it means to use a tablespoon. Can you guess what we might use if we see a lowercase* t?

Cooking Utensils

Today we need to use a hot plate for our recipe. What safety rules do we need to remember? Let's write them on a chart so we won't forget.

We need to turn the mixer on high speed. I wonder which of the words is high. *I know it begins the same way as Hannah's name does.*

How many Cs can you find on this measuring cup?

This special pan is called a wok. The word on the handle: w-o-k. Have you ever heard of a wok before? What kinds of foods can you cook in a wok? Setsuko's family uses a wok often when they cook.

We're going to use a griddle today, just like in the story we read called Pancakes for Breakfast. *Have you ever used a griddle at home? What did you make?*

Tasting

The popcorn tastes very salty. Let's add the word salty *to our list of taste words.*

Which fruit tastes sweet? Which tastes sour?

How do the cooked carrots taste different from the raw carrots?

What is the strangest ice cream flavor you ever tasted?

You said the granola was crunchy. What are some other words that begin the same way as crunchy?

Food Preparation

How is folding eggs into our batter different from folding a napkin?

Knead *sounds just like another word I know. Can you guess what word I'm thinking about? How are these words different?*

Why should we wash the beans?

Can you form a J with your pretzel dough?

Observing Children's Progress

As children explore in the Cooking Area, look for these indications of literacy development:

- using new words as they cook

- following recipe directions and sequence

- using eye-hand coordination to pour, measure, and cut

- building small hand-muscles while kneading, pounding, and squeezing

- making connections with earlier cooking experiences at home

- talking about the letters and words on food containers

- following print from left to right and top to bottom on recipe charts and cards and in cookbooks

Chapter 5, *Literacy Activities*, suggests activities for the Cooking Area.

Literacy in the Computer Area

When used appropriately, the Computer Area can promote language and literacy development. The computer is a tool that helps children learn new words and gain background knowledge. As children work together at the computer, they talk, make predictions, share experiences, and solve problems. They use literacy-related software programs to develop understandings about print concepts and to practice and refine their skills. Computers enable children to both gain and communicate information. With the help of adults, they can use this tool to find the answers to many questions. With word-processing and drawing programs, children can express their ideas and feelings.

Examples of What a Child May Do...	Examples of Related Curriculum Objectives	Examples of How This Relates to Literacy
Type his/her name	46. Demonstrates knowledge of the alphabet	Recognizes letters on the keyboard and makes a connection between uppercase and lowercase letters
Use picture icons to navigate a software program	45. Uses emerging reading skills to make meaning from print	Understands that symbols represent something else, which is a precursor to understanding that letters represent sounds
Use a computer mouse	19. Controls small muscles in hands	Develops the eye-hand coordination and fine motor skills necessary for writing
Write or dictate a story under a picture	49. Understands the purpose of writing	Communicates through writing and begins to consider the audience who will be reading the message
Work with a friend to use a software program	39. Expresses self using words and expanded sentences	Uses language to make predictions, communicate ideas, and solve problems.
Follow along with an interactive storybook on the computer	44. Enjoys and values reading	Develops an understanding of print conventions by following highlighted text from left to right and top to bottom; uses another way to hear stories

The decisions you make about materials and software in the Computer Area affect literacy learning. The chart that follows suggests some materials and books to enhance this area.

materials

- ☐ bookbinding supplies
- ☐ hard copies of books related to interactive storybook software
- ☐ chart with picture and word directions for starting and shutting down the computer
- ☐ colored adhesive labels with words such as *off, on, enter, delete, up, down, forward, backwards, print, stop, go, play, start*
- ☐ individual children's word banks (a collection of words that are important to them, written on cards and held together with a ring)
- ☐ name cards for children to refer to when typing their names or those of their friends
- ☐ picture dictionaries for reference when typing
- ☐ printer, ink, and paper
- ☐ sign-up sheets for computer use
- ☐ sign with rules for Computer Area safety and equipment care

book suggestions

Children's Books Related to Computers

Arthur's Computer Disaster (Marc Brown)

The Computer from A to Z (Bobbie Kalman)

Franklin and the Computer (Paulette Bourgeois and Brenda Clark)

A House With No Mouse (P. S. Tinsley)

Look Inside a Computer (Anna Curti)

The Magic Schoolbus Gets Programmed (Nancy White)

Patrick's Dinosaurs on the Internet (Carol Carrick)

Interactive Storybook Software

The Art Lesson (Riverdeep)

Arthur's Teacher Trouble (Riverdeep)

Cat in the Hat (The Learning Company)

Chicka Chicka Boom Boom (Davidson and Associates)

Dr. Seuss ABCs (The Learning Company)

Green Eggs and Ham (The Learning Company)

The Hare and the Tortoise (Broderbund)

Just Grandma and Me (Broderbund)

Just Me and My Mom (Broderbund)

Little Monster at School (Broderbund)

Mike Mulligan and His Steam Shovel (Simon and Schuster)

Stellaluna (Riverdeep)

Software for Building Early Literacy Skills

Ani's Rocket Ride (Coach)

Bailey's Book House (Edmark)

Bert and Ernie's Computer Phone (Learning Company)

Circletime Tales Deluxe (Don Johnston)

Clifford the Big Red Dog Reading (Scholastic)

Curious George PreK ABCs (Houghton Mifflin)

Dr. Seuss Reading Games (Learning Company)

I Spy Junior (Scholastic)

JumpStart Preschool (Knowledge Adventure)

Kid Pix (Learning Company)

Kid's Work Deluxe (Davidson and Associates)

Learn Together with Ani (Coach)

Monkeys Jumping on the Bed (SoftTouch)

Photo Kit Junior (Coach)

Stanley's Sticker Stories (Edmark)

Using Computers to Teach Literacy Skills

Adult interaction in the Computer Area is just as important as in any other area of the classroom. These interactions help children learn new skills and concepts, collaborate with friends, share discoveries, and solve problems.

Computer Hardware

How do you think this computer works?

Have you ever seen a computer before? What was it used for?

What happens when you move the mouse?

Do you see any letters that you know on the keyboard? What happens if you push them?

That word is backspace, *and the key has an arrow. What do you think* backspace *means?*

Do you think all of the letters of the alphabet are on this keyboard? How can you find out? I wonder why they are not in the right order.

What do you think will happen if we press the escape *key?*

Computer Peripherals (e.g., printers, digital cameras, scanners)

Let's put the photo you took today on the screen so you can write about it.

How many things can you find in the classroom that rhyme with fat? *Would you like to use the camera to take pictures of them? Then we'll make a rhyming book.*

Would you like to scan the paper that you wrote your name on so we can e-mail it to your mom?

Word Processing Software

Would you like to write a story about our field trip? I will help you if you want. Let's think about what we did first.

You covered your screen with many Zs. Do you know any words that begin with the Z sound: /z/?

We call the way the letters and words look on the computer screen the font. *You can make your fonts fancy or plain, large or small. Watch, and I'll show you. How would you like to change the font when you type your name?*

Tell me about the story you just wrote. Would you like to print it for others to enjoy? You may share it at group time if you'd like.

Your name begins with an uppercase letter, and the rest are lowercase letters. On the computer keyboard, I only see uppercase letters. What should we do to write your name just like it is on your name card?

Let's use the computer to write a thank-you letter to the dentist. How should we begin the letter?

Listen to what happens when you type your name using this program. The computer reads it back you! Would you like to type a word and see if the computer can read it?

Let's use this software to write a note to your cousin, who visited our class last week.

Interactive Storybook Software

What do you think this story is about?

Do you see any words (or letters) that you know on this page?

Watch! The words on the screen light up when they are read.

What do you think is going to happen next? Let's click the arrow to turn to the next page to find out.

I wonder why that happened?

Why did you like this story?

This program lets you play on the pages. What do you think will happen when you click on the different pictures?

Other Software

Tell me what you are doing.

How do you know what to do in this program?

What will happen if you click this button?

What words and pictures on the screen tell you what to do next?

I placed the photos we took on our field trip on the computer. Will you tell me about the pictures? I'll type what you say, and we'll print a book for the Library Area.

Internet Sites and E-mail

Would you like to send an e-mail your Mom to tell her what you did today? How would you like to begin your message?

I found an interesting Web site with lots of pictures of worms. Press the page up *or* page down *key to look at them all. How is this worm like the one you found on the playground today? Later, we can write a story about it.*

Observing Children's Progress

As children explore in the Computer Area, look for these indications of literacy development:

- navigating software programs by using picture icons or words

- describing what they are doing and thinking

- using fine motor skills to handle a computer mouse

- attending to the print on the screen

- talking about the letters on the keyboard

- combining letters to make words, using word-processing software.

- following the story line while using interactive books

- tracking print on the screen, from top to bottom and left to right

- using new vocabulary related to computers, such as *disk, CD, mouse, cursor, backspace, enter,* and *delete*

- connecting letter sounds and symbols as they type

Chapter 5, *Literacy Activities*, suggests activities for the Computer Area.

Literacy in the Outdoor Area

The Outdoor Area provides rich opportunities for promoting language skills and for developing the large and small muscle skills necessary for writing and handling print materials. As children play together outdoors, they use language to plan, negotiate, solve problems, and create. They learn new words for what they see (e.g., *cocoon, dandelion, wasp*) and for the what they do (e.g., *gallop, stretch, balance*). Writing in the sand, in dirt, or with sidewalk chalk gives children a chance to practice writing in a different, yet fun, way. Print in the outdoor environment, such as a traffic sign on the tricycle track, a bird identification sign hanging from a tree, and a seed packet label in the garden, helps children understand how print conveys meaning. In addition, every literacy activity that takes place indoors can be brought outdoors. Baskets of books, writing materials, and props for retelling stories can become a part of a literacy-rich Outdoor Area.

Examples of What a Child May Do...	Examples of Related Curriculum Objectives	Examples of How This Relates to Literacy
Run, jump, hop, skip, gallop	14. Demonstrates basic locomotor skills (running, jumping, hopping, galloping)	Develops the gross motor skills that usually precede the fine motor development necessary for writing
Toss a bean bag back and forth with a friend	20. Coordinates eye-hand movement	Develops the coordination that is important for following text across a page
Move through an obstacle course	15. Shows balance while moving 32. Shows awareness of position in space	Follows directions and learns positional concepts and words, such as *over, under, left, right, behind, below, on top*
Play with streamers, moving them up, down, left, and right	14. Demonstrates basic locomotor skills (running, jumping, hopping, galloping)	Makes movements that cross the midline of the body, thus involving both sides of the brain in ways that are important for reading and writing
Watch a butterfly emerge from a cocoon	22. Observes objects and events with curiosity	Develops background knowledge and vocabulary that support listening and reading comprehension
Plan with a group to be circus performers for an audience	10. Plays well with other children	Uses language to plan, negotiate, and communicate
Play a hand-clapping game while singing	38. Hears and discriminates the sounds of language	Develops increased phonological awareness while playfully saying rhymes

Here are suggested materials to enhance your outdoor learning environment. Books can also spark imaginative play and learning outdoors. In addition, children can take books outdoors to read as a quiet activity or a way to be alone. When choosing books for outdoor use, consider informational books about nature as well as storybooks.

materials

- [ ] adhesive labels for Ziploc natural collection bags
- [ ] bird identification charts, laminated and hung in trees
- [ ] blank books or journals
- [ ] clipboards, paper, and writing tools
- [ ] labeled muffin tins, egg cartons, or ice cube trays for collecting and sorting
- [ ] labels for garden plants
- [ ] laminated environmental print signs
- [ ] nature guides, plant and animal identification books
- [ ] pretend driver's licenses
- [ ] props for retelling stories
- [ ] sidewalk chalk
- [ ] traffic signs

book suggestions

Alpha Bugs (David A. Carter)

Around the Pond: Who's Been Here? (Lindsay Barrett George)

Carl's Afternoon in the Park (Alexandra Day)

The Carrot Seed (Ruth Krauss)

Clifford and the Big Storm (Norman Bridwell)

Diary of a Worm (Doreen Cronon)

Franklin and the Thunderstorm (Paulette Bourgeois)

The Giving Tree (Shel Silverstein)

The Grouchy Ladybug (Eric Carle)

Growing Colors (Bruce McMillan)

Henry Hikes to Fitchburg (D.B. Johnson)

I Wish I Were a Butterfly (James Howe)

The Icky Bug Alphabet Book (Jerry Pallotta)

In the Small, Small Pond (Denise Fleming)

It Looked Like Spilt Milk (Charles G. Shaw)

Miss Tizzy (Libba Moore Gray)

Planting a Rainbow (Lois Ehlert)

Roxaboxen (Alice McLerran)

The Snowy Day (Ezra Jack Keats)

The Very Hungry Caterpillar (Eric Carle)

Using the Outdoors to Teach Literacy Skills

Take advantage of outdoor opportunities to enhance language and literacy learning. Help children develop skills by using open-ended questions and prompts.

Gross Motor Equipment

What do you think will happen if you climb on the jungle gym while wearing your gloves?

Do you know what this sign says? You're right: stop. S-T-O-P. *Can you guess why we have that sign on our tricycle track?*

Ben is bouncing a ball. I hear lots of words that begin the same way: Ben, bouncing, *and* ball.

When you hear a word that begins the same way as mouse, *run under the parachute.*

Would you like to walk across the balance beam and pretend to be a tightrope walker, just like in our story, Olivia and the Circus?

Nature Materials and Experiences

You worked hard to plant the seeds. Will you help me find the right seed packet to mark the place where you planted? Look for the packet with a picture of a sunflower and a word that begins with the letter S.

What kind of bird did you see with the binoculars? Why don't we look for its name in our bird book?

Can you guess what letters I am writing with this stick in the dirt? How big can you write your name?

Why do you think the worms crawled under the wet paper towel?

Will you write in our plant journal what you did today, so we can remember?

Group Games

Would you like to join me in a clapping game? We can sing Miss Mary Mack.

Pretend you are driving cars. When I hold up the word STOP, *put on your brakes. When I hold up* GO, *start moving again.*

Will you lead us in a bear hunt, just like in today's story? Where shall we begin?

Here's some sidewalk chalk. Would you like to write letters in the hopscotch squares instead of numbers?

Close your eyes. Let's listen to every sound.

Outdoor Dramatic Play

You're using rocks to make a house with rooms, just as in Roxaboxen. *What else happened in the story? What other materials can you use to create your own Roxaboxen?*

I see you're acting out The Three Little Pigs. *What happened first in the story? What happened next?*

I see that you're pretending to be a police officer. Would you like some paper in case you need to write a traffic ticket?

Observing Children's Progress

As children explore in the Outdoor Area, look for these indications of literacy development:

- following directions

- coordinating movements

- using new vocabulary words

- talking with friends to plan, negotiate play, and communicate

- identifying print in the outdoor environment

- retelling stories or imitating characters from books

Chapter 5, *Literacy Activities*, suggests activities for the Outdoor Area.

inside this chapter

5

Literacy Activities

This section includes activities that use various strategies to help children develop the components of literacy. They are practical ideas to get you started. You can adapt each activity by using different books and materials.

The Appendix includes an Activity Matrix that illustrates how the activities correspond with interest areas. The matrix also shows the association between literacy components and activities. Use this information as you plan. In addition, keep in mind what you know about each child's developmental level, as well as the general level of the children as a group.

Each description is organized in the same way.

Goals and Objectives are from *The Creative Curriculum Developmental Continuum for Ages 3–5*. This list helps teachers observe, document, and assess children's progress on the objectives related to listening and speaking, reading and writing.

Materials and Preparation include the books and materials you will need for the activity and explains anything you need to do to get ready.

Guiding Children's Learning describes how to lead the activity and interact with the children. (See chapter 2 for routines that help children settle themselves for a new activity.)

Closing provides suggestions for ending the activity. In many cases, this section suggests ways for children to use the materials to build comprehension and practice skills independently after they have participated in the teacher-led activity.

Extensions are suggestions for follow-up activities. These activities encourage children to work on the same concepts and skills in different ways.

Modifications include ways to adapt the activity for children who need more assistance. General strategies to assist children who need extra support are discussed in chapter 2; the modifications suggested in this section are more specific to the activity.

At the end of each description is a table indicating the recommended group size, the interest areas where the activity might be conducted, and the length of time the activity might take.

A Bunny's Tale

Goal(s) & Objectives	Listening and Speaking *39. Expresses self using words and expanded sentences* Reading and Writing *44. Enjoys and values reading; 47. Uses emerging reading skills to make meaning from print; 48. Comprehends and interprets meaning from books and other texts*

Materials & Preparation

☐ *The Runaway Bunny* by Margaret Wise Brown (Harper Trophy, 1977)

☐ flannel board pieces or props

The Runaway Bunny is a story about a little bunny who decides to run away. He tells his mother that he is going to turn into a fish in a trout stream, a rock, a crocus, a bird, a sailboat, a bunny on a flying trapeze, and a little boy. His mother tells him that, if he becomes each of these things, she will follow him, becoming a fisherman, a mountain climber, a gardener, a tree, the wind, a tightrope walker, and a mother, because he is "her little bunny." In the end, the bunny decides to stay home.

Create flannel board pieces or collect props to illustrate the story (e.g., a toy fish and fishing rod, a crocus and a hand spade, etc.).

Guiding Children's Learning

Introduce the story to the children and have them predict what will happen.

As you read the story, use the props or arrange the flannel pieces in the order they are mentioned.

After the story, lead a discussion about the words that might be unfamiliar to the children. Refer to the props or pictures to help clarify the meaning of words. Have the children pretend to be tightrope walkers by walking on a balance beam or a piece of masking tape on the floor. They can pretend to be the wind by swaying back and forth.

Discuss the children's earlier predictions. Ask open-ended questions to help children understand and make personal connections to the story, such as, "Why do you think they did that? If you were going to run away, where would you go?"

Closing

Remind the children that their families and teachers love them very much, just as the mother bunny in the story loves her little bunny.

Tell the children that the book, flannel pieces, or props will be available in the Library Area, where they may retell the story on their own at choice time.

Extension(s)

- Invite the children to offer other ideas of what the bunny might think about becoming and what the mother bunny would say. Record their ideas on chart paper.

- Have each child write or dictate and then illustrate a sentence about another character or object the bunny might think about becoming. Bind the pages as a book. Share it at story time and place it in the Library Area for the children to read on their own.

- Cut blank paper in the shape of a bunny. Staple several sheets together to create bunny books and place them in the Library Area. Children may write or draw in them.

- Create "bunny salad" recipe cards with words and pictures. Encourage the children to make the salad by chopping apples, carrots, and celery and mixing them with a little plain yogurt and raisins.

- Read other stories about a family member's love for a child, such as

    Mama, Do You Love Me? by Barbara M. Joosse
    Love You Forever by Robert Munsch
    I Love You, Stinky Face by Lisa McCourt
    I Love You Because You're You by Liza Baker
    You Are My I Love You by Maryann K. Cusimano

Modification(s)

- If a child has difficulty with new activities, preview the book and props with her individually before the small group activity begins.

- For a child who has difficulty focusing on the story, introduce a stuffed or flannel bunny before reading the book. Let the child hold the bunny while you read.

- For children with language or developmental delays, use simple gestures or American Sign Language while you read. Use props for the first readings, and save flannel board pieces for subsequent readings.

- For less experienced listeners, support comprehension by using facial expressions and gestures and by pointing to important parts of the illustrations while reading.

Individual	Small Group	Large Group	Interest Area	Single Day	Multiday	Minutes
	●		Library	●		15–20

All Kinds of Spiders

Goal(s) & Objectives	Listening and Speaking
	38. Hears and discriminates the sounds of language; 39. Expresses self using words and expanded sentences; 43. Actively participates in conversations
	Reading and Writing
	45. Demonstrates understanding of print concepts; 49. Understands the purpose of writing

Materials & Preparation

☐ chart paper and a marker

☐ props to illustrate vocabulary

Use the familiar nursery rhyme *The Itsy-Bitsy Spider*, to introduce children to new vocabulary. Determine which words in the song might be unfamiliar to the children and think of ways to convey their meaning. For example, you might make a small motion with your finger and thumb to show the meaning of *itsy-bitsy* or talk about very small things like ants and ladybugs. You could bring in a section of gutter or various types of spouts to explain the meaning of *waterspout*.

Guiding Children's Learning

Teach or review the rhyme, *The Itsy-Bitsy Spider*. Talk with the children about what they think the words *itsy-bitsy* and *waterspout* mean. Clarify the meaning of the words by using motions, props, and discussion. Have the children think of other words that have the same meaning, for example, *tiny, small, teensy-weensy, teeny-tiny,* or *itty-bitty*.

Explain to the children that you will introduce them to some other kinds of spiders, such as big, fat spiders; quiet, creeping spiders; and long-legged spiders. Change your voice and the motions to help children understand new words.

Invite the children to name other kinds of spiders and to make up appropriate motions to match their suggestions. Write the names of the spiders on a chart to follow as you sing new versions of the rhyme.

Continue the activity as long as the children are interested.

Closing

Dismiss the children, one at a time, by having them walk like spiders.

Extension(s)
- Read Mary Ann Hoberman's adaptation of the rhyme, *The Eensy-Weensy Spider* (Megan Tingley, 2000). She tells what else the spider did: met a baby bug, went swimming in the pool, joined a big parade, shopped for shoes, etc. Invite the children to name other places the spider could go and list them on chart paper.

- Include informational picture books about spiders in the Discovery Area. Share them with the children, encouraging them to talk about the similarities and differences they notice.

- Invite the children to make up new verses for *The Itsy-Bitsy Spider*. Jot down their ideas and sing the new verses at meeting times.

- Encourage children to draw pictures of various kinds of spiders and to write about or dictate their ideas. Combine their pages to make a book. Create a cover that includes a title and the children's names as authors.

Modification(s)
- Have a child with a visual impairment or motor planning problems follow hand and finger movements by placing his hands over an adult's hands. Alternatively, the adult can offer hand-over-hand prompts.

Individual	Small Group	Large Group	Interest Area	Single Day	Multiday	Minutes
		●	Music & Movement, Discovery, Library	●		15–20

Baggie Books

Goal(s) & Objectives	Reading and Writing **45.** *Demonstrates understanding of print concepts;* **46.** *Demonstrates knowledge of the alphabet;* **47.** *Uses emerging reading skills to make meaning from print;* **48.** *Comprehends and interprets meaning from books and other texts*

Materials & Preparation

□ 6-8 Ziplock baggies per book

□ environmental print

□ construction paper sized to fit inside a baggie

□ markers

□ scissors

□ stapler

□ colorful tape

Before this activity, communicate with families to make them aware of their children's likely ability to recognize print in the environment (e.g., signs, labels, and logos). Ask them to help their child identify some items with words they recognize and to send the items to school for their child to read.

Make books by stapling 6-8 baggies together at the bottom, leaving the zipper available for insertions. Further secure the baggies by covering the stapled end with colorful tape.

Guiding Children's Learning

Invite a child to sit with you and read the environmental print he has brought to school. Sweep your fingers under the words as the child reads. Make comments that will help to make the words personal and meaningful to the child [e.g., "Kate, is your favorite cereal *Special K*? Your name has a capital *K* (or uppercase *K*), just like *Special K*. Can you show me the *K*? See if you can find any other *K/ks* on the things you brought."] Call attention to any labels that have the same or similar words (e.g., *corn muffins* and *creamed corn* both include the word *corn*.)

Verbally encourage the child's reading efforts.

Show the child the empty baggie book. Ask if she would like to make a book using the print you just read together. Depending on the type of print the child brought, help her decide what the title of the book should be. For example, the title might be *Words I Can Read, My Favorite Cereals,* or *My Favorite Foods.*

Write the title on a piece of construction paper. Have the child sign her name at the bottom of the paper to indicate the author. Insert this paper into the first baggie.

Have the child choose two pieces of print. Trim them to fit and insert one into the next baggie. Turn this page and insert the second piece of print in the same bag so the two are back-to-back. Seal the bag to make a page in the book. Continue until the baggies are filled or all the print has been used.

The children can change the words as often as they like or create other baggie books.

Closing

Invite the child to read the book aloud. Commend the child for her efforts. The book may be placed in the Library Area where the child can share it with friends or classroom visitors.

Extension(s)

- Help children think about the words that are most meaningful to them, e.g., *Mommy, Daddy*, and so on. Write the words on separate cards. Ask if they would like to draw a picture by each word. Help the children insert the words into their personal *Baggie Book of Special Words*. Refer children to their books when they are writing greeting cards or notes.

Modification(s)

- For an English language learner, write the word in the child's home language on one side of the card and write the English word on the other.

- For a child who finds it difficult to grasp or turn the baggie pages, make the page more rigid by gluing the print on heavy paper or card stock.

Individual	Small Group	Large Group	Interest Area	Single Day	Multiday	Minutes
●			Library	●		20

Be a Word

Goal(s) & Objectives	**Listening and Speaking**
	38. Hears and discriminates the sounds of language; 39. Expresses self using words and expanded sentences
	Reading and Writing
	44. Enjoys and values reading; 48. Comprehends and interprets meaning from books and other texts

Materials & Preparation

☐ *Jump, Frog, Jump!* by Robert Kalan (Harper Trophy, 1989)

☐ frog headbands

Jump, Frog, Jump! is a simple, cumulative story in which a frog, in pursuit of a tasty fly, finds himself a part of the food chain. As new threats appear, there is only one thing for the frog to do: Jump, frog, jump!

Make or purchase frog headbands. Read the story, *Jump, Frog, Jump!* with the children before conducting this activity.

Guiding Children's Learning

Choose three children, each to represent, or "be," one word in the repeated phrase, "Jump, frog, jump!" Give each child a frog headband or a toy frog and have them line up, side by side, facing the rest of the children.

Explain that each child will listen for his assigned word in the phrase, "Jump, frog, jump," and jump when he hears it. Have them practice.

In the beginning, it may be helpful to gently touch the top of each child's head when it is his turn to jump.

Read or retell the story. As you say each word of the phrase, "Jump, frog, jump," have the appropriate child jump. To help the children understand the directionality of print, make sure that the children jump in sequence from the audience's left to the audience's right. Invite the other children to join you in reading or reciting the phrase.

Closing

Explain that the book and headbands will be in the Library Area for children to use during choice time.

Extension(s)

- For variation, use a toy frog and three lily pads made from construction paper or felt (one pad to represent each word of the phrase, "Jump, frog, jump!"). Position the lily pads so all children can see them. Read the story aloud. When you repeat the phrase, "Jump, frog, jump!," make the toy frog jump to each lily pad, beginning with the pad to the children's left. Invite the children to take turns moving the frog from left to right when you come to the phrase.

- Try this "be a word" strategy using other books that repeat simple phrases. Phrases consisting of one syllable words work best with young children. *I Went Walking*, by Sue Williams (Voyager Books, 1992) is another good book to use for this activity.

Modification(s)

- For a child who becomes overstimulated or disorganized by movement activities, or who has difficulty taking turns, preview the activity and ways to participate before the group activity begins.

- To support children who are learning to take turns and to facilitate the expressive language of children with speech delays, teach the group American Sign Language for *jump*. While they wait for their turn to jump on their feet, they may make the sign when they hear the phrase, "Jump, frog, jump!"

Individual	Small Group	Large Group	Interest Area	Single Day	Multiday	Minutes
	●	●	Library	●		15–20

Buried Treasures

Goal(s) & Objectives	Listening and Speaking **40.** *Understands and follows oral directions* Reading and Writing **46.** *Demonstrates knowledge of the alphabet*

Materials & Preparation

☐ magnetic letters

☐ wand magnets

☐ sand table or tubs of sand

Before the activity, bury magnetic alphabet letters in the sandbox or shallow tubs of sand.

Guiding Children's Learning

Invite a child to go on an imaginary treasure hunt to search for "letter treasures."

Show the child how to wave the wand magnet over the sand. Together, identify the letter that is attracted to the wand and talk about its name and features.

Give the child a wand magnet to hunt for letters. Have the child identify each one and talk about its distinguishing features.

Introduce this activity using only a few letters, especially the letters of the child's name.

Continue as long as the child is interested.

Closing

Review the letters the child identified. Suggest that he hunt for letters at choice time.

Extension(s)

- Place containers near the sand table. When a child searches for letters, have her sort them as *letters with curves, letters with straight lines,* and *letters with both curves and straight lines.*

- The child can also sort the letters as *uppercase* (capital) *letters* and *lowercase letters,* or he can match uppercase (capital) letters with the corresponding lowercase letters.

- Laminate children's name cards and store them in the Sand and Water Area. As children discover letters with the wand magnet, have them match the discovered letters to the letters on their name cards.

- Bury the children's laminated name cards in the sand. Show the children how to brush away the sand with a paintbrush to reveal one letter at a time. Until the name is read correctly, have them guess whose name is being uncovered each time a new letter is revealed.

Modification(s)

- Place the sand and buried letters in a plastic bin or baking pan if a child has difficulty standing or reaching the sand table.

- For a child with a weak or inefficient grasp, use a short, stubby wand; thicken the wand handle with tape, foam, elastic bands, playdough, or silly putty; attach the wand to a mitten or glove with Velcro; or use lightweight letters (e.g., made from construction paper or tagboard letters with paper clips attached).

- If a child is unable to use the wand, have her find letter treasures with her hands or a large magnet that can be held with both hands.

- If a child dislikes sand, or if the sand is overstimulating, use a material such as flour, salt, or Easter basket grass.

- For children with visual impairments or fine motor problems, use large magnetic letters.

- If a child requires more instruction and repetition in order to carry out motor tasks, pair the child with a peer who can model the skills.

Individual	Small Group	Large Group	Interest Area	Single Day	Multiday	Minutes
●	●		Sand and Water, Discovery	●		15–20

Can You Do It?

Goal(s) & Objectives	Listening and Speaking *39. Expresses self using words and expanded sentences; 40. Understands and follows oral directions* Reading and Writing *44. Enjoys and values reading; 47. Uses emerging reading skills to make meaning from print; 48. Comprehends and interprets meaning from books and other texts*

Materials & Preparation

☐ *From Head to Toe* by Eric Carle (Harper Trophy, 1999).

From Head to Toe is a simple story in which various animals challenge children to move their bodies in particular ways.

Guiding Children's Learning

Introduce the story by showing the cover (a gorilla touching its head and toe) and the title page (a boy touching his head and toe). Encourage the children to predict what the story is about.

Before you read each page, have the children name the pictured animal and describe what it and the child are doing. Have the children perform the same action. If necessary, demonstrate or explain some of the movements.

As you read, sweep your fingers underneath the text. Invite the children to read the simple, repetitive text with you, "Can you do it? I can do it!"

Closing

Invite the children to repeat some of the new words they learned. Their responses might include

- ways to move: *raise, wriggle, wiggle, thump, bend, arch,* or *stomp*

- animals: *penguin, buffalo, seal, gorilla, camel,* etc.

- body parts: *shoulders, chest, hips*

Extend their responses by asking children questions such as, "What body parts can you raise besides your shoulders?" or, "What's the difference between tiptoeing and stomping?"

Tell the children that the book will be in the Library Area. Suggest that they read it with friends and move their bodies in the same ways as the animals in the story.

Extension(s)

- Have children dictate a list of other ways to move their bodies. Let them take turns leading the other children in moving the ways they listed.

- Use paper plates to create masks of the animals in the story. Put them with the book in the Library Area to encourage the children to reenact the story.

Modification(s)

- Substitute other actions for children who are physically challenged and unable to perform those mentioned in the story.

- To familiarize English language learners with the story vocabulary, introduce the story in their home languages, have families introduce it, or use a taped version of the story that was read by a primary language speaker. You can also introduce key words and phrases in English and scaffold the meaning with gestures, larger actions, and so on.

- For children with hearing impairments or language delays and for English language learners, speak slowly and articulate clearly. Reread the story at a slower rate.

- For a child with language or developmental delays, it is often helpful to add music to help children attend. Use a simple melody to sing repetitive text. After introducing the activity, use it to aid comprehension of the instructions. For example, you might sing these words to the tune of *Row, Row, Row Your Boat*:

  Can you do it?
  I can do it.
  Can you wiggle like this?
  Can you do it? I can do it.
  *Wiggle, wiggle like thi*s.

- If a child becomes overstimulated or disorganized during movement activities, preview the activity and ways to participate. Delineate the child's personal space by using a rug square, by marking the borders of his personal area with tape, or by offering a chair.

- If a child has a language delay or disability, use American Sign Language for the animals as you read the book.

Individual	Small Group	Large Group	Interest Area	Single Day	Multiday	Minutes
		●	Library, Music & Movement, Outdoors	●		15–20

Clap a Friend's Name

Goal(s) & Objectives	Listening and Speaking *38. Hears and discriminates the sounds of language*

Materials & Preparation

None

_____

Guiding Children's Learning

Introduce the following song to the children, inviting them to sing along as they learn the words. Follow the tune of *Mary Had a Little Lamb.*

> *Clap a friend's name with me,*
> *Name with me,*
> *Name with me.*
> *Clap a friend's name with me.*
> *Let's try Shirley.*
> *Shir-ley.*

Clap as you say each syllable of the child's name.

Repeat the song, substituting different children's names.

Try using other movements such as waving, hopping, nodding, or marching.

Closing

Commend the children for listening attentively. Transition them to the next activity by clapping (waving, nodding, or marching) a child's name. For example, clap three times as you direct Jonetta, "Jo-net-ta, you may choose an interest area."

Extension(s)

• Invite the children to suggest other ways to accentuate syllables by moving. List them on chart paper and use them as you sing the song.

• When children are able to identify the syllables in their own names, include other familiar words.

Modification(s)

- For children with auditory processing or attentional difficulties, "warm up" hands for clapping and ears for listening by shaking hands and touching ear lobes.

- For a child with developmental delays or motor planning problems, use hand-over-hand prompts to provide sensory guidance.

- For children who have difficulty clapping, stamp feet instead.

- If a child is reluctant to participate, have her choose a friend to clap her name.

- For a child who benefits from visual input to support receptive language, use pictures (e.g., a black and white illustration of a person speaking and another illustration of clapping hands). Refer to the picture when initially giving the directions, and if needed, as a prompt or cue. Additional pictures could be used to prompt the other movements suggested in the activity, such as waving, hopping, etc.

Individual	Small Group	Large Group	Interest Area	Single Day	Multiday	Minutes
●	●	●	All	●		10–15

Clothesline Storytelling

Goal(s) & Objectives

Listening and Speaking
39. *Expresses self using words and expanded sentences*

Reading and Writing
44. *Enjoys and values reading;* **45.** *Demonstrates understanding of print concepts;* **47.** *Uses emerging reading skills to make meaning from print;* **48.** *Comprehends and interprets meaning from books and other texts*

Materials & Preparation

☐ storybook with a simple plot, such as
Who Took the Farmer's Hat? by Joan L. Nodset
The Wind Blew by Pat Hutchins
The Gingerbread Boy by Paul Galdone
The Three Bears by Paul Galdone
The Three Little Pigs various versions

☐ lamination supplies or clear Contact paper

☐ six feet of clothesline and clothespins

☐ paper star

☐ blank paper and marker

☐ Ziplock bag large enough to store the book and illustrations

Prepare a clothesline story by making illustrations that show the 4-5 major events or characters in the story. Include a picture and words for the title and write the phrase *The end*. Laminate the pieces or cover them with clear Contact paper. Order the illustrations as the events occur, for easy use during storytelling.

Tie a clothesline in the Library Area or another location out of the way of traffic. Write the words *Begin here* on a star and attach it to the left-hand side of the clothesline, to indicate where the story begins.

Guiding Children's Learning

Day 1:
Have a small group of children sit facing the clothesline.

Introduce the story to the children, clipping the title illustration to the clothesline by the star at the children's left. Continue telling the story, clipping each subsequent illustration on the clothesline (from the children's left to the children's right) and concluding with *The end*.

Day 2:
Distribute the illustrations to the children, and discuss each picture to minimize any confusion the children have about how the picture illustrates the text. Retell the story and have the child holding the corresponding illustration clip it to the clothesline. Again, have the children sequence the pictures from left to right, to help them understand the directionality of print.

Closing
Unclip the illustrations and store them in a Ziplock bag with the book. Tell the children that the clothesline illustrations and book will be placed in the Library Area for them to use at choice time.

Extension(s)
- Use a clothesline story to tell different versions of the same story (e.g, a classic folktale). Talk about how each story is similar and different.

- To encourage discussions about the story, think about cooking, art, movement, dramatic play, or writing experiences the children might undertake. For example, they might draw the most exciting part of the story or act out a character's movements.

Modification(s)
- For those children who have difficulty manipulating the clothespins, offer another way to display the illustrations. For example, use Velcro to fasten the pictures to the wall, let the children prop the illustrations on a chalk board tray, or glue felt on the back of the illustrations and use a felt board.

- To help children who need additional support to follow the left-to-right progression of the story, or to help a child with motor planning difficulties, tape paper footprints to the floor. Add arrows to show the direction to walk as the illustrations are displayed.

- Ask a child who has difficulty remaining seated to hold the *Begin here* sign.

- Encourage children who have motor planning problems, developmental delays, or anxiety about participating in group or new activities to watch until they are ready to participate.

- The first time the story is told, or for children who have difficulty participating, seat the children with pictures in the order of story events. This will assist correct picture sequencing and promote the children's understanding of directionality.

- To accommodate children who have difficulty processing visual input or who have visual impairments, modify the illustrations using high/low contrasting colors (fluorescent or dark markers).

- For a child with visual impairments, preview the illustrations. Seat the child close to the clothesline, and let him walk right up to the clothesline if that is helpful.

Individual	Small Group	Large Group	Interest Area	Single Day	Multiday	Minutes
	●		Library		●	15–20

Copy Cat

Goal(s) & Objectives	Listening and Speaking *38. Hears and discriminates the sounds of language; 39. Expresses self using words and expanded sentences; 40. Understands and follows oral directions*

Materials & Preparation

☐ a variety of instruments or other objects that make sounds, e.g., handbell, tone block, maracas, cymbals, sticks, drum, xylophone, tambourine

Guiding Children's Learning

Introduce each instrument or object and demonstrate how to use it to make a sound. In simple language and by demonstrating, explain a few musical terms, such as *pitch, rhythm, percussion, instruments*, etc.

Explain to the children that they are going to play a game using the objects and instruments.

Tell them to close their eyes and listen while you make a sound with one of the instruments. When they open their eyes, they are to guess which one you used. Have the child who guesses play the instrument, and ask the others to decide whether his guess is correct.

Next, make a series of sounds and have the children take turns copying the sounds with the instruments. Start by using two instruments with very different sounds, such as a bell and a drum.

Increase the level of difficulty by adding a third sound to the sequence.

Closing

Explain to the children that the instruments will be in the Music and Movement Area, where they can play the game with a friend at choice time.

Extension(s)

- As children become proficient at discriminating very different sounds, use instruments that have more closely related sounds.

Modification(s)

- For children who are sensitive to sounds, use quiet instruments (e.g., drums with leather or chamois heads, sand blocks, rain sticks).

- If a child is reluctant to close her eyes or is unable to follow directions with closed eyes, cover the instruments with a box so that the children cannot see which are being played.

- If a child is reluctant to participate, let him explore the instruments before beginning the group activity.

- Facilitate the participation of a non-verbal or language-delayed child by encouraging her to point to a photo or drawing of the instrument that she thinks was used, or to the actual instrument.

- For English language learners, introduce (individually or in a small group) the names of the instruments and objects ahead of time.

- Ask English language learners to point to the instrument or object they think was used, and then you supply the name.

Individual	Small Group	Large Group	Interest Area	Single Day	Multiday	Minutes
	●		Music & Movement	●		15–20

Coupon Match

Goal(s) & Objectives	Reading and Writing *45. Demonstrates understanding of print concepts; 46. Demonstrates knowledge of the alphabet; 47. Uses emerging reading skills to make meaning from print*

Materials & Preparation

☐ empty food and other commercial product containers or brand name labels

☐ coupons that correspond to the products (laminated for durability)

☐ grocery bag

☐ envelope

Put a collection of product containers or labels in a grocery bag. Put their corresponding coupons in an envelope and place the envelope in the same bag.

Guiding Children's Learning

Seat the children in a circle on the floor. Take one item out of the sack at a time. Sweep your hand underneath the words on the label and ask, "Can anyone read these words?" Make comments that will help to make the product words personal and meaningful [e.g., point to the *T* and say, "*Tide* and *Tasheen* both start with an uppercase (or capital) *T*. *Total* has two *T*s, an uppercase (or capital) *T* at the beginning and a lowercase *t* in the middle."]

Continue until each child has had a turn. Call attention to similarities in words (e.g., *Wheat Thins* and *Wheaties*).

Take the envelope of coupons out of the bag. Lead a brief conversation about the coupons, asking if children know what they are and what they are used for. Show the children where the value of the coupon is marked.

Explain that there is a coupon to match each product. Spread them out on the floor and have children take turns choosing a coupon, reading it, and matching it to the appropriate product label.

Show children who have difficulty how to look for other visual clues as well as letters.

Closing

Close with comments that encourage children's confidence as readers. Tell them that this matching game will be in the Toys and Games Area to use at choice time.

Extension(s)

- Place coupons in the Dramatic Play Area for children to use in their play. Set up a supermarket where children can use coupons. Also include grocery bags from local supermarkets and supermarket advertisements.

- Share this coupon activity with families and encourage them to involve children in their grocery shopping. Explain how this can support children's literacy learning.

Modification(s)

- Include products and labels that reflect the languages and cultures of the children in your class.

- For children with visual impairments, enlarge the coupons, use black marker to outline letters and numbers, or use fluorescent markers to highlight the print.

- To assist a child who does not understand how to pair the coupons and products, ask a peer partner to demonstrate the task.

- For a child who has difficultly attending and focusing, start with one product and only two coupons. Use a tabletop carrel (3-sided divider) to limit visual stimulation.

- For a child with fine motor problems who has difficulty picking up the coupons, laminate the coupons twice for extra thickness.

Individual	Small Group	Large Group	Interest Area	Single Day	Multiday	Minutes
●	●		Toys & Games, Dramatic Play	●		15–20

Did You Ever See…?

Goal(s) & Objectives	Listening and Speaking *38. Hears and discriminates the sounds of language; 39. Expresses self using words and expanded sentences* Reading and Writing *44. Enjoys and values reading; 45. Demonstrates understanding of print concepts; 47. Uses emerging reading skills to make meaning from print; 48. Comprehends and interprets meaning from books and other texts; 49. Understands the purpose of writing*

Materials & Preparation

☐ book and recording *Down by the Bay* by Raffi and Nadine Bernard Wescott (Crown Books, 1988)

☐ pictures of familiar animals, such as a cat, a dog, a sheep, a mouse, a snake, etc.

Guiding Children's Learning

Sing *Down by the Bay* with the children on multiple occasions, so that they are familiar with it. Here is the first verse:

> *Down by the bay, where the watermelons grow,*
> *Back to my home, I dare not go.*
> *For if I do, my mother will say,*
> *"Did you ever see a goose*
> *Kissing a moose,*
> *Down by the bay?"*

Remind children that rhyming words sound alike at the end. Give some examples of rhyming words in the song. Invite the children to repeat rhymes they heard in the song.

Explain to the children that they are going to make up new verses to the song.

Show the children the pictures and review the names of the animals. Have a child choose a picture. Then ask the group to sing a new verse, inserting the name of the selected animal. Pause appropriately to let the children supply a word that rhymes with the animal's name. Here is an example:

> *Did you ever see a sheep*
> *driving a jeep,*
> *Down by the bay?*

Sing the new verse with the children. Create new verses together as long as the children are interested.

Closing Invite the children to tell which new verse is their favorite. Show them the book, *Down by the Bay*. Demonstrate the directionality of print and the one-to-one correspondence of oral and written words by pointing to the words in the book as you sing the song. Tell them the book and recording will be in the Music and Movement Area to enjoy at choice time.

Extension(s)

- Ask the children if they would like to make their new verses into a book. Write the new verses down and have the children illustrate them. Make copies of the pages and bind them to make several books. Read or sing the verses at group time. Place the books in the Music and Movement Area and the Library Area.

Modification(s)

- For children who need additional support, highlight rhyming words with the same color.

- Have a non-verbal child participate by pointing to the picture of an animal and working with a verbal peer who can supply a word that rhymes with the chosen animal.

- To support the oral language development of children who are reluctant to speak in a group, have children tape-record the new verses.

- For English language learners and children with language delays, the teacher can sing more slowly, accentuating rhyming words by modifying inflection and volume and by exaggerating articulation.

Individual	Small Group	Large Group	Interest Area	Single Day	Multiday	Minutes
	●	●	Music & Movement, Library		●	10–15

Dressing for School

Goal(s) & Objectives	**Listening and Speaking** *39. Expresses self using words and expanded sentences* **Reading and Writing** *44. Enjoys and values reading; 45. Demonstrates understanding of print concepts; 46. Demonstrates knowledge of the alphabet; 47. Uses emerging reading skills to make meaning from print; 48. Comprehends and interprets meaning from books and other texts; 49. Understands the purpose of writing; 50. Writes letters and words*

Materials & Preparation

☐ *Mary Wore Her Red Dress and Henry Wore His Green Sneakers* by Merle Peek (Clarion Books, 1988)

☐ chart paper, blank paper, and card stock or construction paper

☐ colored markers

☐ bookbinding supplies (e.g., brads, metal rings, hole punch, stapler)

Guiding Children's Learning

Introduce the story to the children, stating the title, author, and illustrator. Encourage the children to predict what the story is about.

Read the first few pages aloud, naming and pointing to each new character.

See if the children notice that the text box on each page is the same color as the article of clothing you are reading about. If not, ask a question such as, "Can someone tell me how this box and Mary's dress are the same?" Explain that the text box gives them a clue about what the story will say.

Continue the story, inviting the children to read with you. Help make the story meaningful by discussing what they are wearing.

When the story is over, have each child describe her favorite piece of school clothing. On chart paper, write the child's name and use the corresponding colored maker to record what the child likes to wear and its color. As you write, talk about the letters and words [e.g., names start with uppercase (or capital) letters; you are writing the word *purple* with a purple marker; *turquoise* and *Tasheen* begin with the same letter].

Closing

Review the list with the children, inviting them to read along. Explain that the list will be in the Library Area for them to read.

Ask the children if they would like to make a book about their favorite school clothes.

Explain that they may use the blank paper and markers in the Library Area to draw pictures of themselves wearing their favorite clothes. Encourage them to write or dictate a sentence about their drawing. Suggest that they adapt the text pattern from the book *Mary Wore Her Red Dress and Henry Wore His Green Sneakers*; for example, "Derrick wore his black socks, black socks, black socks. Derrick wore his black socks all day long."

Drawing and dictation may continue over several days. When the children are finished, create a class book by binding their pages with a cover made from card stock or construction paper. Share the book at group time and place it in the Library Area for children to read on their own during choice time.

Extension(s)

- Introduce new vocabulary for clothing mentioned in the story, for example, *sneakers, tennis shoes; bandana, scarf; pants, slacks.*

- The language pattern of the book can be used to make up verses about various topics of study. For example, if children are involved in a study of insects, you might sing a song or write part of a story, "Leo found a ladybug, ladybug, ladybug. Leo found a ladybug outside today."

Modification(s)

- Continue the activity over a period of days in order to reinforce color and clothing vocabulary. You might read the story one day and reread it and create the list on the second day. On the third day, review the list and invite the children to create the book.

- If a child is unable or chooses not to illustrate a page, take a photo of the child. Add a verse about an article of the child's clothing.

- For children who have difficulty attending to the activity, sing the text.

- For English language learners or children with language or developmental delays, point to specific details of the illustrations as you read or sing.

- Make the book pages easier to turn by laminating the pages or by covering them with clear Contact paper.

- For children who have trouble interpreting their peers' drawings, make a similar book using icons and photographs of the children. Big book format is helpful for group reading.

Individual	Small Group	Large Group	Interest Area	Single Day	Multiday	Minutes
●	●		Library, Music & Movement		●	20–25

Feed Me

Goal(s) & Objectives	Listening and Speaking *38. Hears and discriminates the sounds of language; 39. Expresses self using words and expanded sentences* Reading and Writing *44. Enjoys and values reading; 47. Uses emerging reading skills to make meaning from print; 48. Comprehends and interprets meaning from books and other texts*

Materials & Preparation

☐ The Hungry Thing by Jan Slepian and Ann Seidler (Scholarstic Books, 2001).

The Hungry Thing is a story about a creature that wanders into a town wearing a sign that reads, "Feed me." When asked what he wants to eat, he replies, "Shmancakes." The townspeople struggle to figure out what the Hungry Thing wants to eat. Finally a little boy says, "Shmancakes sound like fancakes, sound like pancakes to me." They give the Hungry Thing pancakes, and he eats them up. The Hungry Thing continues asking for foods such as tickles, hookies, and gollilipops, and each time the townspeople must figure out what he wants.

Guiding Children's Learning

Introduce the book to the children, reading the title, authors, and illustrator. Encourage the children to predict what the story is about. Ask questions such as,

Where do you think the Hungry Thing came from?

Why do you think he is wearing a sign around his neck? What do you think it says?

What do you think the Hungry Thing likes to eat?

Read the story aloud. Before revealing the little boy's interpretations of the Hungry Thing's requests, invite the children to guess what the Hungry Thing wants to eat.

Closing

Continue playing with language as you ask a child to put the book in the Library Area on the "delf" (shelf) or as you dismiss the children to go "boutdoors" (outdoors).

Extension(s)

- Create a swallowing puppet of The Hungry Thing. Enlarge a picture of the Hungry Thing; cut it into two pieces; and glue it to the front of a small, empty detergent box.

  Prepare a deck of Hungry Thing cards by cutting pictures of familiar foods from magazines and gluing each on a 3" x 5" index card. Laminate them for durability.

  Review the story of *The Hungry Thing*. Introduce the puppet and explain that they are going to play a game in which they will feed the Hungry Thing.

  Choose a card from the deck, keeping it hidden from the children. Say nonsense words that rhyme with the pictured food and encourage the children to guess what it is. Whoever guesses the food gets to feed the Hungry Thing by placing the card in the puppet's mouth.

  You may use a variety of play food props instead of pictures.

- Use this language play strategy at snack or mealtimes and encourage the children to guess what they will be eating. For example, you might say, "For lunch today we are having *tizza*, *dalad*, and *bilk*," when serving pizza, salad, and milk.

Modification(s)

- For children with visual impairments, enlarge the index cards of familiar foods. Outline the pictures with bold markers or highlighters, and use a contrasting background.

- Use props for children with visual impairments or with developmental or language delays.

- Children who are learning English, have language or developmental delays, or limited phonological awareness would benefit by playing the game using the correct pronunciation of the food words. The teacher should articulate clearly.

- Children who have fine motor or other physical impairments may work with a peer.

Individual	Small Group	Large Group	Interest Area	Single Day	Multiday	Minutes
●	●		Library	●		15–20

Friends

Goal(s) & Objectives	Reading and Writing **45.** *Demonstrates understanding of print concepts;* **46.** *Demonstrates knowledge of the alphabet;* **47.** *Uses emerging reading skills to make meaning from print*

Materials & Preparation

☐ children's name cards (written on sentence strips or card stock and laminated for durability)

☐ bag or container for name cards

☐ tagboard

☐ marker

☐ large paper clip or Velcro

Write the song *Friends* on sturdy tagboard. Cut a slit and insert a large paper clip where the blank appears, or attach adhesive Velcro to both the chart and name cards. This will enable you to insert different name cards.

Friends (Sung to the tune of *Bingo*)

> I have a friend
> Whose name is_____.
> We have fun together.
> We laugh and play at school,
> Laugh and play at school,
> Laugh and play at school,
> In any kind of weather.

Guiding Children's Learning

Sing *Friends* with the children several times, so that it is familiar to them.

Introduce the *Friends* song chart. Explain that you will insert a name card in the blank space on the chart, so everyone will know whose name to sing.

Choose a card from the bag and hold it up so the children can read the name. Provide assistance as needed. Insert the card in the blank.

Sing aloud, sweeping your hand beneath the words as you sing.

Choose, or let a child choose, another name. Insert it in the chart, help the children read the name, and invite the children to sing with you.

Continue as long as the children are enjoying the activity.

Closing

Comment on how well the children are learning to recognize their names. Tell them that the chart and name cards will be placed in the Music and Movement Area, where they may read and sing the song.

Extension(s)

- Sing *I Wish I Had A Little Red Box*, to the tune of *Bingo*. Keep the set of name cards in a little red box or a heart-shaped box. You will also need to make cards with the words *him* and *her*, to insert in the appropriate places on the chart. Children enjoy making smacking sounds instead of saying, "...kiss, kiss, kiss."

  I wish I had a little red box
  To put (child's name) in.
  I'd take her (him) out and kiss, kiss, kiss
  And put her (him) back again.

Modification(s)

- When introducing this activity or with children who have difficulty distinguishing between similar names, add each child's photograph to her name card. Continue to talk about the features of letters and children's names, but keep the experience fun and playful.

Individual	Small Group	Large Group	Interest Area	Single Day	Multiday	Minutes
●	●	●	Music & Movement	●		15

Give a Dog a Bone

Goal(s) & Objectives	Listening and Speaking
	38. Hears and discriminates the sounds of language; 39. Expresses self using words and expanded sentences
	Reading and Writing
	45. Demonstrates understanding of print concepts; 46. Demonstrates knowledge of the alphabet; 49. Understands the purpose of writing

Materials & Preparation

☐ chart paper

☐ marker

Guiding Children's Learning

Sing a familiar song. Invite the children to alter the song by offering new words that rhyme. Try it with a few verses of the children's song, *This Old Man.*

> *This old man*
> *He played one.*
> *He played knick knack*
> *On my _____.*
>
> *With a knick knack Paddy whack,*
> *Give a dog a bone.*
> *This old man came rolling home.*

Continue with subsequent verses. Below is a summary of the words commonly sung:

one...	*drum*
two...	*shoe*
three...	*knee*
four...	*door*
five...	*hive*
six...	*bricks*
seven...	*heaven*
eight...	*gate*
nine...	*line*
ten...	*hen*

Record children's suggestions on chart paper; then sing them. Talk as you write, to call attention to letters and words and to demonstrate the directionality of print and the one-to-one correspondence of oral and written words.

Closing Tell the children that you will sing this song with them and make up other rhymes another day. Suggest that they share the song with their families.

Extension(s)
- Share the book, *This Old Man*, illustrated by Pam Adams (Child's Play International, 1999). Invite the children to make their new version of the song into a book. Record them as they sing their new song, and put the book and tape in the Music and Movement Area for their use.

Modification(s)
- Have a child with attentional or processing difficulties choose and hold a magnetic or foam numeral to guide the group's singing.

- A child with developmental delays can work with a peer to choose a number and create a new verse.

- For children with hearing impairments or with language or developmental delays, use a few American Sign Language signs to increase comprehension and facilitate language development.

Individual	Small Group	Large Group	Interest Area	Single Day	Multiday	Minutes
	●		Music & Movement	●		15–20

Group Sharing

Goal(s) & Objectives

Listening and Speaking

39. Expresses self using words and expanded sentences; 41. Answers questions; 42. Asks questions; 43. Actively participates in conversations

Reading and Writing

45. Demonstrates understanding of print concepts; 49. Understands the purposes of writing; 50. Writes letters and words

Materials & Preparation

☐ chart paper or tagboard for a large schedule

☐ marker

☐ paper log and a pencil for children to sign their names

Establish the rules and procedures for group sharing. For example, explain that children may teach something they know (e.g., a song or dance step), share something they have made (e.g., a greeting card or painting), or share news regarding special events such as the arrival of a new brother or sister. Explain these guidelines to children and families before beginning this routine. Encourage families to talk with their children about what they will teach or share.

Prepare a group sharing schedule and post it where it is visible to the children.

Prepare a log for the children to sign after they have had a turn.

Guiding Children's Learning

Begin by talking about and modeling appropriate speaking and listening skills.

- Ask, "What are some ways we can show (child's name) that we are listening?"

- Help the speaker become aware of the need to speak loudly enough for everyone to hear.

- Encourage the speaker to look at the audience.

- Make sure listeners can see and hear the speaker.

Introduce the child who will be sharing. Extend the child's language as he speaks by

- prompting the child to expand his description and explanation

- rephrasing what the child said

- asking open-ended questions, such as, "What made you decide to share this_____?"

- encouraging other children to ask questions about what the presenter shared

Closing Thank the children for sharing. Have them sign the log to indicate that they had a turn. Read the schedule together to determine who will share next.

Extension(s) • Prepare a journal for each child. Invite them to share personal stories by drawing, writing, or dictating.

Modification(s) • For children with developmental delays or auditory-processing problems and for children who benefit from visual cues, preview the activity with picture cues about group sharing procedures and conversational skills.

• If a child is non-verbal, has language delays, or is learning English, plan ahead and talk to family members or caregivers who can assist with the child's sharing. If they cannot attend the sharing session, they can tell you about the object or photograph that the child wants to share or about what the child wants to teach. You or the family member can model language during the sharing session.

• A child who is not ready to share verbally can dictate to an adult, and the dictation can be read or interpreted to the group. Alternatively, the child can record what she wants to share and play the tape during group time. Take photographs of the child sharing by these alternative methods, to encourage unmodified participation another time.

• For English language learners, create a picture chart that shows the steps in this activity.

Individual	Small Group	Large Group	Interest Area	Single Day	Multiday	Minutes
	●	●			●	15–20

I Spy With My Little Eye

Goal(s) & Objectives	Listening and Speaking
	38. Hears and discriminates the sounds of language; 40. Understands and follows oral directions
	Reading and Writing
	46. Demonstrates knowledge of the alphabet

Materials & Preparation

☐ alphabet cards

☐ binoculars made from two cardboard rolls or a pair of silly glasses

Guiding Children's Learning

Using the binoculars or glasses, look around the room. Then recite,

> *I spy, with my little eye, someone whose name begins with /d/,*
> Dd, *as in* dog.

Hold up the *Dd* card, so children begin to connect the letter symbol with the sound. Ask the children whose names start with the letter to stand up. Ask them to perform an action that begins with the same letter sound. For example, you might ask Dallas to dance. Add comments such as, "Dallas danced. *Dallas, dance,* and *dog* all start with /d/ *Dd*."

If the children's names are listed or their name cards are nearby, point to the *D*s to show that they are the same.

Continue as long as the children are interested or until each child has had a turn.

Closing

Tell the children that you will put binoculars or glasses in several interest areas so they can play *I Spy* with their friends.

Extension(s)
- Use this as a strategy to call attention to rhyming words ("I spy, with my little eye, something that rhymes with *look*.").

- Use this strategy to call attention to words that start with the same sound but not necessarily the same letter ("When I want to know what time it is, I spy, with my little eye, something that starts with the same sound as *key*.").

- Use this strategy to promote children's listening and thinking skills ("I spy, with my little eye, something that's furry, has long floppy ears, and hops.").

- Use this game to help children transition from one activity to the next; for example, "I spy, with my little eye, someone who is wearing a red shirt. That's right, (child's name). You are wearing a red shirt and may choose an interest area."

Modification(s)
- If a child requires assistance in recognizing the first letter of her name, provide her name card during the activity and talk about the location, letter name, and letter sound of the "beginning."

- A child who has difficulties with scanning or who is visually impaired can use both far-point and near-point locations, depending on visual acuity. If the "spy" refers to someone who is across the room from the child, the "spied" person can call out or wave to confirm identification when the child locates him. Children with visual impairments can also be walked around the room to sight spied objects, and objects and people can be positioned within visual range.

Individual	Small Group	Large Group	Interest Area	Single Day	Multiday	Minutes
	●	●	All	●		15

I Went Shopping

Goal(s) & Objectives	Reading and Writing *45. Demonstrates understanding of print concepts;* **46.** *Demonstrates knowledge of the alphabet;* **47.** *Uses emerging reading skills to make meaning from print*

Materials & Preparation

☐ 5 or 6 pieces of environmental print found in a grocery store (e.g., empty product containers or labels)

☐ grocery bag

Place the environmental print in the grocery bag.

Guiding Children's Learning

Assemble a small group of children. Recite the following rhyme:

I went shopping; now I'm back.
Can you help unpack my sack?

Take one item out of the sack and ask for a volunteer to read the label. Sweep your fingers under the word(s) as you ask.

Talk about the print, calling attention to the words, letters, and letter features and helping the children make connections to what they already know. For example:

Do you use Crest toothpaste? What kind do you like best?

Crystal, how is your name like the word Crest? *They begin the same, don't they? They both have an uppercase (capital)* C *and a lowercase* r.

Continue until all the children have had a turn to read, repeating the rhyme each time.

Closing

Comment on the children's competence as readers. Encourage them to bring print that they can read to school.

Extension(s)

- Play a reading and memory game with environmental print. Place the environmental print in the grocery sack. Unpack the sack, one piece at a time, reading and discussing the print with the children. When all the print has been read, explain to the children that they will close their eyes. You will take one item away and put it back into the sack. You will recite the following rhyme, and then invite the children to guess which item is in the sack.

  I went shopping; now I'm back.
  Can you guess what's in my sack?

- Encourage parents to call attention to print in the environment. Invite them to send print that their children can read to school. Allow the children to read their print to others at group meetings or individually. Remove labels from containers and store them in individualized *Words I Can Read* bags. When parents, other adults, or older siblings visit the classroom, have the children read their words. Invite the children to make books, such as *My Favorite Cereals*. Place the books in the Library Area for everyone to read.

Individual	Small Group	Large Group	Interest Area	Single Day	Multiday	Minutes
	●		Library Dramatic Play	●		20

Jumping Beans

Goal(s) & Objectives	Listening and Speaking **40.** *Understands and follows oral directions* Reading and Writing **46.** *Demonstrates knowledge of the alphabet*

Materials & Preparation

□ construction paper

□ marker

□ scissors

□ lamination supplies or clear Contact paper

□ coffee can

Make bean-shaped cards out of construction paper and write one letter of the alphabet on each bean. Create 4–5 special "jumping bean" cards by drawing a bean-shaped character with a funny face on the card. Laminate the cards for durability. Place all of the cards in the coffee can and label it, *Jumping Beans.* For safety, make sure the top edge of the can is smooth.

Guiding Children's Learning

Seat the children in a circle. Ask them if they know what jumping beans are. If you have real ones, share them with the children. Show them the can and tell them they are going to play a game called *Jumping Beans.* Point to the words on the can.

Explain that each child will draw a card out of the can, say the letter on the card, and pass the can to the person sitting next to her. If a child draws one of the special "jumping bean" cards, he calls, "Jumping bean," and all of the children must stand and jump up and down.

Continue until all of the cards have been selected. Keep the game playful, providing assistance to any child who needs it. In the beginning, use letters that are easier to discriminate and identify. Refer to the developmental progression of letter identification that is discussed on page 29.

Closing

Tell the children the *Jumping Bean* game will be in the Toys and Games Area, where they may play it at choice time.

Extension(s) • Create other versions of the *Jumping Bean* game. For example, instead of single letters, use logos or words that the children will recognize from signs and brand name labels (e.g., Cheerios).

Modification(s) • Introduce the game using duplicates of a limited group of letters. Gradually add others as children become more skilled at letter recognition.

• Focus on using the letters of the name of a child who is having difficulty with this activity.

• A child who needs assistance in grasping a jumping bean card or identifying the letter may partner with a peer who has more advanced fine motor or letter-identification skills.

• For children who have visual impairments or who benefit from additional tactile and kinesthetic input, use glue or tape to raise and add texture to the letters on the cards.

Individual	Small Group	Large Group	Interest Area	Single Day	Multiday	Minutes
	●		Toys & Games	●		15–20

Listen for the Word

Goal(s) & Objectives	Listening and Speaking *38. Hears and discriminates the sounds of language* Reading and Writing *44. Enjoys and values reading; 47. Uses emerging reading skills to make meaning from print; 48. Comprehends and interprets meaning from books and other texts*

Materials & Preparation

☐ *Bear Snores On* by Karma Wilson (Simon & Schuster, 2003)

Guiding Children's Learning

Introduce the book *Bear Snores On*. Talk about the cover and ask the children to predict what the story is about.

Lead a brief discussion about snoring. Ask open-ended questions such as these:

> *What does snoring sound like?*
>
> *Do you know anyone who snores?*
>
> *When do people and other animals snore?*
>
> *Why do they snore?*
>
> *Which animal snores more loudly, a mouse or a bear?*
>
> *What do you or others do when you hear someone snoring?*
>
> *What do you think will happen if the animals wake Bear from his winter nap?*

Next, have the children snore their loudest bear snores.

Read a few pages of the story and snore each time you repeat the phrase, "But the bear snores on."

Tell the children that they are to listen carefully for the word *snores*. Each time they hear it, they are to snore.

Closing

End with a discussion to help children think about whether their predictions were correct. Encourage them to explain why the bear is awake while his friends are asleep.

Tell the children the book will be in the Library Area for them to read at choice time.

Extension(s)
- Use this listening strategy with other stories. Encourage the children to perform an action or make a sound whenever they hear a specific word or phrase. Here are some examples:

  The Doorbell Rang by Pat Hutchins (Harper Trophy, 1989): Children say, "Ding, dong!," whenever they hear the phrase *the doorbell rang.*

  The Very Busy Spider by Eric Carle (Scholastic, 1994): Children make a spinning motion with their hands when they hear the word *spinning.*

  Sheep on a Ship or *Sheep in a Shop* by Nancy Shaw (Houghton Mifflin Company, 1992 and 1994, respectively): Give each child a piece of wool yarn to hold up when they hear the word *sheep.*

Modification(s)
- Have children whose attention requires extra support snore first, and then ask them to predict what the story is about.

- For children of varying levels of cognitive, language, and listening comprehension development, and to encourage the participation of all children, ask questions of varying difficulty. Preface some prompts with, "I wonder…," to indicate that there are many possible responses.

- If a child has difficulty answering a question, simplify the question or offer answer choices (e.g., "Do people snore when they are awake or asleep?"). Let children answer by pointing to the book or gesturing.

- Learn and use American Sign Language for *snore* and *bear.*

- For children who need assistance in knowing when to snore, use listening cords. (See the *Listening Cords* activity.)

Individual	Small Group	Large Group	Interest Area	Single Day	Multiday	Minutes
		●	Library	●		10–15

Listening Cords

Goal(s) & Objectives	Listening and Speaking *38. Hears and discriminates the sounds of language;* *39. Expresses self using words and expanded sentences* Reading and Writing *44. Enjoys and values reading*

Materials & Preparation

☐ cord or nylon rope (3–4 feet per child)

☐ scissors

Make "listening cords" by cutting several pieces of cord or nylon rope in lengths of 3–4 feet. Tie the ends of each cord together.

Guiding Children's Learning

Choose a familiar story with repetitive language. Briefly review or encourage the children to recall the characters, sequence of events, and repeated words and phrases.

Show the listening cords to the children and explain that they will be used in retelling the story. Give one cord to each child while you hold the knotted end of each cord.

Explain that you will retell the story, pausing along the way. When you pause, you will tug on the end of a cord a child is holding. This will be the child's cue to provide the missing word or phrase.

Prepare children to listen purposefully, making sure they can each see and hear you as you speak. Make eye contact with the children as you retell the story.

For example, if you retell *The Three Little Pigs*, begin by saying, "Once upon a time, there were three little _____." Tug a cord so the child holding the other end knows when to say *pigs*.

Observe to see which children participate with ease and which have difficulty. Prompt or model language when necessary.

Closing

Explain to the children that the listening cords will be in the Library Area, where they may use them to retell stories on their own during choice time.

Extension(s)
- Use the listening cords with informational books, poems, rhymes, and other word games.

Modification(s)
- For children who have motor planning difficulties, difficulty participating in new activities, or who have problems attending to and following directions, explain the way to use listening cords. Start with a simple story, such as *Bear Snores On*, and have children pull on the cord whenever they hear the designated phrase.

- To accommodate children who have difficulty holding the cord or who are sensitive to touch, adapt the end of the cord by thickening it with tape, elastic, foam, or fabric.

- For children who need to be near the teacher in order to attend, focus, or use the cords appropriately, shorten the cords.

- For children who need help learning to take turns during group discussions, and for children who benefit from kinesthetic input, listening cords provide useful prompts.

Individual	Small Group	Large Group	Interest Area	Single Day	Multiday	Minutes
	●		Library	●		15–20

Making My Name

Goal(s) & Objectives	Reading and Writing *45. Demonstrates understanding of print concepts; 46. Demonstrates knowledge of the alphabet*

Materials & Preparation

☐ small, sturdy envelopes

☐ marker

☐ letter manipulatives

Write each child's name on the outside of a small, sturdy envelope. Put letter manipulatives (letter tiles, letter beads, letter blocks, or magnetic letters) inside the envelope so each child will be able to spell his name. Also prepare an envelope with your name, to demonstrate the activity.

Note: Letter tiles can be made by writing one letter on a one-inch ceramic tile with a fine-tipped permanent marker. Tiles can be purchased from hardware stores.

Guiding Children's Learning

This activity may be introduced to an individual child or a small group of children.

Show the children the envelope with your name. Read your name aloud and say the name of each letter as you point to it.

Take the letter tiles out of the envelope and explain that they are the letters of your name, just as it is written on the envelope.

Demonstrate how to make your name by sequencing the letters appropriately. Demonstrate how to refer to the name written on the envelope for help, talk about the features of the letters, and name the letters as you work.

Give the children their envelopes with the letters inside. Ask them to take the letters out and arrange them to spell, or make, their names. Assist as necessary.

Closing

Tell the children that the envelopes will be placed in the Toys and Games and Library Areas. Suggest that they practice making their names and their friends' names at choice time.

Extension(s)
- Make name puzzles as described below:

   Write each child's name in large print on a 6" x 8" piece of colorful card stock. Laminate the name card and then cut it into 3 jigsaw puzzle pieces. Put the pieces into an envelope with the child's name written on the outside. Place the puzzles in the Toys and Games Area for the children to use at choice time.

- Draw a fat wiggly worm on colored card stock. Draw an eye and mouth and write a child's name on the worm, leaving enough space to cut between each letter. Laminate the worm for durability; then cut the worm into pieces. Repeat this process for several children, using a different color of card stock for each child. Place all of the pieces in a can, making a *Can of worms*. Also make a name card for each child on card stock of the same color as his worm. Store the name cards in the can as well. Place the *Can of worms* in the Toys and Games Area so children can assemble their name worms during choice time.

- Use name cards during transitions. Make a set of name cards for the children and place them in a colorful paper sack. Choose a card and reveal one letter at a time, naming each letter as it becomes visible. Allow children to choose an interest area or move to the next activity when they recognize their names. Assist as necessary.

- Place children's name cards in other interest areas for children to use with other materials. For example, they can be placed in the Art Area for use with sponge and cookie cutter letters, in the Sand and Water Area for use with letter molds, in the Block Area for use with alphabet blocks, and in the Library Area for use with alphabet stamps or textured letters.

Modification(s)
- When just beginning this activity or with children who have difficulty distinguishing between similar names, include each child's photograph on his name card.

Individual	Small Group	Large Group	Interest Area	Single Day	Multiday	Minutes
●	●		Toys & Games Library	●		15

Me, Too!

Goal(s) & Objectives

Listening and Speaking

38. Hears and discriminates the sounds of language; 40. Understands and follows oral directions

Materials & Preparation

None

Guiding Children's Learning

Tell the children that they are going to play a listening game.

Explain that you are going to say several words that begin with the same sound. Give some examples, emphasizing the initial sound of the words. Explain that the children are to listen and determine if the words begin with the same sound as the sound heard at the beginning of their names.

Offer an example like this:

> *If your name begins like* meat, mat, *and* mitt, *please stand up. Mary heard that* meat, mat, *and* mitt *all begin with the same sound: /m/.*

When the children understand the concept of similar beginning sounds, you can make the activity more difficult by asking the children to perform a particular action that also begins with the same sound. For example, you might say,

> *If your name begins like* tiny, tight, *and* telephone, *stand and touch your toes (or tiptoe or twirl). Tasheen was listening carefully;* tiny, tight, telephone, *and* Tasheen *all begin with the same sound: /t/, and so do* touching *and* toes.

Emphasize the beginning sound as you say each of the words that the children should pay particular attention to. Continue until all the children have had a turn. Note those children who have difficulty with this game. If possible, use additional sets of words with the same initial sounds as the names of those children.

Closing

Comment on the children's competence as listeners. Encourage them to play this game with their friends.

Extension(s)

- Use this activity during transitions. For example, "If your name starts like *monkey, milk,* and *marshmallows,* you may get your jacket."

Modification(s)

- For children who have difficulty with auditory discrimination and children who are just beginning to develop phonological awareness, accentuate and repeat the initial letter sounds.

- When a child is just beginning to learn letter sounds and to develop phonological awareness, review the sound of the first letter in his name before starting the activity.

- For English language learners, use alliterative examples in their home languages.

Individual	Small Group	Large Group	Interest Area	Single Day	Multiday	Minutes
	●	●	Library, Outdoors, Music & Movement	●		10–15

Name That Sound

Goal(s) & Objectives	Listening and Speaking **38.** *Hears and discriminates the sounds of language;* **39.** *Expresses self using words and expanded sentences;* **41.** *Answers questions;* **42.** *Asks questions;* **43.** *Actively participates in conversations* Reading and Writing **44.** *Enjoys and values reading;* **47.** *Uses emerging reading skills to make meaning from print*

Materials & Preparation

☐ a book related to listening and noises, such as

The Listening Walk by Paul Showers (Harper Trophy, 1993)

The Noisy Book by Margaret Wise Brown (Harper Trophy, 1993)

The Ear Book by Al Perkins (Random House, 1968)

Too Much Noise by Ann McGovern (Houghton Mifflin Company, 1992)

☐ tape recorder and tape

Guiding Children's Learning

Day 1:
Read one of the suggested stories about listening and noises. Discuss the story briefly.

Day 2:
Take the children on a listening walk around the school/center or nearby neighborhood. Bring a tape recorder to record sounds the children hear.

When you return to the classroom, play the tape to see if children remember what made the sounds.

Invite the children to explain how they know what made each sound.

Closing

Tell the children that the recording will be in the Library Area, where they may listen to it at choice time.

Extension(s)

- Prepare or purchase a recording of environmental sounds that are familiar to the children (e.g., animal sounds, wind, lapping water, rain, laughter, or the children's own voices). Explain to the children that they are going to play a listening game. Have them close their eyes and play a segment of the recording. Call on children to identify the sounds.

Modification(s)

- For children who have auditory-processing, attentional, or hearing difficulties, limit distractions and the general noise level.

- To reduce auditory distractions and to support auditory discrimination and processing, have children wear headphones to listen to a tape of interesting noises.

Individual	Small Group	Large Group	Interest Area	Single Day	Multiday	Minutes
	●		Library		●	15–20

Picture This

Goal(s) & Objectives	Listening and Speaking *39. Expresses self using words and expanded sentences; 41. Answers questions; 42. Asks questions; 43. Actively participates in conversations*

Materials & Preparation

☐ three or four interesting pictures related to one topic

The photos might be of people, unusual land formations, animals, or objects, and they might relate to the latest topic of study. Photos from magazines, wall calendars, and the children's families work well. Laminate them for durability.

Before the activity, think about

> new words to introduce to the children through each picture

> open-ended questions to help extend children's language
> *What do you see in the picture?*
> *What do you think is happening?*
> *What would happen if…?*
> *How would you describe…?*

> prompts to encourage children to elaborate on what they see
> *I wonder if…Why…? How…?*
> *I see. You were thinking…*

Guiding Children's Learning

Explain to the children that you have some interesting pictures to share.

Show the pictures to the children. Then invite them to choose one from the collection to discuss.

Facilitate an informal discussion about the picture, taking the lead from the children and building on what they say. Continue the discussion as long as the children are interested.

Closing

Explain to the children that you will place the pictures in interest areas, where they may continue discussing them with their friends, family members, and other class visitors.

Extension(s)

- Prepare pocket folders by mounting a picture on the outside of each. Place blank paper and pencils inside the folders and place them in various interest areas. Teachers and adult volunteers can invite children to talk about the pictures and record their ideas.

Modification(s)

- For English language learners, consider using shorter sentences during the discussion, learning keys words in the children's home languages to use when you talk about the pictures, and pointing to the important details of the pictures as you talk about them.

- For children with developmental, language, or processing delays, simplify questions by offering answer choices (e.g., "Do you see a mountain or the ocean?" or "Mountain or ocean?"). Provide ample time for the child to process the question and answer.

- Follow the leads of children with language or developmental delays, to encourage social interaction and communication. Recognize and accept as meaningful all of their nonverbal attempts to communicate (e.g., eye gaze, changes in body position, gestures, facial and vocal expressions).

Individual	Small Group	Large Group	Interest Area	Single Day	Multiday	Minutes
	●		All	●		10–20

Pocket Storytelling: *The Mitten*

Goal(s) & Objectives	**Listening and Speaking** *39.* Expresses self using words and expanded sentences **Reading and Writing** *44.* Enjoys and values reading; *45.* Demonstrates understanding of print concepts; *47.* Uses emerging reading skills to make meaning from print; *48.* Comprehends and interprets meaning from books and other texts

Materials & Preparation

☐ *The Mitten* by Alvin Tresselt (Harper Trophy, 1989).

☐ felt or craft foam

☐ Velcro

☐ story props

The Mitten is a traditional Ukrainian folktale about a boy who loses one of his mittens while gathering wood in the forest. A mouse finds the mitten and uses it as shelter from the cold. The mouse allows other animals to share his shelter until the mitten is so full that it bursts, popping the animals back into the snow.

Create a mitten-shaped pocket out of two pieces of felt or craft foam. Use Velcro to hold the two pieces together.

Collect toy props or make picture props of each animal mentioned in the story (a mouse, frog, owl, rabbit, fox, wolf, boar, bear, and cricket).

Guiding Children's Learning

Introduce the story to the children. Explain that it is a folktale, or a story that has been told again and again. Ask the children if their parents or grandparents tell stories to them.

Read or tell the story, placing each animal in the mitten when it is mentioned in the story.

Gradually undo the mitten and, at the appropriate time, pull the mitten apart, spilling the animals onto the floor.

Closing

Close with a discussion about the book. Ask open-ended questions, such as

What happened each time an animal entered the mitten?

A cricket is a very small animal. Why do you suppose the mitten broke when the cricket tried to squeeze in?

Do you think the boy had any idea what had happened to his mitten? Why do you think that?

What did the boy think when he saw the mouse scurry across the snow with the red wool on its head?

Tell the children that the book and props will be in the Library Area for them to use to retell the story during choice time.

Extension(s)

- Have children generate a list of other animals that could have asked to get inside the mitten.

- Cut several sheets of blank paper in the shape of a mitten and put them in the Library Area. Encourage children to write or draw something about the story. Bind their pages as a book.

- Use pocket storytelling with other books, such as

  I Know an Old Lady Who Swallowed a Fly by Simms Taback
  It Looked Like Spilt Milk by Charles G. Shaw
  If You Give a Mouse a Cookie by Laura Joffe Numeroff
  If You Give a Moose a Muffin by Laura Joffe Numeroff

Modification(s)

- Choose stories that reflect the cultures and home languages of English language learners, as well as stories with patterned language and predictable text.

- Simplify questions for children with receptive language difficulties.

- For children with hearing impairments or developmental delays, use American Sign Language for *mitten* and for the story animals.

- Encourage children with developmental delays or attentional difficulties to choose animals and put them in the mitten. Have the child repeat the name of the animal while putting it into the mitten.

- For English language learners and children whose listening comprehension needs extra support, use facial expressions and simple gestures or sign language, and point to key details of the illustrations when reading.

Individual	Small Group	Large Group	Interest Area	Single Day	Multiday	Minutes
	●		Library	●		15–20

Poetry in Motion

Goal(s) & Objectives	Listening and Speaking *38. Hears and discriminates the sounds of language*

Materials & Preparation

Choose a favorite poem, nursery rhyme, or song that is already familiar to the children. (Begin with simple verses and later increase the difficulty of the activity by introducing multiple verses and new vocabulary.) Select a word that rhymes with other words in the text. Decide on a motion the children can perform each time they hear a word in the text that rhymes with the selected word.

This example uses the nursery rhyme *Betty Blue*. The words that rhyme with *blue* are bolded.

*Little Betty **Blue***

*Lost her holiday **shoe**.*

*What shall little Betty **do?***

Give her another

To match the other,

*And then she'll walk upon **two**.*

Guiding Children's Learning

Review or explain that rhyming words are words that sound alike at the end. Give some examples of real and nonsense rhyming words. Invite the children to share some that they know.

Read the poem or a portion of it. Introduce the selected word, *blue*, and invite the children to repeat words they heard that rhyme with it.

Demonstrate the motion you selected; for example, touching one shoe. Explain that you will recite the poem again. When they hear a word that rhymes with *blue*, they should touch a shoe.

Recite the verse again slowly, touching your shoe at the appropriate time.

Continue as long as the children are interested, using new verses, poems, songs, and motions.

Closing   Comment on the children's competence as listeners. Encourage them to play this game with a friend during choice time.

Extension(s)
- Encourage children to identify rhyming nouns (concrete objects or pictured objects) throughout the day. For example, after reading *Big Red Barn* by Margaret Wise Brown (HarperCollins Juvenile Books, 1991), you might ask, "Who can name an animal that rhymes with *wig*?" At mealtime, you might ask, "Who can think of a fruit that rhymes with *zapple*?"

Modification(s)
- A child with a physical limitation may hold or wave a scarf or flag if the selected motion is too difficult.

- For children with auditory discrimination or hearing difficulties, speak slowly, articulate clearly, and exaggerate mouth movements.

- For English language learners, use rhyming poems in their home languages to introduce the concept of rhyming words.

- For English language learners and children whose listening comprehension needs extra support, use facial expressions and simple gestures or sign language, and point to the important details of the illustrations when reading.

Individual	Small Group	Large Group	Interest Area	Single Day	Multiday	Minutes
●	●	●	Library, Music & Movement	●		10–15

Rhyme Time

Goal(s) & Objectives	Listening and Speaking *38. Hears and discriminates the sounds of language*

Materials & Preparation

☐ simple rhymes (poems, chants, songs, other rhyming texts)

☐ chart paper

☐ marker

Read, sing, and recite rhyming language regularly at various times of the day. Once children are familiar with rhymes, you will want to try the activities below.

Guiding Children's Learning

First:

Introduce rhyming words by reciting a rhyme or poem or reading a book with rhyming text. Explain that rhyming words are words that sound alike at the end. For example, if you are reciting *Little Bo Peep*, you might say, "*Peep* sounds like *sheep*. They both end with the same sound: *-eep*. *Peep* and *sheep* rhyme." Over time, discuss many different examples to help all children understand the concept of rhyming words.

When you read or recite a familiar rhyme or poem, invite the children to identify the rhyming words they hear. For example, recite,

> *Humpty Dumpty sat on a wall;*
> *Humpty Dumpty had a great fall.*

Ask, "Which words rhyme?" Depending on the children's developmental levels, you might want to change the tone, pitch, or volume level of your voice to call attention to the rhyming words.

After the children have become familiar with a rhyme, pause to let them fill in the rhyming word; for example, *Little Jack Horner sat in a _____.*

At other times, recite a familiar verse, inserting a word that doesn't rhyme. See if the children notice. Ask them to supply a word that does rhyme. For example, you might say,

> *Little Miss Muffet sat on a* log,
> *Eating her curds and whey.*

Have children listen for pairs of rhyming words. If the words rhyme, they give a "thumbs up." If they do not rhyme, they give a "thumbs down." You might begin by using the children's names. For example,

> *Zack, truck (thumbs down)*
> *Zack, sack (thumbs up)*

Later:
Invite the children to help make new rhymes for a familiar verse. For example, you might begin the new rhyme and ask children to supply a rhyming word when you pause.

> *Hickory, dickory, dog!*
> *The mouse sat on a _____.*
> *The frog did jump,*
> *And hit a _____,*
> *Hickory, dickory, dog!*

Write the new rhymes on chart paper and post them in the classroom.

Closing   Comment on the children's competence as listeners. Explain where you will post their new verses, so they can reread them.

Extension(s)   Bind the new rhymes as a book and let the children illustrate it. Place it in the Library Area for the children to read at choice time.

Individual	Small Group	Large Group	Interest Area	Single Day	Multiday	Minutes
●	●	●	Library	●		10–15

Rhyming Riddles

Goal(s) & Objectives	Listening and Speaking **38.** *Hears and discriminates the sounds of language*

Materials & Preparation

None

Guiding Children's Learning

Tell the children that they are going to play a game called *Rhyming Riddles*. Explain that rhyming words sound alike at the end. Offer some examples and invite children to say some rhyming words they know.

Explain that a riddle is a word puzzle or a word problem that they must figure out.

Pose a riddle that prompts the children to supply a rhyming word. For example, you might ask,

> *I'm thinking of something that you wear on your hands in the winter and that rhymes with* kittens. *What am I thinking about?* (mittens)

> *For lunch we will be having a fruit that rhymes with* danana. *What are we having for lunch?* (banana)

If a child gives an inappropriate response, offer comments or questions to help him think. For example, if a child responds to the first riddle with *gloves*, you might say,

> *You are really thinking! We do wear gloves on our hands in winter. Listen as I say the two words: kittens, gloves. Do they rhyme, or sound the same at the end? Can you think of something else you might wear on your hands? How about mittens? Do the words* kittens *and* mittens *rhyme? Yes, they sound the same at the end.*

Closing

Help the children transition to the next activity using name riddles, such as,

> *I'm thinking of someone whose name rhymes with* skate. *Yes,* Kate *and* skate *rhyme. Kate, you may choose an interest area.*

Extension(s)

- Create a class book of riddles that are answered correctly with rhyming words. Invite children to illustrate the book and place it in the Library Area for everyone to enjoy.

Modification(s)

- For children who have auditory-processing, attentional, or hearing difficulties, limit distractions and the general noise level.

- To help English language learners develop an understanding of rhyming words and riddles, offer examples in their home languages.

- For English language learners and children with language delays, articulate clearly and speak slowly.

- For children who benefit from concrete cues, pull an object out of a box and then ask for a rhyming word.

- When a child benefits from peer modeling and collaboration, pair her with a peer. One child can pull an object out of a box, and the other can respond with a rhyming word.

Individual	Small Group	Large Group	Interest Area	Single Day	Multiday	Minutes
		●	All	●		10–15

Rhyming Tubs

Goal(s) & Objectives	Listening and Speaking *38. Hears and discriminates the sounds of language; 40. Understands and follows oral directions*

Materials & Preparation

☐ plastic tub

☐ bag or small box

☐ pairs of small toys that rhyme (e.g., duck/truck, hat/cat)

Before the activity, place one toy from each pair in the tub and place the others in a bag or small box.

Guiding Children's Learning

Seat a small group of children in a circle.

Explain that they are going to play a rhyming game using the "rhyming tub." Offer some examples of words that rhyme.

Show the children the two collections of toys (one in the tub and one in the bag or box). Explain that the name of each toy in the tub rhymes with a toy in the other collection.

Show and name each toy, one at a time. This will help minimize confusion about the names of the objects.

Explain that they will pass the tub around the circle as you recite,

> *A rub-a-dub, dub, rhyming things in the tub. Let's see if (child's name) can name one.*

The child whose name is called will hold the tub. Then you will choose an object from the other collection, show it to the child, and have her find its rhyming match in the tub. Demonstrate if necessary.

Have the children confirm or reexamine their choices, using such prompts as,

> *Do* duck *and* truck *rhyme? Listen,* duck...truck. *Yes, Crystal, they do because they sound alike at the end. Listen carefully. Do* truck *and* hat *sound the same at the end?*

Continue until each child has had a turn or until the children are no longer interested.

Closing Tell the children that the rhyming tub will be in the Toys and Games Area, where they may play the game with their friends at choice time.

Extension(s)
- Make several small rhyming tubs that contain pairs of rhyming objects. Place the tubs in the Toys and Games Area. At choice time, children may make rhyming pairs on their own.

Modification(s)
- Start with just a few objects and gradually increase the rhyming pairs as children's skills develop.

- For children who have auditory-processing, attentional, or hearing difficulties, limit distractions and the general noise level.

- For English language learners, give examples of rhymes in the children's home languages.

- For a child with fine motor difficulties, provide a scoop or mitt to pick up desired objects from the tub, or put objects on a tray so that they can be pushed off. A child who needs physical assistance could also work with a peer.

- To simplify the activity, each child in the group can hold an object and decide whether it rhymes with a designated word.

Individual	Small Group	Large Group	Interest Area	Single Day	Multiday	Minutes
	●		Toys & Games	●		15–20

Silly Names

Goal(s) & Objectives	**Listening and Speaking** *38. Hears and discriminates the sounds of language; 39. Expresses self using words and expanded sentences* **Reading and Writing** *44. Enjoys and values reading; 45. Demonstrates understanding of print concepts; 47. Uses emerging reading skills to make meaning from print*

Materials & Preparation

☐ *Silly Sally* by Audrey Wood (Harcourt Big Books, 1994)

☐ chart paper

☐ markers

☐ sentence strips or Post-it notes

Silly Sally is the story of a girl who goes to town, "walking backwards, upside down." On her way, she dances a jig with a silly pig, plays leapfrog with a silly dog, sings a tune with a silly loon, and falls asleep with a silly sheep. Fortunately, Neddy Buttercup, who is "walking forwards, right side up," comes along and tickles Sally and her friends awake so they can continue their parade into town in this most unusual way.

Guiding Children's Learning

Read *Silly Sally* aloud, sweeping your fingers under the text as you read.

Call attention to the fact that *silly* and *Sally* begin with the same sound.

Explain to the child that you are going to read the story again, but substitute his name for Silly Sally's.

Help the child think of a descriptive word that begins with the same sound as his name (e.g., Laughing Leo). Write the child's name on a sentence strip or Post-it note.

Reread the story, placing the child's name card over the name *Silly Sally* each time it appears in the book.

If you are working with a small group of children, alternate children's names as you reread the story.

Closing

Lead a brief discussion with the children to help them understand how using these new and sometimes silly names in a teasing manner outside of story time can hurt children's feelings.

Explain that the book and name cards will be in the Library Area to read at choice time.

Extension(s)

- Use children's descriptive names during transitions; for example, "Laughing Leo may choose where he would like to work," or, "Dancing Dallas may get his jacket to go outside."

- Have each child name something she likes to do that begins with the same sound as her name, for example, "Tonya likes to tumble. Derek likes to dig." Take a photo of each child performing that action. Post the pictures in a prominent area of the classroom. From time to time, have children recall what they were doing in the photos. At a later time, make a class book with the photos and place it in the Library Area.

- Read *Ellsworth's Extraordinary Electric Ears and Other Amazing Alphabet Anecdotes* by Valorie Fisher (Atheneum, 2003). This unique alphabet book has alliterative text on every page, perfect for drawing children's attention to the beginning sounds of words.

Modification(s)

- Use children's photographs along with name cards, to assist those children who do not yet recognize their written names.

- Some English language learners will have difficulty identifying an appropriate descriptive word. Preview the activity with an individual child or small group. Plan in advance to have pictures or objects available to illustrate word choices; e.g., to help Ben make a choice, have a blue card and a picture of someone bending.

- For children who have language delays or who are just beginning to develop phonological awareness, articulate clearly and exaggerate tongue and lip movements.

- For children who need extra time for auditory processing, record *Silly Sally* at a slower reading rate.

- If a child is apprehensive or especially sensitive to the use of his name, encourage him to rename a doll or puppet.

- For children with visual impairments and children who benefit from additional sensory experience, provide magnetic or foam letters for them to handle as you discuss letter sounds.

Individual	Small Group	Large Group	Interest Area	Single Day	Multiday	Minutes
●	●		Library	●		20

Story Aprons

Goal(s) & Objectives	Listening and Speaking **39.** *Expresses self using words and expanded sentences* Reading and Writing **44.** *Enjoys and values reading;* **48.** *Comprehends and interprets meaning from books and other texts*

Materials & Preparation

☐ story apron (purchased or made; see instructions below)

☐ Velcro

☐ scissors

☐ story props to represent the events in the story (e.g., small objects; simple, bold illustrations that have been laminated; or felt figures).

Purchase a bibbed apron, which can be found in many kitchen supply stores or departments. Decorate the bib to suit the retelling of a particular kind of story (e.g., a country scene picturing a barnyard and pond for retelling stories such as *In the Big Red Barn*, *The Gingerbread Boy*, *The Little Red Hen*, or *Chicken Little*). Alternatively, sew buttons at the top of the apron to attach different background panels for changes of scenery. Attach Velcro to the apron skirt and to the back of the props, so that the props can be attached and removed. Aprons can also be made of felt or vinyl.

Guiding Children's Learning

Wear the story apron and gather a small group of children.

Explain that a story can be told without a book, as well as read, and that you will tell a story using the story apron and props.

Tell the story, attaching the appropriate prop to the apron as it is mentioned in the story.

Involve children in the storytelling as much as possible, by inviting them to repeat a refrain, make sound effects, or predict words when you pause.

Closing

Lead a brief discussion about the story, asking children to share what they liked or what they found interesting, funny, or frightening.

If the story is available in book form, share it with the children and tell them that it will be in the Library Area to read on their own during choice time.

Extension(s)	•	Make a child-size story apron for the children to retell the story on their own or to a small group of friends.
Modification(s)	•	For children with developmental delays, keep the story short and simple.
	•	For English language learners, learn some key words of the story in their home languages. Preview the story using these key words. Use gestures and facial expressions when telling the story.
	•	To support comprehension and language development, use American Sign Language for key words in the story; use props such as stuffed toys and meaningful objects; and speak clearly, varying your rate of speech as necessary. Monitor the children's comprehension and adjust vocabulary and sentence length as needed.
	•	For children who have difficulty with new experiences, preview the book and props.
	•	For children who need additional support, provide opportunities for them to attach or detach the props as you tell the story.

Individual	Small Group	Large Group	Interest Area	Single Day	Multiday	Minutes
	●		Library	●		15–20

Walk a Letter

Goal(s) & Objectives	Listening and Speaking *40. Understands and follows oral directions* Reading and Writing *46. Demonstrates knowledge of the alphabet*

Materials & Preparation

- ☐ masking tape
- ☐ alphabet cards or an alphabet chart
- ☐ chart paper
- ☐ marker

Guiding Children's Learning

Have the children choose one or two letters from the cards or chart and, together, mark large versions on the floor using masking tape. Name the letters and talk about their features.

Next, have the children walk (hop, skip, jump, glide, tiptoe, or crawl) along the tape.

Closing

Invite the children to suggest other ways they might move along the letters and list them on chart paper. Encourage them to move along the letters in different ways during choice time.

Extension(s)

- Provide rolls of masking tape for the children to use. Encourage them to form letters on their own. Provide assistance as needed.

Modification(s)

- For a child who has difficulty handling a roll of tape, consider pre-cutting strips of tape or holding the roll.

- Pair a child in a wheelchair with a partner to move along the letters. Make sure the letters are large enough for the child to maneuver the wheelchair.

- If a child has difficulty focusing on the activity, offer to hold his hand and move along the letter together.

- For English language learners, say the letter and its sound as you move along the letter. Relate the letter to a word in the child's home language that begins with the same sound, e.g., /t/ as in *tortilla*.

- For a child who has a visual impairment or motor-planning difficulties, use colored tape to accentuate the letters.

Individual	Small Group	Large Group	Interest Area	Single Day	Multiday	Minutes
●	●		Music & Movement, Outdoors	●		20

What's for Breakfast?

Goal(s) & Objectives

Listening and Speaking

39. *Expresses self using words and expanded sentences;* **41.** *Answers questions;* **42.** *Asks questions;* **43.** *Actively participates in conversation*

Reading and Writing

44. *Enjoys and values reading;* **45.** *Demonstrates understanding of print concepts;* **46.** *Demonstrates knowledge of the alphabet;* **47.** *Uses emerging reading skills to make meaning from print;* **48.** *Comprehends and interprets meaning from books and other texts;* **49.** *Understands the purpose of writing*

Materials & Preparation

☐ *Pancakes for Breakfast* by Tomie DePaola (Voyager Books, 1978)

☐ Post-it notes

☐ pen or pencil

Pancakes for Breakfast is a wordless picture book about a little old lady who attempts to make pancakes for breakfast.

Guiding Children's Learning

Day 1:

Introduce the book *Pancakes for Breakfast*. Show the book to the children and encourage them predict what it is about. Lead a discussion about the children's favorite breakfast foods. Ask if anyone has helped make pancakes. If so, have them recall the steps.

Explain that the book doesn't have words, but they will be able to tell the story by looking at the pictures.

Take a walk through the book, inviting children to comment on what they see on each page and predict what will happen next. Extend children's language and thinking by using prompts such as,

> *Why do you think there is a picture of pancakes here?* (Point to the thought bubble in the picture.)

> *Have you ever wanted something so much you couldn't stop thinking about it?*

> *What kind of book do you think she is getting from the shelf?*

> *It looks like her egg tray is empty. I wonder where she will go to get eggs.*

Day 2:
Assemble a small group of children who were introduced to the book previously. During this reading, invite children by turns to tell you what the lady might be saying in each picture.

Write their ideas on Post-it notes and stick them to the pages.

Return to the beginning and read the text the children created for the story.

Closing

Ask the children if they would like to share their story with other friends in the class. Designate a time to read it to the class.

Explain that you will place the book in the Library Area, where they may read and discuss it with their friends.

Extension(s)

- Use this strategy with other wordless picture books, such as

    Changes, Changes by Pat Hutchins
    Good Dog, Carl; Carl Goes Shopping; Carl Goes to Daycare; Carl's Afternoon in the Park; and *Carl's Birthday* by Alexandra Day

    Place plenty of Post-its in the Library Area so children can write or dictate their own text for picture stories during choice time.

- Write the recipe for pancakes on chart paper and make them with the children in the Cooking Area.

Modification(s)

- Some children will require more explicit explanation of the illustrations. Offer open-ended prompts and give children chances to ask questions as well as to articulate their ideas about the illustrations.

- For children with developmental, language, or processing delays, simplify questions by offering answer choices. For example, if the egg tray in an illustration is empty, you might say "No eggs." Shake your head from side to side and point to the empty egg tray. "Where are the eggs? In the ____ or the ____?" Point to the illustrations of the choices you offer.

- To support comprehension and language development, model story language and use props, gestures, and facial expressions when offering prompts.

Individual	Small Group	Large Group	Interest Area	Single Day	Multiday	Minutes
●	●		Library		●	15–20

What's for Snack?

Goal(s) & Objectives	Reading and Writing **45.** *Demonstrates understanding of print concepts;* **46.** *Demonstrates knowledge of the alphabet;* **47.** *Uses emerging reading skills to make meaning from print*

Materials & Preparation

☐ food product labels

☐ large paper or tagboard

☐ marker

☐ recipe cards or charts

☐ two cans with smooth edges

☐ tongue depressors or large craft sticks

☐ small photo of each child

☐ lamination supplies or clear Contact paper

☐ staples or glue

Create a snack menu using food product labels and food preparation pictures (e.g., *Today's snack is Cheerios and apple juice.*)

For foods that the children will prepare, make picture and word recipes using labels from products (e.g., labels from cereal, pretzels, and raisins for a trail mix recipe).

Create a system for children to record whether or not they had snack. Write *Yes* on one can and *No* on the other. Write each child's name on a tongue depressor or large craft stick. Then laminate a small photo of each child and staple or glue it to the top of the tongue depressor. At the beginning of each day, place all names in the *No* can.

Guiding Children's Learning

Read the snack menu with the children, sweeping your fingers under the words. If the children will be preparing a snack independently, also read the recipe and procedure for preparing the snack.

Call attention to similarities in words or letters. For example, *Cheerios* and *Chex* both begin with *ch*, /ch/.

Tell the children that the menu, recipe, and ingredients will be placed in the Cooking Area to use as they prepare snack.

Closing

Explain to the children and demonstrate how to move their names from the *No* can to the *Yes* can after they have prepared or eaten snack.

Assure them that you will be available at choice time to provide any help they need.

Extension(s)
- Invite children to create menus using environmental print and food labels and pictures. Place them in the Dramatic Play Area for the children to use in restaurant play.

Modification(s)
- For children with motor delays and disabilities, include adaptive plates, cups, and utensils to make cooking activities more manageable.

- For children with visual impairments or processing difficulties, adapt the picture and word recipe and the name and photo sticks by enlarging and highlighting the print and by adding texture or Braille.

Individual	Small Group	Large Group	Interest Area	Single Day	Multiday	Minutes
●	●	●	Cooking, Dramatic Play		●	10–15

Which Friend Did You See?

Goal(s) & Objectives	Listening and Speaking
	39. *Expresses self using words and expanded sentences*
	Reading and Writing
	44. *Enjoys and values reading;* **45.** *Demonstrates an understanding of print concepts;* **46.** *Demonstrates knowledge of the alphabet;* **47.** *Uses emerging reading skills to make meaning from print;* **48.** *Comprehends and interprets meaning from books and other texts;* **49.** *Understands the purpose of writing*

Materials & Preparation

☐ *I Went Walking* by Sue Williams (Voyager Books, 1992)

☐ camera

☐ glue

☐ blank paper

☐ cardboard or card stock for a bookcover

☐ marker

☐ bookbinding supplies

I Went Walking uses repetitive, rhyming text to tell the story of a young child who encounters a variety of animals while taking a walk. By the end of the story, there is a colorful parade of animals following the child, including a black cat, brown horse, red cow, green duck, pink pig, and yellow dog.

Guiding Children's Learning

Read *I Went Walking* with the children. When they are familiar with the text pattern, invite them to make a class book titled *Which Friend Did You See?*

Take a picture of each child and one of the entire class. Put each photograph on a separate page.

Over the course of several days, invite each child to dictate sentences with a pattern much like *I Went Walking*, inserting his or her own name and a friend's name where appropriate. Here are examples:

> *Kate went walking.*
> *Which friend did you see?*
> *I saw Sonya looking at me.*

> *Sonya went walking.*
> *Which friend did you see?*
> *I saw Carlos looking at me.*

Read the new sentences with the child, pointing to each word as you read. Have the children sign their names on an authors' page.

Combine the pages to form a book, ending with a photo of the entire class. Make a cover for the book with the title, *Which Friend Did You See?*

Closing

Read the book to the children at story time. Have them decide what the last page should say and write it to complete the book. Let them know that their book will be in the Library Area to read and enjoy.

Extension(s)

- Create a class book based on a study topic. For example, in a gardening study, the pattern of your book might be,

    Dallas was digging.
    What did you see?
    I saw a wiggly worm looking at me.

    Crystal was watering.
    What did you see?
    I saw a ladybug looking at me.

Modification(s)

- For children with hearing impairments or developmental delays, use American Sign Language for important words in the text.

- For English language learners, translate the book in their home languages if possible. For vocabulary development, the translation does not have to rhyme. You may also send copies of the book home in advance, so families can talk with their children about the pictures.

- For a child who is visually impaired, highlight illustrations by outlining the animals with a wide black marker or using a high-contrast background. Highlight print, or use a contrasting color to bring attention to repeated words.

- Make teacher-made books more durable by using baggie pages, by laminating the pages, or by covering them with clear Contact paper. (See the *Baggie Books* activity for an explanation of baggie pages.)

- For a child with fine motor difficulties, provide adaptive page-turners (e.g., dried glue, a paper clip, Velcro, or a clothespin).

Individual	Small Group	Large Group	Interest Area	Single Day	Multiday	Minutes
●		●	Library, Outdoors	▲	●	10

Who Ate the Cookies?

Goal(s) & Objectives	Listening and Speaking **38.** *Hears and discriminates the sounds of language;* **41.** *Answers questions;* **42.** *Asks questions;* **43.** *Participates in conversations* Reading and Writing **45.** *Demonstrates understanding of print concepts;* **46.** *Demonstrates knowledge of the alphabet;* **47.** *Uses emerging reading skills to make meaning from print*

Materials & Preparation

☐ rhyme written on tagboard

☐ Velcro

☐ construction paper or tagboard

☐ marker

☐ lamination supplies or clear Contact paper

☐ children's and teachers' name cards

☐ cookie jar (or empty cookie box or picture of cookie jar attached to a container)

Write the rhyme below on sturdy tagboard. Place half of an adhesive Velcro dot where a child's name would appear. This will enable you to switch name cards.

Make a set of cookie-shaped name cards for the children in your class, laminate them, and attach Velcro on the back of each. Store them in the cookie jar.

Guiding Children's Learning

Have your assistant teacher or another adult help you introduce the rhyme by demonstrating the actions and exchanges.

> *Who Ate the Cookies?*
>
> *Who ate the cookies from the cookie jar?*
> (<u>Child's name</u>) *ate the cookies from the cookie jar.*
> *Who, me?* (Selected child points to self and responds.)
> *Yes, you.* (Rest of children respond in unison.)
> *Couldn't be.* (Selected child responds, shaking his head, no.)
> *Then who?* (Selected child chooses a name from the cookie jar and inserts it into the pocket.)

Give children time to recognize the name. If they have difficulty, offer help by asking them to identify the beginning letter or by saying the beginning sound and asking them to think of a child's name that begins with that sound.

Invite the children to read the rhyme with you as you sweep your fingers under the words from left to right. Continue changing the names and reciting the rhyme as long as the children remain interested.

Closing   Tell the children that the rhyme chart will be available in the Library Area for them to read at choice time.

Extension(s

- Discuss taking turns in conversations.

  Talk about the punctuation mark that signals a question.

- Read *Who Took the Cookies from the Cookie Jar?* by Rozanne Lanczak Williams (Creative Teaching Press, 1995). Compare this version to the rhyme on the chart. With the children, brainstorm other ways to change the poem and write the new poem on large paper.

- Bake cookies or visit a bakery to watch cookies being made.

Modification(s)

- For children who are visually impaired, write names in large print or provide them in Braille.

- Read a book version of the rhyme first, to stimulate interest.

- Make and eat cookies to stimulate interest.

- For children with language delays and English language learners, use gestures and facial expressions. Point to concrete objects or key details of the illustrations when reading the book and asking questions.

- For English language learners, find a traditional name game with rhymes in the children's home languages.

Individual	Small Group	Large Group	Interest Area	Single Day	Multiday	Minutes
	●	●	Library	●		15–20

Who Will Jump the Candlestick?

Goal(s) & Objectives	Listening and Speaking **40.** *Understands and follows directions* Reading and Writing **45.** *Demonstrates understanding of print concepts;* **46.** *Demonstrates knowledge of the alphabet;* **47.** *Uses emerging reading skills to make meaning from print*

Materials & Preparation

☐ candlestick

☐ children's name cards (written on sentence strips or card stock)

☐ tagboard

☐ scissors

☐ paper clip

☐ marker

☐ adhesive Velcro dots

Write the nursery rhyme *Jack Be Nimble* on sturdy tagboard. Attach Velcro where the word *Jack* appears. This will enable you to attach children's name cards.

Guiding Children's Learning

Review the nursery rhyme or introduce it if the children are not familiar with it.

Read the rhyme, sweeping your hand under the words.

Place the candlestick on the floor where there is enough space for a child to jump over it without hurting himself or others.

Explain to the children that you will replace Jack's name with one of their names.

When a child recognizes her name, she should stand while the new rhyme is recited and jump over the candlestick when her name is read.

Continue as long as children are enjoying the activity. Offer assistance as needed.

Closing

Comment on how well the children are learning to recognize their names. Tell them that the rhyme board, candlestick, and name cards will be placed in the Music and Movement Area, where they can read and act out the rhyme. If children are interested, take the candlestick outdoors.

Extension(s)
- Write this altered rhyme on a piece of sturdy tagboard:

    Jack was nimble, Jack was quick.
    He (<u>number</u>) times jumped the candlestick.

    Make number word–number cards, 0–10. Insert a different card each time the rhyme is recited and have the children jump that number of times. For example, recite,

    Jack was nimble, Jack was quick.
    He <u>two–2</u> times jumped the candlestick.

    The children would jump twice.

Modification(s)
- For English language learners and children with language delays or impairments, read the rhyme several times. Read slowly and articulate clearly.

- If possible, translate the rhyme into the home languages of children who are learning English. For the purpose of helping children count and develop concepts such as *over/under*, the translation does not need to rhyme.

- For a child who needs assistance in recognizing his name, review his written name with him before the activity. Put his photo on his name card and let him hold the card while you talk about some of the distinguishing features of his name. For children with visual impairments, highlight the letters or use a contrasting background.

Individual	Small Group	Large Group	Interest Area	Single Day	Multiday	Minutes
	●		Music & Movement, Outdoors	●		15

Appendix

Literacy Implementation Checklist: Literacy in the Overall Environment

Do Teachers		
	YES	**NO**

1. Include print that ☐ ☐

    a. **labels objects** (e.g., names on cubbies),
    b. **provides information** (e.g., daily schedule, recipe, instructions on how to wash hands),
    c. **provides narrative descriptions** (e.g., dictation about artwork), and
    d. **identifies classroom practices** (e.g., waiting lists, job charts)?

2. Provide a variety of books (3 or more in each category) including ☐ ☐

    a. Narrative ☐ ☐ ☐
    b. Predictable ☐ ☐ ☐
    c. Alphabet ☐ ☐ ☐
    d. Number/counting ☐ ☐ ☐
    e. Informational ☐ ☐ ☐
    f. Rhyming ☐ ☐ ☐
    g. Other texts (e.g., magazines, signs, charts) ☐ ☐ ☐

3. Include a variety of materials written in English and other languages spoken by the children in the class: ☐ ☐

    a. Books (3 or more) in at least 5 interest areas
    ☐ Blocks ☐ Dramatic Play ☐ Toys & Games ☐ Art ☐ Library
    ☐ Discovery ☐ Sand & Water ☐ Music & Movement ☐ Cooking ☐ Computers
    ☐ Outdoors
    b. Other texts (3 or more) in at least 3 interest areas
    ☐ Blocks ☐ Dramatic Play ☐ Toys & Games ☐ Art ☐ Library
    ☐ Discovery ☐ Sand & Water ☐ Music & Movement ☐ Cooking ☐ Computers
    ☐ Outdoors

4. Offer a variety of writing materials (e.g., paper, notepads, markers, appointment books, envelopes, chalkboards, wipe-off boards, sign-up sheets) in at least 5 interest areas? ☐ ☐

    ☐ Blocks ☐ Dramatic Play ☐ Toys & Games ☐ Art ☐ Library
    ☐ Discovery ☐ Sand & Water ☐ Music & Movement ☐ Cooking ☐ Computers
    ☐ Outdoors

5. Display the alphabet at the children's eye level? ☐ ☐

Literacy Implementation Checklist: Literacy in the Library Area

1. Make the Library Area available as a choice activity on a daily basis? ☐ ☐

2. Provide a variety of materials and furnishings to make the space comfortable and attractive (e.g., carpeted floor, good lighting, beanbag chairs, child-size rocker) where children can look at books? ☐ ☐
    a. Feature #1: _____
    b. Feature #2: _____
    c. Feature #3: _____

3. Provide space and materials for listening (e.g., books stored together with tapes or CDs, cassette recorder or CD players, two headphones)? ☐ ☐

4. Include a ☐ ☐
    a. Bookshelf to display books facing out?
    b. Table and chairs for writing?
    c. Shelf for writing materials?

5. Provide a variety of materials to ☐ ☐
    a. **Write on** (e.g., assorted lined and unlined paper, chalkboards, envelopes, stationery)
        1) _____
        2) _____
        3) _____
    b. **Write with** (e.g., pencils, pens, markers, chalk)
        1) _____
        2) _____
        3) _____
    c. **Letter and Word Manipulatives** (e.g., letter stamps, name cards, alphabet cards for children to handle and use as models)?
        1) _____
        2) _____
        3) _____

6. Display (with covers facing out) at least 25 children's books (e.g., storybooks; nursery rhymes; and informational, predictable, alphabet, and number/counting books)? ☐ ☐

7. Provide books and related props for retelling stories (e.g., hand puppets, flannel board, magnetic board, or story apron related to a particular story?) ☐ ☐

Literacy Implementation Checklist: Guiding Children's Literacy Learning

Do Teachers

		YES	NO
1.	Read books to individuals as well as to large and small groups at least twice every day, and prompt children to interact and respond (e.g., take a picture walk through the story before reading, leave out a word so children can fill it in, ask open-ended questions, relate the story to prior experiences)?	☐	☐
2.	Engage children in retelling a story using puppets, flannel board figures, or props?	☐	☐
3.	Draw children's attention to the sounds of language through playful songs, stories, rhymes, and chants to help develop **phonological awareness**?	☐	☐
4.	Draw children's attention to a. **concepts of print** (e.g., left to right, top to bottom) and b. **concepts of books** (e.g., author, illustrator, book-handling skills, turning pages)?	☐	☐
5.	Draw children's attention to **letters and words** (e.g., reading big books and pointing to words, taking a walk to look for signs, writing a group thank-you letter)?	☐	☐
6.	**Talk with children** throughout the day, **modeling correct grammar, introducing new vocabulary** and **asking questions** to encourage children to express their ideas in words?	☐	☐
7.	**Write with children** (e.g., record their ideas and stories, write experience charts, write a thank you note to a visitor) and **encourage children to write** (e.g., put their names on artwork, create a shopping list in dramatic play, make signs for a block structure)?	☐	☐

Activity Matrix

Activities	Blocks	Dramatic Play	Toys & Games	Art	Library	Discovery	Sand & Water	Music & Movement	Cooking	Computer	Outdoors	Vocabulary & Language	Phonological Awareness	Knowledge of Print	Letters & Words	Comprehension	Books & Other Texts
A Bunny's Tale					•							•				•	•
All Kinds of Spiders					•	•		•				•	•	•	•		
Baggie Books					•							•		•	•		•
Be a Word					•							•	•	•	•	•	
Buried Treasures						•	•							•			
Can You Do It?					•			•			•	•		•			•
Clap a Friend's Name	•	•	•	•	•	•	•	•	•	•	•		•				
Clothesline Storytelling					•									•		•	•
Copy Cat								•				•					
Coupon Match		•	•											•	•		•
Did You Ever See…?					•			•				•	•		•		•
Dressing for School					•			•				•		•	•		
Feed Me					•								•		•		•
Friends								•				•		•	•		
Give a Dog a Bone								•				•	•	•			•
Group Sharing												•		•	•		
I Spy with My Little Eye	•	•	•	•	•	•	•	•	•	•	•		•		•		
I Went Shopping		•			•									•	•		•
Jumping Beans			•											•			
Listen for the Word					•							•	•				
Listening Cords					•								•			•	
Making My Name		•			•									•	•		
Me, Too!					•			•			•		•				
Name that Sound					•							•	•			•	
Picture This	•	•	•	•	•	•	•	•	•	•	•	•		•	•		
Pocket Storytelling: *The Mitten*					•							•				•	•
Poetry in Motion					•			•					•				
Rhyme Time					•								•				
Rhyming Riddles	•	•	•	•	•	•	•	•	•	•	•	•	•				
Rhyming Tubs			•										•				
Silly Names					•							•	•	•	•		
Story Aprons					•							•				•	
Walk a Letter								•			•	•			•		
What's for Breakfast?					•							•		•	•		•
What's for Snack?		•							•					•	•		•
Which Friend Did You See?					•					•		•		•	•		•
Who Ate the Cookies?					•							•		•	•		•
Who Will Jump the Candlestick?								•			•	•	•	•	•		

LANGUAGE DEVELOPMENT
Listening and Speaking

Developmental Continuum for Ages 3–5

Curriculum Objectives	Forerunners	I	II	III
38. **Hears and discriminates the sounds of language**	**Forerunners** Notices sounds in the environment *e.g., pays attention to birds singing, sirens* Joins in nursery rhymes and songs	Plays with words, sounds, and rhymes *e.g., repeats songs, rhymes, and chants; says, "Oh you Silly Willy"*	Recognizes and invents rhymes and repetitive phrases; notices words that begin the same way *e.g., makes up silly rhymes ("Bo, Bo, Biddle, Bop"); says, "My name begins the same as pop-corn and pig"*	Hears and repeats separate sounds in words; plays with sounds to create new words *e.g., claps hands 3 times when saying "Su-zan-na"; says, "Pass the bapkin [napkin]"*
39. **Expresses self using words and expanded sentences**	**Forerunners** Uses non-verbal gestures or single words to communicate *e.g., points to ball* Uses 2-word phrases *e.g., "All gone"; "Go out"*	Uses simple sentences (3–4 words) to express wants and needs *e.g., "I want the trike"*	Uses longer sentences (5–6 words) to communicate *e.g., "I want to ride the trike when we go outside"*	Uses more complex sentences to express ideas and feelings *e.g., "I hope we can go outside today because I want to ride the tricycle around the track"*
40. **Under stands and follows oral directions**	**Forerunners** Associates words with actions *e.g., says "throw" when sees ball thrown; throws when hears the word* Follows oral directions when combined with gestures *e.g., "come here" accompanied with gesture*	Follows one-step directions *e.g., "Please get a tissue"*	Follows two-step directions *e.g., "When you get inside, please hang up your coat"*	Follows directions with more than two steps *e.g., follows directions to put clay in container, wipe table, and wash hands when activity is finished*
41. **Answers questions**	**Forerunners** Answers yes/no questions with words, gestures, or signs *e.g., points to purple paint when asked what color she wants*	Answers simple questions with one or two words *e.g., when asked for name says, "Curtis"; says, "Purple and blue" when asked the colors of paint*	Answers questions with a complete thought *e.g., responds, "I took a bus to school"; "I want purple and blue paint"*	Answers questions with details *e.g., describes a family trip when asked about weekend; says, "I want purple and blue like my new shoes so I can make lots of flowers"*

Listening and Speaking (continued)

Developmental Continuum for Ages 3–5

Curriculum Objectives		I	II	III
42. **Asks questions**	**Forerunners** Uses facial expressions/gestures to ask a question Uses rising intonation to ask questions *e.g., "Mama comes back?"* Uses some "wh" words (*what* and *where*) to ask questions *e.g., "What that?"*	Asks simple questions *e.g., "What's for lunch?" "Can we play outside today?"*	Asks questions to further understanding *e.g., "Where did the snow go when it melted?" "Why does that man wear a uniform?"*	Asks increasingly complex questions to further own understanding *e.g., "What happened to the water in the fish tank? Did the fish drink it?"*
43. **Actively participates in conversations**	**Forerunners** Initiates communication by smiling and/or eye contact Responds to social greetings *e.g., waves in response to "hello" or "bye-bye"*	Responds to comments and questions from others *e.g., when one child says, "I have new shoes," shows own shoes and says, "Look at my new shoes"*	Responds to others' comments in a series of exchanges *e.g., makes relevant comments during a group discussion; provides more information when message is not understood*	Initiates and/or extends conversations for at least four exchanges *e.g., while talking with a friend, asks questions about what happened, what friend did, and shares own ideas*

LANGUAGE DEVELOPMENT
Reading and Writing

Developmental Continuum for Ages 3–5

Curriculum Objectives		I	II	III
44. **Enjoys and values reading**	**Forerunners** Looks at books and pictures with an adult or another child Chooses and looks at books independently Completes phrases in familiar stories	Listens to stories being read *e.g., asks teacher to read favorite story; repeats refrain when familiar book is read aloud*	Participates in story time interactively *e.g., answers questions before, during, and after read-aloud session; relates story to self; acts out familiar story with puppets*	Chooses to read on own; seeks information in books; sees self as reader *e.g., gives reasons for liking a book; looks for other books by favorite author; uses book on birds to identify egg found on nature walk*
45. **Demonstrates understanding of print concepts**	**Forerunners** Points to print on page and says, "Read this" Recognizes logos *e.g., McDonald's* Recognizes book by cover	Knows that print carries the message *e.g., points to printed label on shelf and says, "Cars go here"; looking at the name the teacher has written on another child's drawing, says, "Whose is this?"*	Shows general knowledge of how print works *e.g., runs finger over text left to right, top to bottom as he pretends to read; knows that names begin with a big letter*	Knows each spoken word can be written down and read *e.g., touches a written word for every spoken word in a story; looking at a menu asks, "Which word says pancakes?"*
46. **Demonstrates knowledge of the alphabet**	**Forerunners** Participates in songs and fingerplays about letters Points out print in environment *e.g., name on cubby, exit sign*	Recognizes and identifies a few letters by name *e.g., points to a cereal box and says, "That's C like in my name"*	Recognizes and names many letters *e.g., uses alphabet stamps and names the letters— "D, T, M"*	Beginning to make letter-sound connections *e.g., writes a big M and says, "This is for Mommy"*
47. **Uses emerging reading skills to make meaning from print**	**Forerunners** Uses familiar logos and words to read print *e.g., cereal logos, "exit" and "stop" signs* Recognizes own name in print and uses it as a cue to find possessions *e.g., cubby, cot, placemat*	Uses illustrations to guess what the text says *e.g., looking at The Three Pigs, says, "And the wolf blew down the pig's house"*	Makes judgements about words and text by noticing features (other than letters or words) *e.g., "That must be Christopher's name because it's so long"; "You didn't write enough words. I said, 'A Book about the Dog Biff,' and you just wrote three words"*	Uses different strategies (known words, knowledge of letters and sounds, patterns in text) to make meaning from print *e.g., "That word says book"; anticipates what comes next based on pattern in Brown Bear; figures out which word says banana because he knows it starts with b*

Reading and Writing (continued)

Developmental Continuum for Ages 3–5

Curriculum Objectives		I	II	III
48. **Comprehends and interprets meaning from books and other texts**	**Forerunners** Repeats words and actions demonstrated in books *e.g., roars like a lion* Relates story to self and shares information *e.g., after hearing a story about snow says, "I made a snowman"*	Imitates act of reading in play *e.g., holds up book and pretends to read to baby doll; takes out phonebook in dramatic play area to make a phone call*	Compares and predicts story events; acts out main events of a familiar story *e.g., compares own feelings about baby brother to those of character; re-enacts Three Billy Goats Gruff*	Retells a story including many details and draws connections between story events *e.g., says, "The wolf blew the house down because it wasn't strong"; uses flannel board to retell The Very Hungry Caterpillar*
49. **Understands the purpose of writing**	**Forerunners** Watches when others write Pretends to write (scribble writes)	Imitates act of writing in play *e.g., pretends to write a prescription while playing clinic; scribble writes next to a picture*	Understands there is a way to write that conveys meaning *e.g., tells teacher, "Write this down so everyone can read it"; asks teacher, "How do I write Happy Birthday?"; says, "That's not writing, that's scribble-scrabble"*	Writes to convey meaning *e.g., on drawing for sick friend, writes own name; copies teacher's sign, "Do Not Disturb," to put near block pattern; makes deliberate letter choices during writing attempts*
50. **Writes letters and words**	**Forerunners** Scribbles with crayons Experiments with writing tools such as markers and pencils Draws simple pictures to represent something	Uses scribble writing and letter-like forms	Writes recognizable letters, especially those in own name	Uses letters that represent sounds in writing words

Alphabet Knowledge Observation Form

Child's Name: _____

Directions: Use this form to record your observations about a child's alphabetic knowledge. You may choose to either check or date the appropriate boxes as you observe the child demonstrate this knowledge.

Note: It is not expected that preschool children recognize and/or write all upper- and lowercase letters or make all letter-sound connections.

	Recognizes Letters		Writes Letters		Letter-Sound Connection
	Uppercase	**Lowercase**	**Uppercase**	**Lowercase**	
A					
B					
C					
D					
E					
F					
G					
H					
I					
J					
K					
L					
M					
N					
O					
P					
Q					
R					
S					
T					
U					
V					
W					
X					
Y					
Z					

Print and Book Concepts Observation Form

Child's Name: _____

Knows that print carries the message.

☐ Notices and reads environmental print.

☐ Knows that the pictures are related to what is written in print.

☐ Knows that it is the print that is read.

Shows general knowledge of how print works in English.

☐ Knows that print is read from left to right.

☐ Knows that print is read from top to bottom.

☐ Understands that different forms of print are used for different functions (e.g., lists for shopping)

☐ Notices various features of print (punctuation, spaces, upper- /lowercase letters).

Knows each spoken word can be written down and read.

☐ Understands the concept of a letter and a word.

☐ Matches spoken word to written word, one-to-one.

Shows general knowledge of book concepts.

☐ Knows a book has information or a story to tell.

☐ Understands the concept of title, author, and illustrator.

☐ Holds the book right side up.

☐ Turns pages from the front of the book to the back.

☐ Knows where to begin reading.

☐ Pretends to read.

Phonological Awareness Observation Form

Child's Name: _____

Listening

☐   Notices and recognizes sounds in the environment.

☐   Discriminates sounds that are the same and different.

☐   Remembers sounds heard.

☐   Discriminates one sound out of many.

Rhyming

☐   Joins in and repeats rhyming songs, fingerplays and poems.

☐   Fills in missing rhyming word of a song, fingerplay, or story.

Alliteration

☐   Participates in songs, stories, and rhymes with alliterative text (e.g., Silly Sally).

☐   Recognizes that a group of words all begin with the same sound(s).

☐   Identifies many beginning sounds of familiar words.

Sentences and Words

☐   Claps separate words in a sentence

☐   Listens for a particular word or phrase

Syllables

☐   Claps syllables of own name.

☐   Claps syllables of familiar words.

Onset and Rime

☐   Recites rhymes, songs, or fingerplays that focus on onset and rime (e.g., rub-a-dub).

☐   Begins to separate initial sound from rest of word (e.g., writes the letter *m* when adding milk to a shopping list).

Phonemes

☐   Plays with the sounds of words.

Bibliography & References

Adams, M. J. (1990). *Beginning to read: Thinking and learning about print.* Cambridge, MA: MIT Press.

Adams, M. J., Treiman, R., & Pressley, M. (1998). Reading, writing, and literacy. In I. E. Sigel & K. A. Renninger (Eds.), *Handbook of child psychology: Vol. 4: Child psychology in practice* (5th ed.)(pp. 275–355). New York: Wiley.

Alexander, A., Anderson, H., Heilman, P., Voeller, K., & Torgesen, J. (1991). Phonological awareness training and the remediation of analytic decoding deficits in a group of severe dyslexics. *Annals of Dyslexia, 41,* 193–206.

Allen, L., Cipielewski, J., & Stanovich, K. E. (1992). Multiple indicators of children's reading habits and attitudes: Construct validity and cognitive correlates. *Journal of Educational Psychology, 84,* 489–503.

Anderson, R. C., & Freebody, P. (1981). Vocabulary knowledge. In J. Guthrie (Ed.), *Comprehension and teaching: Research reviews* (pp. 77–117). Newark, DE: International Reading Association.

Anderson, R. C., & Pearson, P. D. (1984). A schema–thematic view of basic processes in reading comprehension. In P. D. Pearson, R. Barr, M. L. Kamil, & P. Mosenthal (Eds.), *Handbook of reading research* (pp. 255–290). New York: Longman.

Anderson, R.C., Reynolds, R. E., & Montague, W. E. (1977). *School and the acquisition of knowledge.* Hillsdale, NJ: Erlbaum.

Anderson, R. C., Reynolds, R. E., Schallert, D. L., & Goetz, E. T. (1977). Frameworks for comprehending discourse. *American Educational Research Journal, 14*(4), 367–381.

Apel, K. (1997, June 17). *Metalinguistic skills in school-age children: Building blocks for literacy.* Presentation at the Montana Speech, Language, and Hearing Association Summer Institute, Great Falls, MT.

Baker, L., Fernandez-Fein, S., Scher, D., & Williams, H. (1998). Home experiences related to the development of word recognition. In J. L. Metsala & L. C. Ehri (Eds.), *Word recognition in beginning literacy* (pp. 263–287). Mahwah, NJ: Erlbaum.

Baker, L., Scher, D., & Mackler, K. (1997). Home and family influences on motivations for literacy. *Educational Psychologist, 32,* 69–82.

Ball, E. (1993). Assessing phoneme awareness. *Language, Speech, and Hearing Services in Schools, 24*(3), 130–139.

Bishop, D. V. M., & Adams, C. (1990). A prospective study of the relationship between specific language impairment, phonological disorders and reading retardation. *Journal of Child Psychology and Psychiatry and Allied Disciplines, 31,* 1027–1050.

Bloodgood, J. W. (1999). What's in a name? Children's name writing and literacy acquisition. *Reading Research Quarterly, 34*(3), 342–367.

Bond, G. L., & Dykstra, R. (1967). The cooperative research program in first-grade reading instruction. *Reading Research Quarterly, 2,* 5–142.

Bowey, J. A. (1994). Phonological sensitivity in novice readers and nonreaders. *Journal of Experimental Psychology, 58*, 134–159.

Bradley, L., & Bryant, P. E. (1978). Difficulties in auditory organization as a possible cause of reading backwardness. *Nature, 271*, 746–747.

Bradley, L., & Bryant, P. E. (1983). Categorizing sounds and learning to read: A causal connection. *Nature, 310*, 419–421.

Bransford, J. D., & Johnson, M. K. (1972). Contextual prerequisites for understanding: Some investigations of comprehension and recall. *Journal of Verbal Learning and Verbal Behavior, 11*, 717–726.

Braunger, J., Lewis, J., & Hagans, R. (1997). *Building a knowledge base in reading*. Portland, OR: Northwest Regional Educational Laboratory, National Council of Teachers of English.

Burgess, S. R., & Lonigan, C. J. (1998). Bidirectional relations of phonological sensitivity and prereading abilities: Evidence from a preschool sample. *Journal of Experimental Child Psychology, 70*, 177–141.

Burns, M. S., Griffin, P., & Snow, C. E. (Eds.). (1999). *Starting out right*. Washington, DC: National Academy Press.

Butler, S. R., Marsh, H. W., Sheppard, M. J., & Sheppard, J. L. (1985). Seven-year longitudinal study of the early prediction of reading achievement. *Journal of Educational Psychology, 77*, 349–361.

Campbell, C. (Ed.). (1998). *Facilitating preschool literacy*. Newark, DE: International Reading Association.

Chall, J. S. (1967). *Learning to read: The great debate*. New York: McGraw-Hill.

Chall, J. S., Jacobs, V. A., & Baldwin, L. E. (1990). *The reading crisis: Why poor children fall behind*. Cambridge, MA: Harvard University Press.

Christie, F. (1984). Young children's writing development: The relationship of written genres to curriculum genres. In N. B. Bartlett & J. Carr (Eds.), *Language in education conference: A report of proceedings* (pp. 41–69). Brisbane, CAE, Australia: Mt. Gravatt Campus.

Christie, F. (1987). Factual writing in the first years of school. *Australian Journal of Reading, 10*, 207–216.

Christie, J. F. (1983). The effects of play tutoring on young children's cognitive performance. *Journal of Educational Research, 76*, 326–330.

Christie, J., Roskos, K., Vukelich, C., Enz, B., & Neuman, S. (1995). *Linking literacy with play*. Newark, DE: International Reading Association.

Clay, M. M. (1979a). *The early detection of reading difficulties* (2nd ed.). Auckland, New Zealand: Heinemann.

Clay, M. M. (1979b). *Reading recovery: A guidebook for teachers in training*. Auckland, New Zealand: Heinemann.

Clay, M. M. (1981). *Becoming literate*. Portsmouth, NH: Heinemann.

Clay, M. M. (1991). *Becoming literate: The construction of inner control*. Auckland, New Zealand: Heinemann.

Clay, M. (1993). *An observation survey of early literacy achievement*. Portsmouth, NH.: Heinemann.

Cochran-Smith, M. (1984). *The making of a reader*. Norwood, NJ: Ablex.

Collier, V. P. (1995). *Promoting academic success for ESL students: Understanding second language acquisition for school* (No. 1-883514-00-2). Jersey City, NJ: New Jersey Teachers of English to Speakers of Other Languages–Bilingual Educators.

Crain-Thoreson, C., & Dale, P. S. (1992). Do early talkers become early readers? Linguistic precocity, preschool language and emergent literacy. *Developmental Psychology, 50*, 429–444.

Cunningham, A. E., & Stanovich, K. E. (1991). Tracking the unique effects of print exposure in children: Associations with vocabulary, general knowledge and spelling. *Journal of Educational Psychology, 83*, 264–274.

Cunningham, A. E., & Stanovich, K. E. (1998). Early reading acquisition and its relation to reading experience and ability 10 years later. *Developmental Psychology, 33*, 934–945.

Daniels, M. (1994). The effect of sign language on hearing children's language development. *Communication Education, 43*(4), 291–298.

Daniels, M. (1996). Bilingual, bimodal education for hearing kindergarten students. *Sign Language Studies, 90*, 25–37.

Davis, F. B. (1968). Research in comprehension in reading. *Reading Research Quarterly, 3*, 499–545.

Dickinson, D. K., & DeTemple, J. (1998). Putting parents in the picture: Maternal reports of preschoolers' literacy as a predictor of early reading. *Early Childhood Research Quarterly, 13*, 241–261.

Dickinson, D. K., & Smith, M. W. (1994). Long-term effects of preschool teachers' book readings on low-income children's vocabulary and story comprehension. *Reading Research Quarterly, 29*, 104–122.

Dickinson, D. K., & Tabors, P. O. (1991). Early literacy: Linkages between home, school and literacy achievement at age five. *Journal of Research in Childhood Education, 6*, 30–46.

Dickinson, D. K., & Tabors, P. O. (Eds.). (2001). *Building literacy with language: Young children learning at home and school*. Baltimore: Brookes.

Dole, J. S., Sloan, C. J., & Trathen, W. (1995). Teaching vocabulary within the context of literature. *Journal of Reading, 38*, 444–451.

Downing, J. (1986). Cognitive clarity: A unifying and cross-cultural theory for language awareness phenomena in reading. In D. B. Yaden, Jr. &. S. Templeton (Eds.), *Metalinguistic awareness and beginning literacy* (pp. 13–29). Portsmouth, NH: Heinemann.

Drevno, G. E., Dimball, J. W., Possi, M. K, Heward, W. L., Gardner, R., & Barbetta, P. M. (1994). Effects of active student response during error correction on the acquisition, maintenance and generalization of science vocabulary by elementary students: A systematic replication. *Journal of Applied Behavior Analysis, 27*(1), 179–180.

Duke, N. K., & Kays, J. (1998). "Can I say 'once upon a time'?": Kindergarten children developing knowledge of informational book language. *Early Childhood Research Quarterly, 13*(2), 295–318.

Durkin, D. (1966). *Children who read early*. New York: Teacher's College Press.

Echols, L. D., West, R. F., Stanovich, K. E., & Zehr, K. S. (1996). Using children's literacy activities to predict growth in verbal cognitive skills: A longitudinal investigation. *Journal of Educational Psychology, 88*, 296–304.

Ehri, L. C. (1984). How orthography alters spoken language competencies in children learning to read and spell. In J. Downing & R. Valtin (Eds.), *Language awareness and learning to read*. New York: Springer Verlag.

Ehri, L., & Wilce, L. (1985). Movement into reading: Is the first stage of printed word learning visual or phonetic? *Reading Research Quarterly, 20*, 163–179.

Espinosa, L. (in press). Curriculum and assessment considerations for young children from culturally, linguistically, and economically diverse backgrounds. *Psychology in the Schools.*

Fowler, A. E. (1991). How early phonological development might set the stage for phoneme awareness. In S. A. Brady & D. A. Shankweiler (Eds.), *Phonological processes in literacy* (pp. 97–117). Hillsdale, NJ: Lawrence Erlbaum Associates.

Galda, L., & Cullinan, B. E. (1991). Literature for literacy: What research says about the benefits of using trade books in the classroom. In J. Flood, J. Jensen, D. Lapp, & J. R. Squire (Eds.), *Handbook of research on teaching the English language arts*. New York: Macmillan.

Gambrell, L. B., Palmer, B. M., & Coding, R. M. (1993). *Motivation to read*. Washington, DC: Office of Educational Research and Improvement.

Gibson, E., & Levin, E. (1975). *The psychology of reading*. Cambridge, MA: MIT Press.

Goatly, V. J., Brock, C. H., & Raphael, T. E. (1995). Diverse learners participating in regular education book clubs. *Reading Research Quarterly, 30*, 352–380.

Goatly, V. J., & Raphael, T. E. (1992). Non-traditional learners' written and dialogic response to literature. *Learner factors/teacher factors: Issues in literacy research and instruction: 40th yearbook of the National Reading Conference* (pp. 313–322). Chicago: National Reading Conference.

Goswami, U., & Bryant, P. E. (1990). *Phonological skills and learning to read*. Hillsdale, NJ: Erlbaum.

Griffith, P. O., & Olson, W. (1992). Phoemic awareness helps beginning readers break the code. *The Reading Teacher, 45*(7), 516–523.

Gundlach, R., McLane, J., Scott, F., & McNamee, G. (1985). The social foundations of early writing development. In M. Farr (Ed.), *Advances in writing research: Vol. 1: Children's early writing development*. Norwood, NJ: Ablex.

Gunn, B., Simmons, D., & Kameenui, E. (1995). *Emergent literacy: Synthesis of the research* (Tech. Rep. No. 19). Retrieved June 2004, from http://idea.uoregon.edu/~ncite/documents/techrep/tech19.html

Hall, S. L., & Moats, L. C. (1999). *Straight talk about reading: How parents can make a difference during the early years*. Lincolnwood, IL: NTC/Contemporary Publishing.

Hart, T., & Risley, B. (1995). *Meaningful differences in the everyday experience of young children*. Baltimore: Paul H. Brookes Publishing Co.

Heath, S. B., Branscombe, A., & Thomas, C. (1986). The book as a narrative prop in language acquisition. In B. Schieffelin & P. Gilmore (Eds.), *The acquisition of literacy: Ethnographic perspectives* (pp. 16–34). Norwood, NJ: Ablex.

Hicks, D. (1995). The social origins of essayists writing. *Builletin Suisse de Linguistique Applique, 61*, 61–82.

Hiebert, E. H. (1981). Developmental patterns and interrelationships of preschool children's print awareness. *Reading Research Quarterly, 16*, 236–260

Holdaway, D. (1979). *The foundations of literacy*. Portsmouth, NH: Heinemann.

Huck, C. (1976). *Children's literature in the elementary school* (3rd ed.). New York: Holt, Rinehart & Winston.

Jenkins, R., & Bowen, L. (1994). Facilitating development of preliterate children's phonological abilities. *Topics in Language Disorders, 14*(2), 26–39.

Johnston, M. (2002). Assessment in reading. In R. Barr, M. L. Kamil, & P. Mosenthal (Eds.), Handbook of *Reading Research* (pp. 147–182). Mahwah, NJ: Lawrence Erlbaum Associates.

Johnston, R. S., Anderson, M., & Holligan, C. (1996). Knowledge of the alphabet and explicit awareness of phonemes in prereaders: The nature of the relationship. *Reading and Writing: An Interdisciplinary Journal, 8*, 217–234.

Kameenui, E. J., Carnine, D. W., & Freschi, R. (1982). Effects of text construction and instructional procedures for teaching word meanings on comprehension and recall. *Reading Research Quarterly, 17*, 367–385.

Leung, C. B. (1992). Effects of word-related variables on vocabulary growth repeated read-aloud events. In C. K. Kinzer & D. J. Leu (Eds.), *Literacy research, theory, and practice: Views from many perspectives: 41st yearbook of the National Reading Conference* (pp. 491–498). Chicago, IL: The National Reading Conference.

Lonigan, C. J., Burgess, S. R., & Anthony, J. L. (2000). Development of emergent literacy and early reading skills in preschool children: Evidence from a latent-variable longitudinal study. *Developmental Psychology, 36*, 596–613.

Lonigan, C. J., Burgess, S. R., Anthony, J. L., & Barker, T. A. (1998). Development of phonological sensitivity in 2- to 5-year-old children. *Journal of Educational Psychology, 90*(2), 294–311.

MacLean, M., Bryant, P., & Bradley, L. (1987). Rhymes, nursery rhymes, and reading in early childhood. *Merrill-Palmer Quarterly, 33*, 255–281.

Mason, J. M. (1980). When do children begin to read? An exploration of four-year-old children's letter and word reading competencies. *Reading Research Quarterly, 15*, 203–227.

Mason, J. M. (1992). Reading stories to preliterate children: A proposed connection to reading. In P. B. Gough, L. C. Ehri, & R. Treiman R. (Eds.), *Reading acquisition* (pp. 215–241). Mahwah, NJ: Lawrence Erlbaum Associates.

Mason, J., & Allen, J. B. (1986). A review of emergent literacy with implications for research and practice in reading. *Review of Research in Education, 13*, 3–47.

Mattingly, I. (1984). Reading linguistic awareness, and language acquisition. In J. Downing & R. Caltin (Eds.), *Language awareness and learning to read*. New York: Springer-Verlag.

McCormick, C. E., & Mason, J. M. (1986). Intervention procedures for increasing preschool children's interest in and knowledge about reading. In W. H. Teale & E. Sulzby (Eds.), *Emergent literacy: Writing and reading* (pp. 90–115). Norwood, NJ: Ablex.

McKeon, M. G., Beck, I. L., Omanson, R. C., & Pople, M. T. (1985). Some effects of the nature and frequency of vocabulary instruction on the knowledge and use of words. *Reading Research Quarterly, 20*(5), 522–535.

McGee, L., & Richgels, D. (1996). *Literacy's beginnings: Supporting young readers and writers*. Needham Heights, MA: Allyn and Bacon.

McGee, L. M., Richgels, D., & Charlsworth, R. (1986). Emerging knowledge of written language: Learning to read and write. In S. J. Kilmer (Ed.), *Advances in early education and day care* (Vol. IV)(pp. 67–121). Greenwich, CT: JAI Press.

Moats, L. (1998, July). *Achieving research-based practice: Replacing romance with reality*. Presentation at Sopris West Summer Institute, A Summit on Literacy, Snowmass, CO.

Morrow, L. M. (1983). Home and school correlates of early interest in literature. *Journal of Educational Research, 76*, 221–230.

Morrow, L. M. (1985). Retelling stories: A strategy for improving children's comprehension, concept of story structure and oral language complexity. *The Elementary School Journal, 85*, 647–661.

Morrow, L. M. (1987). The effect of small group story reading on children's questions and comments. In S. McCormick & J. Zutell (Eds.), *Cognitive and social perspectives for literacy research and instruction: 37th yearbook of the National Reading Conference* (pp. 77–86). Chicago: National Reading Conference.

Morrow, L. M. (1987). Promoting voluntary reading: The effects of an inner city program in summer day care centers. *The Reading Teacher, 41,* 266–274.

Morrow, L. M. (1988). Young children's responses to one-to-one story readings in school settings. *Reading Research Quarterly, 23,* 89–107.

Morrow, L. M. (1990). Preparing the classroom environment to promote literacy during play. *Early Childhood Research Quarterly, 5,* 537–554.

Morrow, L. M. (2001). *Literacy development in the early years: Helping children read and write.* Needham Heights, MA: Allyn and Bacon.

Morrow, L. M., & Smith, J. K. (1990). The effects of group size on interactive storybook reading. *Reading Research Quarterly, 25,* 214–231.

Morrow, L. M., & Weinstein, C. S. (1982). Increasing children's use of literature through program and physical design changes. *The Elementary School Journal, 83,* 131–137.

Morrow, L. M., & Weinstein, C. S. (1986). Encouraging voluntary reading: The impact of a literature program on children's use of library centers. *Reading Research Quarterly, 21,* 330–346.

Murray, B. A., Stahl, S. A., & Ivey, M. G. (1996). Developing phoneme awareness through alphabet books. *Reading and Writing, 8,* 307–322.

Nagy, W. E., & Anderson, R. C. (1984). How many words are there in printed school English? *Reading Research Quarterly, 19,* 304–330.

Naslund, J. C., & Schneider, W. (1996). Kindergarten letter knowledge, phonological skills, and memory processes: Relative effects on early literacy. *Journal of Experimental Child Psychology, 62,* 30–59.

National Early Literacy Panel. (2004). *A synthesis of research on language and literacy.* Retrieved June 2004, from http://www.famlit.org/ProgramsandInitiatives/FamilyPartnershipinReading/index.cfm

National Institute of Child Health and Human Development. (2000a). *Report of the National Reading Panel. Teaching children to read: An evidence-based assessment of the scientific research literature on reading and its implications for reading instruction* (NIH Publication No. 00-4769). Washington, DC: U.S. Government Printing Office.

National Institute of Child Health and Human Development. (2000b). *Why children succeed or fail at reading. Research from NICHD's program in learning disabilities.* Retrieved June 2004, from http://www.nichd.nih.gov/publications/pubs/readbro.htm

Neuman, S. B., Copple, C., & Bredekamp, S. (2000). *Learning to read and write.* Washington, DC: National Association for the Education of Young Children.

Neuman, S. B., & Roskos, K. (1990). Play, print and purpose: Enriching play environments for literacy development. *Reading Teacher, 44*(3), 214–221.

Neuman, S. B., & Roskos, K. (1991). The influence of literacy-enriched play centers on preschoolers' conceptions of the functions of print. In J. Christie (Ed.), *Play and early literacy development* (pp. 167–187). Albany, NY: State University of New York Press.

Neuman, S. B., & Roskos, K. (Eds.). (1998). *Children achieving*. Newark, DE: International Reading Association.

Ninio, A., & Bruner, J. (1978). The achievements and antecedents of labeling. *Journal of Child Language, 5*, 5–15.

Noble, E., & Foster, J. E. (1993). Play centers that encourage literacy development. *Day Care and Early Education, 21*(2), 22–26.

Olfman, S. (Ed.). (2003). *All work and no play…: How educational reforms are harming our preschoolers*. Westport, CT: Praeger.

Owocki, G. (1999). *Literacy through play*. Portsmouth, NH: Heinemann.

Owocki, G. (2001). *Make way for literacy! Teaching the way young children learn*. Portsmouth, NH: Heinemann; Washington, DC: National Association for the Education of Young Children.

Pappas, C. C. (1991). Fostering full access to literacy by including information books. *Language Arts, 68*, 449–462.

Pappas, C., & Brown, E. (1987). Learning to read by reading: Learning how to extend the functional potential of language. *Research in the Teaching of English, 21*(2), 160–184.

Pellegrini, A. D., & Galda, L. (1982). The effects of thematic fantasy play training on the development of children's story comprehension. *American Educational Research Journal, 19*, 443–452.

Pickett, L. (1998). Literacy learning during block play. *Journal of Research in Childhood Education, 12*(2), 225–230.

Pikulski, J. J., & Tobin, A. W. (1989). Factors associated with long-term reading achievement of early readers. In S. McCormick, J. Zutell, P. Scharer, & P. O'Keefe (Eds.), *Cognitive and social perspectives for literacy research and instruction* (pp. 123–133). Chicago: National Reading Conference.

Purcell-Gates, V. (1988). Lexical and syntactic knowledge of written narrative held by well-read-to kindergartners and second graders. *Research in the Teaching of English, 22*, 128–160.

Rawson, R. M., & Goetz, E. M. (1983). *Reading-related behavior in preschoolers: Environmental factors and teacher modeling*. Unpublished manuscript.

Read, C. (1971). Preschool children's knowledge of English phonology. *Harvard Educational Review, 41*, 1–34.

Robbins, C., & Ehri, L. C. (1994). Reading storybooks to kindergarteners help them learn new vocabulary words. *Journal of Educational Psychology, 86*(1), 54–64.

Roser, N., & Martinez, M. (1985). Roles adults play in preschoolers' response to literature. *Language Arts, 62*(5), 485–490.

Roser, N. L., & Martinez, M. G. (Eds.). (1995). *Book talk and beyond: Children and teachers respond to literature*. Newark, DE: International Reading Association.

Roskos, K. A., & Christie, J. F. (Eds.). (2000). *Play and literacy in early childhood: Research from multiple perspectives*. Mahwah, NJ: Lawrence Erlbaum.

Sawyer, W. (2004). *Growing up with literature* (4th ed.). Clifton Park, NY: Delmar Learning.

Saltz, E., Dixon, D., & Johnson, J. E. (1997). Training disadvantaged preschoolers on various fantasy activities: Effects on cognitive functioning and impulse control. *Child Development, 48*, 367–380.

Scarborough, H. (1989). Prediction of reading dysfunction from familial and individual differences. *Journal of Educational Psychology, 81*, 101–108.

Schickedanz, J. (1999). *Much more than the ABCs: The early stages of reading and writing*. Washington, DC: National Association for the Education of Young Children.

Sénéchal, M. (1997). The differential effect of storybook reading on preschoolers' acquisition of expressive and receptive vocabulary. *Journal of Child Language, 24*(1), 123–138.

Sénéchal, M., & Cornell, E. H. (1993). Vocabulary acquisition through shared reading experiences. *Reading Research Quarterly, 28*(4), 360–374.

Share, D. L., & Jaffe-Gur, T. (1999). How reading begins: A study of preschoolers' print identification strategies. *Cognition and Instruction, 17*, 177–213.

Share, D. L., Jorm, A. F., MacLean, R., & Mathews, R. (1984). Sources of individual differences in reading acquisition. *Journal of Educational Psychology, 76*, 1309–1324.

Share, D. L., & Silva, P. (1987). Language deficits and specific reading retardation: Cause or effect? *British Journal of Disorders of Communication, 22*, 219–226.

Silvern, S., Williamson, P., & Waters, B. (1983). Play as a mediator of comprehension: An alternative to play training. *Educational Research Quarterly, 7*, 16–21.

Snow, C. E., Barnes, W. S., Chandler, J., Goodman, I. F., & Hemphill, L. (1991). *Unfulfilled expectations: Home and school influences on literacy*. Cambridge, MA: Harvard University Press.

Snow, C. E., Burns, M. S., & Griffin, P. (Eds.). (1998). *Preventing reading difficulties in young children*. Washington, DC: National Academy Press.

Snowling, M., & Stackhouse, J. (1996). *Dyslexia speech and language: A practitioner's handbook*. San Diego, CA: Singular Publishing Group.

Snyder, L., & Downey, D. (1997). Developmental differences in the relationship between oral language deficits and reading. *Topics in Language Disorders, 17*(3), 27–40.

Stahl, S. A., & Murray, B. A. (1994). Defining phonological awareness and its relationship to early reading. *Journal of Educational Psychology, 86*, 221–234.

Stanovich, K. E. (1986). Matthew effects in reading: Some consequences of individual differences in the acquisition of literacy. *Reading Research Quarterly, 21*, 360–407.

Stanovich, K. E. (1994). Romance and reality. *The Reading Teacher, 47*(4), 280–291.

Stanovich, K. E. & West, R. F. (1989). Exposure to print and orthographic processing. *Reading Research Quarterly, 24*, 402–433.

Stevenson, H. W., & Newman, R. S. (1986). Long-term prediction of achievement and attitudes in mathematics and reading. *Child Development, 57*, 646–659.

Stewig, J. W., & Sebesta, S. (Eds.). (1978). *Using literature in the elementary classroom.* Urbana, IL: National Council of Teachers of English.

Strickland, D., & Morrow, L. (Eds.). (1989). *Emerging literacy: Young children learn to read and write.* Newark, DE: International Reading Association.

Strickland, D., & Morrow, L. (Eds.). (2000). *Beginning reading and writing.* New York, NY: Teachers College Press.

Sulzby, E. (1985). Children's emergent reading of favorite books: A developmental study. *Reading Research Quarterly, 20*(4), 458–481.

Sulzby, E. & Teale, W. H. (1987). *Young children's storybook reading: Longitudinal study of parent-child interaction and children's independent functioning. Final report to the Spencer Foundation.* Ann Arbor: University of Michigan.

Sulzby, E., & Teale, W. H. (1991). Emergent literacy. In R. Barr, M. Kamil, P. Mosenthal, & P. Pearson (Eds.), *Handbook of Reading Research* (Vol. 2) (pp. 727–757). New York: Longman.

Taylor, D. (1983). *Family literacy.* Exeter, NH: Heinemann.

Teale, W. (1984) Reading to young children: Its significance for literacy development. In H. Goelman, A. Oberg, & F. Smith (Eds.), *Awakening to literacy* (pp.110–121). Portsmouth, NH: Heinemann.

Teale, W., & Yokota, J. (2000). Beginning reading and writing: Perspectives on instruction. In D. S. Strickland & L. M. Morrow (Eds.), *Beginning reading and writing* (pp. 3–21). New York: Teachers College Press.

Torgesen, J. K. (1998, Spring/Summer). Catch them before they fall: Identification and assessment to prevent reading failure in young children. *American Educator, 22*, 32–39.

Treiman, R. (1993). *Beginning to spell.* New York: Oxford University Press.

Vukelich, C. (1990). Where's the paper? Literacy during dramatic play. *Childhood Education, 66*(4), 205–209.

Vukelich, C. (1994). Effects of play interventions on young children's reading of environmental print. *Early Childhood Research Quarterly, 9,* 153–170.

Vygotsky, L. S. (1978). *Mind in society: the development of psychological processes.* Cambridge, MA: Harvard University.

Wagner, R. K., Torgesen, J. K., Laughon, P., Simmons, K., & Rashotte, C. A. (1993). The development of young readers' phonological processing abilities. *Journal of Educational Psychology, 30,* 73–87.

Wagner, R. K., Torgesen, J. K., Rashotte, C. A., Hecht, S. A., Barker, T. A., Burgess, S. R., Donahue, J., & Garon, T. (1997). Changing relations between phonological processing abilities and word-level reading as children develop from beginning to skilled readers: A 5-year longitudinal study. *Developmental Psychology, 33,* 468–479.

Wells, G. (1985). Preschool literacy-related activities and success in school. In D. R. Olance, N. Torrance, & A. Hildyard (Eds.), *Literacy, language and learning* (pp. 229–255). Cambridge, England: Cambridge University Press.

Wells, G. (1986). *The meaning makers: Children learning language and using language to learn.* Portsmouth, NH: Heinemann.

Weitzman, E., & Greenberg, J. (2002). *Learning language and loving it.* Toronto, Ontario: The Hanen Centre.

Whitehurst, G., & Lonigan, C. (1998). Child development and emergent literacy. *Child Development, 69*(3), 848–872.

Yopp, H. K. (1992). Developing phonemic awareness in young children. *The Reading Teacher, 45*(9), 696–703.